TODAY
MATTERS

TODAY
MATTERS

12 DAILY PRACTICES TO
GUARANTEE TOMORROW'S SUCCESS

JOHN C. MAXWELL

WARNER
Faith

NEW YORK BOSTON NASHVILLE

Page 315 is a continuation of this copyright page.

Warner Faith

Time Warner Book Group
1271 Avenue of the Americas, New York, NY 10020

The Warner Faith name and logo are registered trademarks of Warner Books.

Visit our Web site at www.twbookmark.com.

Printed in the United States of America

First Warner Books printing: May 2004

10 9 8 7 6 5 4 3 2

Text design by Meryl Sussman Levavi/Digitext

Library of Congress Cataloging-in-Publication Data

Maxwell, John C., 1947–
   Today matters : 12 daily practices to guarantee tomorrow's
success / John C. Maxwell.
    p. cm.
   ISBN 0-446-52958-3
  1. Success—Psychological aspects.   I. Title.
   BF637.S8M3423   2004
   158—dc22   2003023070

Today Matters is dedicated to Madeline Elizabeth Miller,
our first grandchild. Her mother is the apple of my eye, and
Madeline is our sunshine. As she grows, it is our desire that she
value the potential of each of her days.

Contents

Acknowledgments   ix

Just for Today . . .   xi

1. Today Often Falls to Pieces—What Is the Missing Piece?   1

2. Today Can Become a Masterpiece   18

3. Today's ATTITUDE Gives Me Possibilities   39

4. Today's PRIORITIES Give Me Focus   62

5. Today's HEALTH Gives Me Strength   83

6. Today's FAMILY Gives Me Stability   105

7. Today's THINKING Gives Me an Advantage   128

8. Today's COMMITMENT Gives Me Tenacity   152

9. Today's FINANCES Give Me Options   176

10. Today's FAITH Gives Me Peace   197

11. Today's RELATIONSHIPS Give Me Fulfillment   217

12. Today's GENEROSITY Gives Me Significance   239

13. Today's VALUES Give Me Direction   259

14. Today's GROWTH Gives Me Potential   278

Conclusion: Making Today Matter   300

Notes   303

Acknowledgments

I'd like to say thank you to:

Margaret Maxwell, who makes every day of my life a masterpiece;

Charlie Wetzel, my writer;

Kathie Wheat, who does my research;

Stephanie Wetzel, who proofs and edits every manuscript page;

and Linda Eggers, my assistant.

Just for Today . . .

Just for today . . . I will choose and display the right attitudes.

Just for today . . . I will determine and act on important priorities.

Just for today . . . I will know and follow healthy guidelines.

Just for today . . . I will communicate with and care for my family.

Just for today . . . I will practice and develop good thinking.

Just for today . . . I will make and keep proper commitments.

Just for today . . . I will earn and properly manage finances.

Just for today . . . I will deepen and live out my faith.

Just for today . . . I will initiate and invest in solid relationships.

Just for today . . . I will plan for and model generosity.

Just for today . . . I will embrace and practice good values.

Just for today . . . I will seek and experience improvements.

Just for today   I will act on these decisions and practice these disciplines, and

Then one day . . . I will see the compounding results of a day lived well.

TODAY
MATTERS

CHAPTER 1

Today Often Falls to Pieces— What Is the Missing Piece?

A few weeks ago I was going through a box of old books in the basement looking for something to read to my grandchildren, and I came across a book my wife, Margaret, and I used to read to my daughter, Elizabeth, when she was little. It's called *Alexander and the Terrible, Horrible, No Good, Very Bad Day* by Judith Viorst. It's the story of a little boy whose day falls to pieces. It begins,

> I went to sleep with gum in my mouth and now there's gum in my hair and when I got out of bed this morning I tripped on the skateboard . . . and I could tell it was going to be a terrible, horrible, no good, very bad day.[1]

From there, Alexander's day just keeps getting worse as he goes to school, finds himself at the dentist's office, and has to go shopping for clothes with his mother. He has a miserable day. Even the family cat seems to be against him.

What Is the Missing Piece?

Our kids always liked Viorst's book. And I think we adults had as much fun reading little Alexander's grumpy complaints as they did listening. But it's no fun when your own day feels like Alexander's. Who looks forward to a day filled with obstacles, trials, and setbacks, where each bend in the road seems to hold something worse?

When it comes to approaching the day, we often are more like Alexander than we would care to admit. We may not wake up with gum in our hair or feel that our family and friends are out to get us, but our days often fall to pieces. And, as a result, they seem like very bad days.

How often do you have a *great* day? Is it the norm or the rare exception for you? Take today, for example. How would you rate it? So far, has today been a great day? Or has it been less than wonderful? Perhaps you haven't even thought about it until now. If I asked you to rate today on a scale of 1 to 10 (with 10 being perfect), would you even know how to score it? Upon what would you base your rating? Would it depend on how you feel? Would it be determined by how many items you've checked off your to-do list? Would you score your day according to how much time you've spent with someone you love? How do you define success for today?

How Does Today Impact Tomorrow's Success?

Everyone wants to have a good day, but not many people know what a good day looks like—much less how to create one. And even fewer people understand how *the way you live today impacts your tomorrow.* Why is that? The root of the problem is that most people misunderstand success. If we have a faulty view of success, we take a faulty approach to our day. As a result, today falls to pieces.

Look at these common misconceptions concerning success and the responses that often go with them:

WE BELIEVE SUCCESS IS IMPOSSIBLE— SO WE CRITICIZE IT

Psychiatrist M. Scott Peck opened his best-selling book *The Road Less Traveled* with the words "Life is difficult." He went on to say, "Most do not fully see this truth that life is difficult. Instead they moan more or less incessantly . . . about the enormity of their problems, their burdens, and their difficulties as if life were generally easy, as if life *should* be easy."[2] Because we want to believe life should be easy, we sometimes assume anything that's difficult must be impossible. When success eludes us, we are tempted to throw in the towel and assume it's unattainable.

That's when we begin to criticize it. We say, "Who wants success anyway?!" And if success is achieved by anyone whom we consider less worthy than ourselves, then we *really* get steamed. Like journalist and short-story writer Ambrose Bierce, we see success as "the one unpardonable sin against one's fellows."[3]

WE BELIEVE SUCCESS IS MYSTICAL— SO WE SEARCH FOR IT

If success has escaped us, yet we haven't entirely given up on it, then we often see it as a big mystery. We believe that all we have to do to succeed is find the magic formula, silver bullet, or golden key that will solve all our problems. That's why there are so many diet books on the best-seller lists and so many management fads employed in corporate offices each year.

The problem is that we want the rewards of success without paying the price. Seth Godin, author of *Permission Marketing*, recently wrote about this problem in the business world. He believes that business leaders frequently look for quick fixes for their companies. But he admonishes that "we need to stop shopping for lightning bolts."

"You don't win an Olympic gold medal with a few weeks of intensive training," says Godin. "There's no such thing as an overnight opera sensation. Great law firms or design companies don't spring up overnight. . . . Every great company, every great brand, and every great career has been built in exactly the same way: bit by bit, step by step, little by little."[4] There is no magic solution to success.

WE BELIEVE SUCCESS COMES FROM LUCK— SO WE HOPE FOR IT

How many times have you heard people say something like "He was just in the right place at the right time" to explain away someone else's success? It's a myth, just like the idea of the overnight success. The chances of becoming a success due to luck are about as good as of winning the lottery—50 million to 1.

Every now and then, we hear about a Hollywood star who was discovered while working as a drugstore clerk or an athlete drafted by a pro team even though he didn't begin playing the sport until late in high school and we get excited. What luck, we think. That could happen to me! But those are rare occurrences. For every person who makes it under such circumstances, there are thousands and thousands of people who have spent a dozen years toiling at a craft to get their chance. And there are tens of thousands more who have put in the years of work but who still aren't good enough to make it. When it comes to success, you're better off hopping to it than hoping for it.

We Believe Success Is Productivity— So We Work for It

I once saw a sign posted in a small business that said,

> The 57 Rules of Success
> #1 Deliver the goods.
> #2 The other 56 don't matter.

There's something about working hard and producing results that feels very rewarding. And many people regard that feeling so highly that they define it as success. Former U.S. President Theodore Roosevelt observed, "Far and away the best prize that life offers is the chance to work hard at work worth doing."

But seeing hard work as success is one-dimensional. (Is a day that contains no work unsuccessful? Is someone who retires unsuccessful?) Besides, it's not always true. A strong work ethic is an admirable trait, but hard work alone doesn't bring success. There are plenty of people who work hard and never see success. Some people give their energy to dead-end jobs. Others work so hard that they neglect important relationships, ruin their health, or burn out. Success may not come to those who don't work hard, but hard work and success are not one and the same.

We Believe Success Comes from an Opportunity— So We Wait for It

Many of the people who work very hard yet don't seem to get anywhere believe that the only thing they need is a break. Their motto begins with the words "if only." If only my boss would cut me some slack . . . If only I could get a promotion . . . If only I had some start-up capital . . . If only my kids would behave . . . then life would be perfect.

The truth is that people who do nothing more than wait for an opportunity won't be ready to capitalize on one if it *does* appear. As basketball legend John Wooden says, "When opportunity comes, it's too late to prepare." And for those who receive their wish—of a promotion, start-up money, or anything else—it rarely changes anything in the long term if they haven't already done all the groundwork to be successful.

> "When opportunity comes, it's too late to prepare."
>
> —JOHN WOODEN

Besides, we're all fickle. The thing we believe will solve our problems or make us happy isn't lasting. It's like when I was eight years old and I said, "If only I had a new bike." When Christmas rolled around, I got my new Schwinn with all the bells and whistles. And I loved it—for about a month. Then I had a new "if only" that I thought would make me happy. An opportunity may help you, but it won't guarantee your success.

WE BELIEVE SUCCESS COMES FROM LEVERAGE— SO WE POWER UP FOR IT

Some people associate success with power. Their viewpoint is reinforced by the words of powerful people like industrialist Andrew Carnegie, who asserted, "Success is the power with which to acquire whatever one demands of life without violating the rights of others." Many people take their view of success and power one step further, assuming that successful people have taken advantage of others to get where they are. So to get what they want, they look for an angle to exploit or for leverage over someone else. They believe they can force their way to success.

Saddam Hussein, Iraq's longtime dictator, took that approach by using power, manipulation, and brute force. He got his start politically as an enforcer. He committed murder for the Ba'ath Party in order to rise through its ranks, eventually becoming vice president of Iraq following a coup by the Ba'aths. When Hussein grew unsatisfied with serving as vice president, he simply seized power and made himself president.

For decades he used torture, oppression, and murder to retain power. His vision was to become the hero of the Middle East, its unifying ruler, a modern-day Nebuchadnezzar. But like all people who use and abuse power to get ahead—whether an arrogant corporate CEO or a bloody dictator—he failed in the end. No amount of power, no matter how ruthlessly wielded, can guarantee success.

WE BELIEVE SUCCESS COMES FROM CONNECTIONS— SO WE NETWORK FOR IT

Which do you think is more important for getting what you want in life: *what* you know or *who* you know? If you believe the answer is *who,* then you probably believe that success comes from connections.

People who believe in connections think they would have it made if only they had been born into the right family. Or they think their fortunes would suddenly improve if they met the right person. But those beliefs are misplaced. Relationships are certainly satisfying. And knowing good people has its rewards. But connections alone will neither improve the life of someone who is off track nor guarantee success. If they did, the children of every successful businessperson would have it made. And the siblings of every U.S. president would be highly successful. But you know that's not true. Remember Billy Carter? Ultimately, no one can network himself to success unless he has something to offer in the first place.

WE BELIEVE SUCCESS COMES FROM RECOGNITION— SO WE STRIVE FOR IT

In your profession, is there a sure sign that you've made it? Would your peers be impressed if you were recognized by *Fortune* magazine, became a chess grand champion, or won the Lombardi Trophy? If you were named teacher of the year or awarded an honorary doctorate by a prestigious university, would that mean success? Perhaps you have quiet dreams of someday winning an Oscar, an Emmy, or a Grammy. Or do you picture yourself accepting a Pulitzer prize, Fields Medal, or Nobel prize? Every profession or discipline has its own form of recognition. Are you striving to achieve recognition in yours?

In France, a nation of food lovers where chefs receive the highest honors, one of the highest marks of recognition anyone can receive is a three-star rating for his restaurant from the Michelin guide. At present, only twenty-five restaurants in all of France hold that honor. One of them is an establishment in the Burgundy region owned by Bernard Loiseau called the Côte d'Or.

For decades, Chef Loiseau was said to be obsessed with creating the perfect restaurant and receiving the highest rating awarded by Michelin. He worked tirelessly; it takes great work to earn even a two-star rating, but Loiseau achieved it in 1981. And then he worked harder. He perfected each dish on his menu. He improved the restaurant's service. And he went $5 million in debt to improve and expand his facility. And finally, in 1991, he received his third star. He had accomplished what only a handful of others could.

"We are selling dreams," he once said. "We are merchants of happiness."[5] But the recognition he received didn't keep him happy. In the spring of 2003, after the lunch service, he committed suicide by shooting himself. He didn't warn anyone, nor did he leave a note. Some say he was disconsolate because his rating in another restaurant guide had fallen from nineteen to seventeen (out of twenty). Others described him as a manic-depressive. No one will ever know why he killed himself, but we can be sure that the great recognition he had received in his profession wasn't enough for him.

WE BELIEVE SUCCESS IS AN EVENT— SO WE SCHEDULE IT

I've dedicated more than thirty years of my life to speaking at events and putting on conferences to help people be more successful and become better leaders. But I'm very realistic about the limited impact an event can make in a person's life, and I frequently remind conference attendees of those limitations. Events are great places for receiving inspiration and encouragement. They often prompt us to make important decisions to change. And they can even provide knowledge and tools to get us started. However, real, sustainable change doesn't happen in a moment. It's a process. Knowing that has always compelled me to write books and record lessons so that people who have made the decision to change have access to tools they can use after the event to help facilitate the process.

We use that process orientation at EQUIP, the nonprofit organization I

> Real, sustainable change doesn't happen in a moment. It's a process.

founded in 1996 with the goal of training and resourcing one million leaders overseas. We don't simply drop in, put on an event, and disappear. We use a three-year strategy. We begin by translating books and lessons into the local language. After the first teaching event, we give leaders books and tapes to use for their ongoing growth. And teams go back to the country every six months to teach more skills and follow up with leaders.

Don't get me wrong. Events can be very helpful—as long as we understand what they can and cannot do for us. I want to encourage you to attend events that can be catalysts for change in your life. Just don't expect them to suddenly bring you success. Growth comes from making decisions *and* following through on them. And that's what this book is all about.

Today Matters

People create success in their lives by focusing on *today*. It may sound trite, but today is the only time you have. It's too late for yesterday. And you can't depend on tomorrow. That's why **today matters.** Most of the time we miss that. Why? Because . . .

WE OVEREXAGGERATE YESTERDAY

Our past successes and failures often look bigger to us in hindsight than they really were. Some people never get over their past accomplishments: the high school basketball stars or homecoming queens look back at their glory days and define themselves by those accomplishments for the next two decades. The person who receives a patent for an invention might live off the proceeds for the rest of his life and never work another day. A salesperson stays in a five-year slump after being recognized as Employee of the Year. Why? Because he'd rather spend more time thinking about when he was at the top instead of trying to reach that level again.

> It may sound trite, but today is the only time you have. It's too late for yesterday. And you can't depend on tomorrow. That's why **today matters.**

Even worse are the people who exaggerate what they *could have* done. You've probably heard the saying "The older I am, the better I was." It's a curious phenomenon: People who were mediocre high school athletes reach their thirties, and they suddenly believe they could have gone pro. Average businesspeople in dead-end careers at forty believe they could have been Wall Street tycoons if only they had been given a chance. Almost any opportunity that went unpursued looks golden now that it's too late to go after it.

Then there are the people whose negative experiences shape them for their entire lives. They relive every rejection, failure, and injury they've received. And they let those incidents tie them into emotional knots. My friend's mother still laments that on her fifth birthday, her father gave the best lollipop to her younger sister instead of to her as a present. It still bothers her—and she's eighty-three years old!

For years I kept a sign on my desk that helped me maintain the right perspective concerning yesterday. It simply said, "Yesterday Ended Last Night." It reminded me that no matter how badly I might have failed in the past, it's done, and today is a new day. Conversely, no matter what goals I may have accomplished or awards I

> Yesterday ended last night.

may have received, they have little direct impact on what I do today. I can't celebrate my way to success either.

WE OVERESTIMATE TOMORROW

What is your attitude toward the future? What do you expect it to hold? Do you think things will get better or worse for you? Answer the following questions related to your expectations for the coming two to three years:

1. Do you expect your annual income to go
   up or down?   Up / Down
2. Do you expect your net worth to increase
   or decrease?   Increase / Decrease

3. Do you expect to have more or fewer
opportunities?   More / Fewer
4. Do you expect your marriage (or most
significant relationship) to get better or worse?   Better / Worse
5. Do you expect to have more or fewer
friendships?   More / Fewer
6. Do you expect your faith to be stronger
or weaker?   Stronger / Weaker
7. Do you expect to be in better or worse
physical condition?   Better / Worse

If you're like most people, your answers reflect that you expect the days ahead to be better. Now, let me ask you one more question: *Why* do you think that? Is your expectation based on anything other than a vague hope that your life will get better? I trust it is. For many people, it's not. They just figure that tomorrow is bound to be better, but they have no strategy for *making* it better. In fact, the worse some people feel about today, the more they exaggerate how good tomorrow is likely to be. They have a lottery mind-set.

Pulitzer prize–winning journalist William Allen White observed, "Multitudes of people have failed to live for today. They have spent their lives reaching for the future. What they have had within their grasp today they have missed entirely, because only the future has intrigued them . . . and the first thing they knew the future became the past." Hoping for a good future without investing in today is like a farmer waiting for a crop without ever planting any seed.

WE UNDERESTIMATE TODAY

Have you ever asked someone what he was doing and heard him respond, "Oh, I'm just killing time"? Have you ever really thought about that statement? A person might as well say, "I'm throwing away my life" or "I'm killing myself," because, as Benjamin Franklin asserted, time is "the stuff life is made of." Today is the only time we have within our grasp, yet many people let it slip through their fingers. They recognize neither today's value nor its potential.

A friend named Dale Witherington recently e-mailed to me a poem he wrote called "The Lifebuilder's Creed." In part, this is what it says:

> Today is the most important day of my life.
> Yesterday with its successes and victories, struggles and failures
> is gone forever.
> The past is past.
> Done.
> Finished.
> I cannot relive it. I cannot go back and change it.
> But I will learn from it and improve my Today.
>
> Today. This moment. NOW.
> It is God's gift to me and it is all that I have.
>
> Tomorrow with all its joys and sorrows, triumphs and
> troubles isn't here yet.
> Indeed, tomorrow may never come.
> Therefore, I will not worry about tomorrow.
>
> Today is what God has entrusted to me.
> It is all that I have. I will do my best in it.
> I will demonstrate the best of me in it—
> my character, giftedness, and abilities—
> to my family and friends, clients and associates.
> I will identify those things that are most important
> to do Today,
> and those things I will do until they are done.
> And when this day is done
> I will look back with satisfaction at that
> which I have accomplished.

Then, and only then, will I plan my tomorrow,
Looking to improve upon Today, with God's help.

Then I shall go to sleep in peace . . . content.[6]

The Missing Piece Has Been Discovered!

If we want to do something with our lives, then we must focus on today. That's where tomorrow's success lies. But how do you win today? How do you make today a great day instead of one that falls to pieces?

> The secret of your success is determined by your daily agenda.

Here's the missing piece: *The secret of your success is determined by your daily agenda.*

How would you like every day to . . .

- ◆ Possess possibilities?
- ◆ Remain focused?
- ◆ Enjoy good health?
- ◆ Exhibit stability?
- ◆ Hold an advantage?
- ◆ Possess tenacity?
- ◆ Exercise options?
- ◆ Sense inner peace?
- ◆ Experience fulfillment?
- ◆ Feel significant?
- ◆ Receive direction?
- ◆ Learn and grow?

Wouldn't that make today a great day?

It all comes down to what you do today. When I talk about your daily "agenda," I *don't* mean your to-do list. Nor am I asking you to adopt a particular kind of calendar or computer program to manage your time. I'm focusing on something bigger. I want you to embrace what may be a whole new approach to life.

Make the Decision Once . . . Then Manage It Daily

There are only a handful of important decisions people need to make in their entire lifetimes. Does that surprise you? Most people complicate life and get bogged down in decision making. My goal has always been to make it as simple as possible. I've boiled the big decisions down to twelve things. Once I've made those decisions, all I have to do is manage how I'll follow through on them.

If you make decisions in those key areas once and for all—and then manage those decisions daily—you can create the kind of tomorrow you desire. ***Successful people make right decisions early and manage those decisions daily.*** The earlier you make those right decisions and the longer you manage them, the more successful you can become. The people who

> Successful people make right decisions early and manage those decisions daily.

neglect to make those decisions and to manage them well often look back on their lives with pain and regret—no matter how much talent they possessed or how many opportunities they once had.

Regret in the End

A classic example of such a person was Oscar Wilde. A poet, playwright, novelist, and critic, Wilde was a man of unlimited potential. Born in 1854, he won scholarships and was educated in Britain's best schools. He excelled in Greek, winning the Gold Medal at

Trinity College for his studies. He was awarded the Newdigate Prize and was honored as "First in Greats" at Oxford. His plays were popular, earned him lots of money, and he was the toast of London. His talent seemed limitless. Karen Kenyon, writer for *British Heritage* magazine, called Wilde "our most quotable writer" after Shakespeare.[7]

Yet at the end of his life, he was broken and miserable. His wanton living landed him in prison. From jail, he wrote a perspective on his life. In it, he said,

> I must say to myself that I ruined myself, and that nobody great or small can be ruined except by his own hand. I am quite ready to say so. I am trying to say so, though they may not think it at the present moment. This pitiless indictment I bring without pity against myself. Terrible as was what the world did to me, what I did to myself was far more terrible still.

> I was a man who stood in symbolic relations to the art and culture of my age. I had realised this for myself at the very dawn of my manhood, and had forced my age to realise it afterwards. Few men hold such a position in their own lifetime, and have it so acknowledged. It is usually discerned, if discerned at all, by the historian, or the critic, long after both the man and his age have passed away. With me it was different. I felt it myself, and made others feel it. Byron was a symbolic figure, but his relations were to the passion of his age and its weariness of passion. Mine were to something more noble, more permanent, of more vital issue, of larger scope.

> The gods had given me almost everything. But I let myself be lured into long spells of senseless and sensual ease. I amused myself with being a FLANEUR, a dandy, a man of fashion. I surrounded myself with the smaller natures and the meaner minds. I became the spendthrift of my own genius, and to waste an eternal youth gave me a curious joy. Tired of being on the heights, I deliberately went to the depths in the search for new sensation. What the paradox was to me in the sphere of thought, perversity

became to me in the sphere of passion. Desire, at the end, was a malady, or a madness, or both. I grew careless of the lives of others. I took pleasure where it pleased me, and passed on. I forgot that *every little action of the common day makes or unmakes character*, and that therefore *what one has done in the secret chamber one has some day to cry aloud on the housetop*. I ceased to be lord over myself. I was no longer the captain of my soul, and did not know it. I allowed pleasure to dominate me. I ended in horrible disgrace. There is only one thing for me now, absolute humility.[8] (emphasis added)

By the time Wilde saw where his inattention to the day was going to land him, it was too late. He lost his family, his fortune, his self-respect, and his will to live. He died bankrupt and broken at age forty-six.

I believe that everyone has the power to impact the outcome of his life. The way to do it is to focus on today. Benjamin Franklin rightly observed, "One today is worth two tomorrows;

> "One today is worth two tomorrows; what I am to be, I am now becoming."
> —BENJAMIN FRANKLIN

what I am to be, I am now becoming." You can make today a good day. In fact, you can make it a masterpiece. That is the subject of the next chapter.

CHAPTER 2

Today Can Become
a Masterpiece

How would you describe your life? Are you achieving what you desire? Are you accomplishing the things that are important to you? Do you consider yourself a success? How do your prospects look for the future?

If I could come to your house and spend just one day with you, I would be able to tell whether or not you will be successful. You could pick the day. If I got up with you in the morning and went through the day with you, watching you for twenty-four hours, I could tell in what direction your life is headed.

When I tell this to people at conferences, there's always a strong reaction. Some people are surprised. Some get defensive because they think I would be making a snap judgment about them. A few get ticked off because they think my claim sounds arrogant. Others are simply intrigued and desire to know why I make such a statement.

The Advantage of Today

The answer lies in what I mentioned in the previous chapter. The secret of your success is determined by your daily agenda. If you make a few key decisions and then manage them well in your daily agenda, you will succeed.

You will never change your life until you change something you do daily. You see, success doesn't just suddenly occur one day in someone's life. For that matter, neither does failure. Each is a process.

> You will never change your life until you change something you do daily.

Every day of your life is merely preparation for the next. What you become is the result of what you do today. In other words . . .

YOU ARE PREPARING FOR SOMETHING

The way you live your life today is preparing you for your tomorrow. The question is, What are you preparing for? Are you grooming yourself for success or failure? As my father used to tell me when I was growing up, "You can pay now and play later, or you can play now and pay later. But either way, you are going to pay." The idea was that you can play and take it easy and do what you want today, but if you do, your life will be harder later. However, if you work hard now, on the front end, then you will reap rewards in the future.

It's the old ant and grasshopper story. During the summer and fall, the ant is constantly working, gathering food. Meanwhile, the grasshopper is playing all summer long. When winter's chill sets in, the ant retires to his home and enjoys life. He's paid the price for his leisure. But now it's time for the grasshopper, who played on the front end, to pay a price. He starves out in the cold because he has been preparing to fail, not succeed. He doesn't understand that the only adequate preparation for tomorrow is the right use of today.

One of the ways I "pay" today so that I can have a better tomorrow comes in my practice of filing away quotes and thoughts. From the time I was seventeen, I knew I was going to become a pastor.

> The only adequate preparation for tomorrow is the right use of today.

I knew that meant I would be writing and speaking to people every week of my life. If you've ever needed to write and present more than one hundred new lessons in a year, you know how hard it is to find good fresh material for an audience.

In 1964, I started the regular discipline of reading with an eye for finding good quotes, ideas, and illustrations for sermons and lessons. As I found good material (on any subject), I'd cut it out, decide what topic best described it, and file it away. That's something I have done every day for forty years!

Is it fun to do? Not especially. Often the practice is quite tedious. Does it work? Absolutely. The twelve hundred files in my office containing thousands of quotes are evidence of its success. Any time I need to write a lecture or want to work on a chapter for a book, instead of spending countless hours over the course of several weeks searching for high-quality material, I go to my files, and in *minutes* I put my hands on great quotes and stories I've collected. I simply look at reading and filing as a price I pay every day to make tomorrow better. It's a way of preparing to succeed.

PREPARATION TODAY GIVES CONFIDENCE TOMORROW

I always try to look at today as preparation for the future, and as a result it paves the way for my success tomorrow. One benefit of that mind-set is confidence. When you were in school, did you ever study so well for an exam that you walked into the classroom with absolute confidence, knowing you would ace the test? Or have you ever rehearsed a song or practiced a basketball shot so thoroughly that you just *knew* you would be able to deliver at crunch time?

You can bring that same kind of confidence to your everyday life, if you keep in mind that today matters. Legendary New York Jets quarterback Joe Namath explained it this way: "What I do is prepare myself until I know I can do what I have to do." When you invest in today, it's like putting money in the bank. It's like studying for the test of tomorrow. You're just better prepared to meet life's challenges.

PREPARATION TODAY GIVES SUCCESS TOMORROW

Not long ago I was chatting with John Kotter, the Harvard Business School professor and author of *Leading Change*. We were preparing to speak at a simulcast to thousands of businesspeople, and I told him about the idea for *Today Matters*. His response was, "Most people don't lead their own lives—they accept their lives." I believe that is true.

> "Most people don't lead their own lives—they accept their lives."
>
> —JOHN KOTTER

Unfortunately, many people approach their lives very passively. They take a reactive approach to living instead of a proactive one. It's as if they're waiting for something. But life is not a dress rehearsal. You won't get a second chance to relive today! I believe that everyone chooses how to approach life. If you're proactive, you focus on *preparing*. If you're reactive, you end up focusing on *repairing*.

Preparing	Repairing
Lets you focus on today	Makes you focus on yesterday
Increases efficiency	Consumes time
Increases confidence	Breeds discouragement
Saves money	Increases costs
Pays now for tomorrow	Pays now for yesterday
Takes you to a higher level	Becomes an obstacle to growth

"The secret of success in life is for a man to be ready for his time when it comes."

—BENJAMIN DISRAELI

To become a preparer, heed the advice of nineteenth-century British prime minister Benjamin Disraeli, who said, "The secret of success in life is for a man to be ready for his time when it comes."

The Makings of a Masterpiece

In February of 2003, I fulfilled a lifelong dream. I was privileged to spend some time with one of my idols: John Wooden, UCLA's Hall of Fame basketball coach. I'll tell you more about that later. One of Wooden's sayings provides the missing piece for how we should handle today. He frequently exhorted his players to make each day their masterpiece:

> When I was teaching basketball, I urged my players to try their hardest to improve on that very day, to make that practice a masterpiece. Too often we get distracted by what is outside our control. You can't do anything about yesterday. The door to the past has been shut and the key thrown away. You can do nothing about tomorrow. It is yet to come. However, tomorrow is in large part determined by what you do today. So make today a masterpiece. . . . This rule is even more important in life than in basketball. You have to apply yourself each day to become a little better. By applying yourself to the task of becoming a little better each and every day over a period of time, you will become a *lot* better. Only then will you be able to approach being the best you can be.[1]

Isn't the idea of making today a masterpiece appealing? The question is, How? What does it take? I believe there are two ingredients necessary to make every day a masterpiece: decisions and discipline. They are like two sides of the same coin; you could call them "goal setting" and "goal getting." And they can't be separated because one is worthless without the other. I say that because . . .

Good Decisions – Daily Discipline = A Plan without a Payoff
Daily Discipline – Good Decisions = Regimentation without Reward
Good Decisions + Daily Discipline = A Masterpiece of Potential

Time is an equal opportunity employer, but how we treat time is not equal. Time is like a block of marble. Give a block of marble to an average person, and you end up with . . . a block of marble. But put it in the hands of a master sculptor, and watch what happens! The sculptor looks at it with an artist's eye. First, he makes decisions about what it will be. Then he practices the disciplines of his craft until he has transformed lifeless stone into a masterpiece. I believe you and I can become like the sculptor. We can learn to become master craftsmen, not of stone but of our lives.

GOOD *DECISIONS* TODAY WILL GIVE YOU A BETTER TOMORROW

It seems obvious to say that good decisions help to create a better tomorrow, yet many people don't appear to connect their lack of success to their poor decision making. Some people make choices, then experience negative consequences, yet wonder why they can't seem to get ahead in life. They never figure it out. Others know their choices may not be good for them, but they make them anyway. Such is the case with the alcoholic who keeps drinking excessively or the person who engages in one abusive relationship after another.

Nobody says that good decisions are always simple, but they are necessary for success. Theodore Hesburgh, former president of Notre Dame University, admonished:

You don't make decisions because they're EASY;
You don't make decisions because they're CHEAP;
You don't make decisions because they're POPULAR;
You make decisions because they're RIGHT.

You begin to build a better life by determining to make good decisions, but that alone is not enough. You need to know *what* decisions to make. I've given the subject a lot of thought, talked to many successful people, and narrowed down the list of critical areas for success to twelve. I call them the "Daily Dozen":

1. Attitude: Choose and display the right attitudes daily.
2. Priorities: Determine and act on important priorities daily.
3. Health: Know and follow healthy guidelines daily.
4. Family: Communicate with and care for my family daily.
5. Thinking: Practice and develop good thinking daily.
6. Commitment: Make and keep proper commitments daily.
7. Finances: Make and properly manage dollars daily.
8. Faith: Deepen and live out my faith daily.
9. Relationships: Initiate and invest in solid relationships daily.
10. Generosity: Plan for and model generosity daily.
11. Values: Embrace and practice good values daily.
12. Growth: Seek and experience improvements daily.

If you settle these twelve issues by making the right decision in each area and then manage those decisions daily, you can be successful.

Before going any further, I need to make something clear: Please don't let the length of the list bother you. I'm not trying to add twelve more things to your daily to-do list. What I'm suggesting is that you take some time to think through these areas and make a major decision in each that will be lifelong. You can settle an issue once and for all, and you won't have to revisit it daily. That's a good idea for two reasons:

1. **It Takes the Emotion Out of the Decision:** We often make decisions in the heat of the moment. If we're not careful, we can make a life-altering decision based on a temporary situation rather than on our values. Or we can base it on our feelings. Instead, if we make critical decisions before we *have* to, then we can make them without our emotions controlling us. When we do that, we are more likely to make decisions with integrity.

2. **It Makes Managing Your Life Easier:** If you nail down the critical decisions in your life, then you just have to manage yourself based on those decisions. For example, let's say you discover that you have an innate desire to gamble, causing you to make bets that lose lots of money. If you make the decision not to do any kind of betting, then in the future, your task will be to manage yourself in the light of that decision. That may mean avoiding visits to racetracks, removing Las Vegas from your list of potential vacation spots, and passing on an invitation to a friendly poker game. Once the big decision has been made, you rarely need to revisit it.

The most successful people in life are the ones who settle their critical issues early and manage them daily. The earlier you settle the critical issues in your life, the greater your potential for success.

> The most successful people in life are the ones who settle their critical issues early and manage them daily.

THE *DISCIPLINES* YOU PRACTICE TODAY WILL GIVE YOU A BETTER TOMORROW

The first ingredient of success—making good decisions—has no real value without the second, which is practicing good discipline. Let's face it: Everyone wants to be thin, but nobody wants to diet. Everyone wants to live long; not many want to exercise. Everybody

wants money, yet few want to work hard. Successful people conquer their feelings and form the habit of doing things unsuccessful
people do not like to do.
The bookends of success
are starting and finishing.

> Decisions help us start. Discipline helps us finish.

Decisions help us start. Discipline helps us finish.

Most people want to avoid pain, and discipline is often painful.
But we need to recognize that there are really two kinds of pain
when it comes to our daily conduct. There's the pain of self-
discipline and the pain of regret. Many people avoid the pain of
self-discipline because it's the easy thing to do. What they may not
realize is that the pain of self-discipline is momentary but the payoff is long-lasting.

If we've made a decision to try to be healthy, but we put off exercising, it's true that we avoid thirty minutes of unpleasantness.
But then we feel guilty because we've violated the decision we
know was right for us. Then we regret not having exercised. And if
we consistently avoid exercise, we end up paying a price later.

On the other hand, when we do practice the discipline of exercise for thirty minutes, we feel good about ourselves *the entire day*.
That's a great trade-off. We get sixteen hours of positive feelings
about ourselves for half an hour of work. And if we consistently
practice the discipline of exercise, we also receive a health benefit
that can literally save—and extend—our lives. When we subject
ourselves to the pain of discipline, the rewards are great and our
opportunities increase. However, if we repeatedly compromise our
discipline, we not only receive fewer opportunities, but the regret
grows.

I have to give my parents a lot of credit for training me to be
self-disciplined. One of the ways they did that was to use my chores
to teach me. Every Sunday my father gave me a list of chores for
the week. Some I had to do on a particular day, such as taking out
the garbage the night before pickup. Others I could do anytime I

wanted, as long as they were done by noon on Saturday. At first, I would put off as many tasks as possible. That was, until one week during the summer when I neglected to clean out the basement by the deadline. At noon that day, the whole family loaded into the car to go swimming. When I arrived there with my towel, my father asked me, "John, did you clean out the basement as you were supposed to?"

I hemmed and hawed for a moment and then finally confessed, "No, sir, I didn't." Then I thought fast: "But I'll do it as soon as we get back from swimming!"

My father looked at me and said kindly but firmly, "That's not what you agreed to. You chose to play all week instead of finishing your chores. We're going swimming, but you're staying home to finish the basement. I'm sorry, son, but those are the rules."

I spent that afternoon working in the smelly basement while my brother and sister swam and had fun. I stopped procrastinating after that. I wasn't about to miss out on all the fun again. Someone once defined hard work as the accumulation of the easy things you didn't do when you should have. The work just didn't seem quite as hard when I stopped putting it off. And I soon discovered that the quicker I got my work done, the better I enjoyed the week.

The First Step toward Success

Getting started is often the hardest part of making changes in your life, whether it's an exercise regimen, a personal growth plan, a diet, or a program to quit smoking. Because we already have so many reasons *not* to start in the back of our minds, let me encourage you by giving you some compelling ideas about getting started:

START WITH YOURSELF

A few years ago on a trip to India, I got the opportunity to visit the home of that nation's great leader, Mahatma Gandhi. The house has been turned into a museum, and it contains some of his personal possessions as well as artifacts from his time of leadership. It also teaches much of his philosophy. One of his statements

> "Be the change you want to see in the world."
>
> —MAHATMA GANDHI

that I saw there struck me: "Be the change you want to see in the world." What a great statement! So often we want to change the world. But it's easier to talk about the change someone else should make than to roll up our sleeves and do it ourselves.

If you desire for just one person close to you—your spouse, your child, a close friend, an employee—to change in some way, then become a model of change yourself. When that happens—

- You gain experience, confidence, integrity, and influence.
- You become content with yourself. (As the popular psychologist Dr. Phil McGraw would say, "You need to be there for you first.")
- You must have something to give before you can give to others.

I started learning these lessons the hard way early in my career. Back then I often tried to *push* people forward. Today, I work at *leading* people forward by trying to set the example.

START EARLY

There's an old saying that Noah didn't wait for his ship to come in; he built one! If you take a proactive approach to changing your life and you start early, you increase your odds for success—and you create more options for yourself later in life.

One of the people I greatly admire is Pat Summit, basketball coach of the University of Tennessee Lady Volunteers. She has been named Naismith Women's Collegiate Coach of the Century, inducted into the Basketball Hall of Fame, and given the John Bunn Award. Her teams have won six NCAA titles. As a head coach, she has won more than eight hundred games. Only a handful of coaches at any level have accomplished such a feat. How did she do it? Well, first of all, she's just good! Nobody achieves that many victories without talent and drive. But the other secret of her success is that she started at age twenty-six.

As you read the chapters ahead, you will become acquainted with my personal history and how I came to make each decision for practicing one of the Daily Dozen. I share it because I want to flesh out the process for you and let you know that I'm trying to live out the principles I write about. And I'll tell you where I struggle—I'm not pretending that I do all this perfectly. But you'll also find that I had the good fortune to make many of these decisions early in life:

In my teens—4 decisions
In my 20s—5 decisions
In my 30s—2 decisions
In my 50s—1 decision

The earlier I made the decision and consistently practiced the discipline, the greater the compounding effect on my life. The same will be true for you!

If you happen to be young, then you have an advantage older people don't. The earlier you start, the more your odds for success increase. Beginning early is like getting a head start in the 100-yard dash. As a result, your performance may surpass even hardworking people with much more talent than you.

START SMALL

The bigger the change, the more intimidating it can be. That's why I recommend starting small. Just about everyone believes he can take a small step. That's encouraging. When you start small and succeed, it helps you believe you can accomplish the next step. (Besides, you can't do step two until you've completed step one, right?) It also helps you to prioritize your actions and focus your energy. But here's a piece of advice: As you get ready to begin, don't expect to understand all of what it will take to get to the top. Just focus on the next step.

START NOW

My friend Dick Biggs, author of *Burn Brightly Without Burning Out*, says, "The greatest gap in life is the one between knowing and doing." Deep down, we all know that if we want to change and grow, we need to get started. Yet we sometimes hesitate.

> "The greatest gap in life is the one between knowing and doing."
>
> —DICK BIGGS

That's why Maureen Falcone says, "Most people fail in the starting."

A few weeks ago, Sammy Poole e-mailed me something that captures the heart of the excuses we make for not beginning what we know we should. In part it said,

So stop waiting . . .
Until your car or home is paid off.
Until you get a new car or home.
Until your kids leave the house.

Until you go back to school.
Until you finish school.
Until you lose ten pounds.
Until you gain ten pounds.
Until you get married.
Until you get a divorce.
Until you have kids.
Until you retire.
Until summer.
Until spring.
Until winter.
Until fall.
Until you die.

You may have a million reasons not to get started now. But deep down, none of them can be as compelling as your desire to change, grow, and succeed. In a month or a year or five years from now, you may have only one regret—that you didn't start now. Today matters. The way you spend today really can change your life. But the first decision you must make is to begin.

How to Make These Decisions a Reality in Your Life

Cartoonist Charles Schulz, the creator of *Peanuts,* quipped, "Life is easier if you dread only one day at a time." But the truth is that you don't have to dread your days if you settle the decisions you need to make and the disciplines you need to practice in the critical areas of your life. You've probably already noticed that this book contains a chapter concerning each of the twelve critical areas in the Daily Dozen. After reading through the chapters, do the following to begin turning today into your masterpiece:

REVIEW THE DECISIONS AND ASK YOURSELF, "WHICH GOOD DECISIONS HAVE I ALREADY MADE?"

Undoubtedly, you will have already made decisions in many of the critical areas discussed in this book. Some you've made without really knowing it. Others you may have thought through very carefully. You may even have put some decisions in writing at certain points in your life. Begin the process by recognizing and acknowledging the positive steps you've already taken. At the end of each chapter, I'll prompt you to do that.

IDENTIFY THE DECISIONS YOU STILL MUST MAKE

There will also be areas to which you've not given any consideration before now. As you read some chapters, you may even find that there are a few you thought you'd settled but haven't. Don't get discouraged, but do acknowledge your need to change. You can't improve in an area if it's not on your radar.

CHOOSE ONE OF THOSE DECISIONS AND DETERMINE TO MAKE IT THIS WEEK

When it comes to change, there are really only three kinds of people:

1. Those who don't know what to do
2. Those who know what to do but don't do it
3. Those who know what to do and follow through

This book has been written to help you be the third kind of person.

I've attempted to be thorough in this book, so that individuals who have given no attention to one of the twelve areas will have everything they need to tackle it and make it a success asset. However, one of the dangers of a book like this is that it covers so much ground that you may be tempted to go in too many directions at once. Just focus on one area at a time to make the greatest progress. And remember, when it comes to the big decisions in life, once you make them, you won't have to keep dealing with them in that way again.

LEARN THE DISCIPLINES THAT GO WITH EACH DECISION

Most people can make good decisions once they know what the issues are. But character and perseverance determine what happens *after* the decision is made. To help you follow through in each critical area, I've recommended disciplines for you to practice so that you can manage the decision well in your life.

As you proceed, remember that while decisions can be made quickly, adopting disciplines in your life takes more time. If you've lived without much self-discipline in the past, you'll need more time to learn them. However, if you are already a highly disciplined person, you will find it easier to adopt new disciplines. A victory of discipline in one area of life can carry over and help you win in other areas.

REPEAT THE PROCESS UNTIL YOU'VE MASTERED EACH OF THE DAILY DOZEN

Once you've settled a critical decision and have a handle on its disciplines, then move on to another one. That's what I'm doing. I have to admit, I'm still working at this myself. For example, I didn't make the decision to exercise consistently until I was in my fifties. And I'm still learning the

> What I do in the future depends on what I already am; and what I am is the result of previous years of discipline.

discipline of it. Do I have it down? No, I'm still fighting the fight. I'm getting better over time; I'm a work-in-progress. As I strive to move forward, I keep in mind that what I do in the future depends on what I already am; and what I am is the result of previous years of discipline.

His Life Is a Masterpiece

I mentioned earlier in the chapter that I fulfilled my lifelong dream of spending half a day with John Wooden. He is an amazing man. He coached basketball for over forty years. And, in all those years, he had only *one* losing season (his first). He led his UCLA teams to four undefeated seasons and a record ten NCAA championships, including seven in a row. No wonder he is called the Wizard of Westwood (the Los Angeles suburb where the UCLA campus is situated).

Before I went to see him, I spent three weeks rereading his books and devouring every bit of information I could about him. Then, on the appointed day, I met him for lunch at a little diner near his home where he eats regularly. When we met, he was ninety-two years old. But you wouldn't know it to talk to him. He's alert. And he is sharp!

As we ate, I must have asked him a thousand questions, and he answered them all graciously. I wanted to learn as much as I could about his leadership. I wanted to know why he thought he had been able to win as he did. He said he attributed it to four things: (1) analyzing players, (2) getting them to fulfill their roles as part of the team, (3) paying attention to fundamentals and details, (4) working well with others. I also wanted to know what he missed most about coaching. At first his answer surprised me.

"Practice," he said. It wasn't the acclaim or the championships.

Then I remembered a quote from him I had read before our meeting. I later went back to reread it:

> I have often been asked when I first started dreaming about winning a national championship. Was it at Indiana State Teachers College or after I arrived at UCLA? Perhaps while I was a college player? I never dreamed about winning a national championship.
>
> What I was dreaming about each year, if you want to call it that, was trying to produce the best basketball team we could be. My thoughts were directed toward preparation, our journey, not the results of the effort (such as winning national championships). That would simply have shifted my attention to the wrong area, hoping for something out of my control. Hoping doesn't make it happen.
>
> Mix idealism with realism and add hard work. This will often bring much more than you could ever hope for.[2]

We talked more about practice, and he said, "What you do in practice is going to determine your level of success. I used to tell my players, 'You have to give 100 percent every day. Whatever you don't give, you can't make up for tomorrow. If you give only 75 percent today, you can't give 125 percent tomorrow to make up for it.'"

As I listened to him speak, something steeled inside me. Before I met Coach Wooden, I had wanted to write *Today Matters*. After meeting him, I felt I *had* to write it. Everything he was saying to me seemed to confirm what I believed about how tomorrow's success can be found in what you do today.

After lunch, Coach Wooden invited me to his home. It's a small, unassuming place. I got very excited when he took me into his office. He must have had a thousand awards and mementos on the walls—so many you could hardly see the wallpaper. And any time I asked him about an item on the wall, he would deflect the honor from himself and talk about the team. For a while, he read poetry aloud to me. His love for verse was evident as he read each with great expression. After about an hour, he said, "Just one more," and read the following poem written by Swen Nader, one of his former players:

> I saw love once, I saw it clear.
> It had no leash. It had no fear.
> It gave itself without a thought.
> No reservation had it brought.
> It seemed so free to demonstrate.
> It seems obsessed, to orchestrate.
> A symphony designed to feed.
> Composed to lift the one in need.
> Concern for others was its goal.
> No matter what would be the toll.
> It's strange just how much care it stores.
> To recognize its neighbor's sores.
> And doesn't rest until the day.
> It's helped to take the sores away.
> Its joy retains and does not run.
> Until the blessing's job is done.
> I saw love once. 'Twas not pretend.
> He was my coach. He is my friend.[3]

The poem touched me, and I mentioned that I knew Swen because our daughters had gone to school together. "He's a good man, and he was a good ballplayer," Coach Wooden responded. "You know, many of my players still come visit me."

We talked for probably another hour and a half, and I began thinking that it was about time for me to go. But before I did, I said, "I've read that you carry something with you that contains your philosophy. Can I see it?"

He smiled and said, "I'll give you one."

He pulled out a card, a duplicate of one that he carries with him always. And he signed it for me. On the card is this statement:

"Success is peace of mind, which is a direct result of self-satisfaction in knowing you did your best to become the best that you are capable of becoming."

I thanked him for his time and I left, grateful that I had been allowed the privilege of being with and learning from someone I greatly respected as

> "Success is peace of mind, which is a direct result of self-satisfaction in knowing you did your best to become the best that you are capable of becoming."
>
> —JOHN WOODEN

a coach, a leader, and a human being. As I walked back to my car, I looked down at the card. And there it was, along with other favorite maxims of John Wooden: "Make each day your masterpiece."

APPLICATION AND EXERCISES

Since I will not have the opportunity to spend a day with you personally, I'm going to share with you the questions I would have asked as I went through the day with you:

1. Is your attitude a plus or a minus today?
2. Are your priorities keeping you focused today?
3. Is your health enabling you to succeed today?
4. Does your family situation provide support today?
5. Is your thinking mature and productive today?
6. Have your commitments been kept today?
7. Have your financial decisions been solid today?
8. Has your faith been active today?
9. Are your relationships being strengthened today?
10. Has your generosity added value to others today?
11. Are your values giving you direction today?
12. Is your growth making you better today?

Spend some time asking yourself these same questions, and be brutally honest in your answers. You'll have more time to think about them as you read through the next twelve chapters. I want you to see the whole process, looking at each of the areas in turn. Each chapter will have an "Application and Exercises" section to help you improve in that critical area. At the end of the book, I'll also give you the kind of plan I would provide if I were to spend the day with you.

CHAPTER 3

Today's **ATTITUDE** Gives Me Possibilities

Is it possible for an individual to have success without a good attitude? The answer is yes, but their attitude will determine how much they enjoy the success. I once read an account in which Clarence Darrow told an audience in Lincoln, Nebraska, "If I were a young man in my twenties and knew what I do now, I would commit suicide." Darrow was a successful lawyer and author, but based on that statement, I'd say his attitude was pretty grim.

Sigmund Freud is another example of someone with a poor attitude who was otherwise able to achieve. The father of modern psychotherapy was hailed as a groundbreaking genius during his lifetime, wrote numerous books, and influenced several generations of physicians, artists, and thinkers. He has been called one of the most influential people of the twentieth century. Yet from the time he was a teenager, he was pessimistic, skeptical, and often depressed.

For thirty years, Armand M. Nicholi Jr., an associate professor of clinical psychiatry at Harvard Medical School, has taught a class on Sigmund Freud at Harvard. He has also written a book about Freud in which he describes the chronic "pessimism, gloom, and general state of unhappiness" communicated in Freud's letters and autobiography. Freud, who tried to relieve his distress with cocaine beginning at twenty-eight years of age,[1] believed that happiness was difficult to experience, and unhappiness was the lot of most people. He remarked,

> We are threatened with suffering from three directions: from our own body, which is doomed to decay and dissolution and which cannot even do without pain and anxiety as warning signals; from the external world, which may rage against us with overwhelming and merciless forces of destruction; and finally from our relations with other men. The suffering which comes from this last source is perhaps more painful to us than any other.[2]

And in his book *Civilization and Its Discontents,* Freud wrote, "What good to us is a long life if it is difficult and barren of joys, and if it is so full of misery that we can only welcome death as a deliverer?"[3] Without a doubt, his attitude, not his accomplishments, influenced his outlook on life. He was a miserable person who was unhappy his entire life. What's sad is he chose his discontent.

Why Attitude Matters Today

While it is possible for people with great talent or drive to achieve with a bad attitude, it doesn't happen very often, and it takes an incredible amount of effort. And even if they do achieve some degree of success, they aren't happy. (And they make the people around them miserable too.) Most often, people with bad attitudes don't get very far in life.

On the other hand, even barely average people can do great things when their attitudes are great. In *The Winner's Edge,* Denis Waitley observed, "The winner's edge is not in a gifted birth, a high IQ, or in talent. The winner's edge is all in the attitude, not aptitude. Attitude is the criterion for success. But you can't buy an attitude for a million dollars. Attitudes are not for sale."[4]

Here's why attitude makes such a difference as you approach your day:

YOUR ATTITUDE AT THE BEGINNING OF A TASK AFFECTS ITS OUTCOME MORE THAN ANYTHING ELSE

You've heard the phrase "All's well that ends well." Here's another that I believe is equally true: All's well that begins well! Look at successful people and you'll see that they em-

> All's well that begins well!

braced this truth, whether it's a doctor going into surgery, a coach readying his team for a game, a pastor preparing a sermon, or a businessperson entering negotiations before a big deal. The confident person increases his chances for success. The pessimist invites the negative outcome he expects.

What is your attitude at the beginning of a new experience? Are you excited, cautious, or negative? Are there particular experiences that cause you to feel negative? If those experiences are areas critical to your success, then you need to make an adjustment in your attitude. Charlie Wetzel, who works with me on my books, recently underwent a change in attitude in his thinking concerning the process of editing. Charlie believes that most people in writing and publishing naturally gravitate to either writing or editing. He is a writer and has never particularly enjoyed the editing process. It reminds him of when he graded students' papers as an English composition teacher.

Recently, when we were working on my book *There's No Such*

Thing as "Business" Ethics, he received the edited manuscript from the publisher and was asked to review it, check the editor's changes, verify facts, etc. It's a process he normally hates because he thinks it takes time away from the writing he should be doing. But this time, he decided to change his attitude as he approached the task. Rather than performing the task in short blocks of time during afternoons (mornings are prime writing times), he blocked off an entire week just for editing, and he looked at the task as an opportunity to refine the manuscript and take it to the next level. As a result, the job was more enjoyable and the results were more effective.

When you approach a task—especially an important one you don't relish—fix your mind on the facts, not on your feelings. Focus on the possibilities, not the problems. That will put your attitude on the right track. And if it starts on the right track, it's more likely to end up at the right destination.

YOUR ATTITUDE TOWARD OTHERS OFTEN DETERMINES THEIR ATTITUDE TOWARD YOU

A mother and her adult daughter were out shopping one day, trying to make the most of a big sale weekend before Christmas. As they went from store to store in the mall, the older woman complained about everything: the crowds, the poor quality of the merchandise, the prices, and her sore feet. After the mother experienced a particularly difficult interaction with a clerk in one department store, she turned to her daughter and said, "I'm never going back to that store again. Did you see that dirty look she gave me?"

The daughter answered, "She didn't give it to you, Mom. You had it when you went in!"

When we interact with others, our attitudes often set the tone for how we treat one another. Smile at people when you meet them, and they often smile back. Act combative, and they are likely to snap back at you. If you want to enjoy mostly pleasant interaction with people as you go through your day, treat others well. It works more often than not.

Your Attitude Can Give You a Winner's Perspective

On June 28, 1939, Joe Louis defended his heavyweight boxing title against Tony "Two-Ton" Galento in Yankee Stadium. Galento wasn't a particularly talented fighter, but he could take a punch and he was a big hitter. In the second round, Louis knocked Galento down and seemed to be controlling the fight. But in the third round, Galento knocked the champ down.

Louis immediately jumped back to his feet and went after his opponent. When Louis went to his corner, his trainer chastised him: "You know you're supposed to take the full count when you go down. Why didn't you stay down for nine?"

"What!" answered Louis, "and give him a chance to rest?" Louis pummeled Galento so badly in the fourth round that the referee stopped the fight.

In today's competitive culture, everybody is looking for an edge. Top athletes and top businesspeople alike know that—all things being equal—attitude wins. But this is also true: All things not being equal, attitude sometimes still wins. Possessing a great attitude is like having a secret weapon.

> All things being equal, attitude wins. All things not being equal, attitude sometimes still wins.

Your Attitude—Not Your Achievements— Gives You Happiness

Samuel Johnson, the eighteenth-century poet and critic, stated, "He who has so little knowledge of human nature as to seek happiness by changing anything but his own disposition will waste his life in fruitless efforts and multiply the grief which he purposes to remove." He understood that contentment was generated internally, based on attitude.

The thoughts in your mind will always be more important than the things in your life. Fame and fortune are fleeting. The satisfaction that comes from achievement is momentary. The author of the Biblical book of Ecclesiastes observed, "He who loves silver will not be satisfied with silver; nor he who loves abundance, with increase."[5] You cannot buy or win happiness. You must choose it.

> The thoughts in your mind will always be more important than the things in your life.

YOUR ATTITUDE IS CONTAGIOUS

While it's true that you choose your attitude, you also need to keep in mind that the choices you make influence other people around you. In the Law of the Bad Apple in *The 17 Indisputable Laws of Teamwork,* I explain,

> Several things on a team are not contagious. Talent. Experience. Willingness to practice. But you can be sure of one thing: Attitude is catching. When someone on the team is teachable and his humility is rewarded by improvement, others are more likely to display similar characteristics. When a leader is upbeat in the face of discouraging circumstances, others admire that quality and want to be like her. When a team member displays a strong work ethic and begins to have a positive impact, others imitate him. . . . People have a tendency to adopt the attitudes of those they spend time with—to pick up on their mind-set, beliefs, and approaches to challenges.[6]

One of my mentors, Fred Smith, once told me there are two kinds of people in any organization: polluters and purifiers. Polluters are like smokestacks, belching out dirty smoke all the time. They hate clear skies, and no matter how good it gets, they can find a way to make it gloomy. When the people around them in the organization "breathe" their toxins, they feel sicker and sicker. Purifiers, on the other hand, make everything around them better. It doesn't matter what kind of rotten atmosphere they encounter. They take in the toxic words of polluters in the organization just as everyone else does, but they filter the words before passing them on. What goes in may be gloomy and negative, but when it comes back out, it's fresh and clear.

When you spend time with others, do they walk away feeling better or worse? Do you clear the air, giving them a fresh perspective and positive encouragement? Or do they go away feeling gloomy? Watch how people respond to you, and you'll know which kind of person you are.

The bottom line on attitude is that a good one helps to increase your possibilities. Pessimists usually get what they expect. So do optimists. Believing in yourself increases your chances of success. Looking for the positive in every situation helps you see opportunities that you would otherwise miss. Being positive with people prompts them to be positive with you—and individuals who interact well with others have a leg up on people who don't. I can't think of one legitimate criticism of positive thinking. It's all good.

Making the Decision to Choose and Display the Right Attitudes Daily

I discovered the importance of attitude in 1964 when I was seventeen years old. My high school basketball coach, Don Neff, took me aside at the beginning of my senior season and told me that he wanted me to be captain of the team. I was excited, but I was also a little surprised, because I knew that my teammate John Thomas was a better player than I was. But then Coach Neff said something that explained it. "John," he said, "you have the best attitude on the team, and it influences the other players."

Just a few weeks later, I was named "Citizen of the Month" at my school. Why? Once again, it was because of my attitude. My teachers said they loved my attitude. Then it sank in. My attitude was making a difference in my life. And it was making an impact on the people around me. That's when I made my attitude decision: *I am going to keep a positive attitude and use it to influence others.*

Many people in this world mistakenly believe their attitude is set. It has become such a habit for them that they believe it can't be changed. They see it as one of the "cards" of life they've been dealt, such as height or a history of cancer in the family. But that's not true. Your attitude is a choice. If you desire to make your day a masterpiece, then you need to have a great attitude. If it's not good now, you need to change it. Make the decision. Here's how:

> Many people in this world mistakenly believe their attitude is set.

TAKE RESPONSIBILITY FOR YOUR ATTITUDE

After my wife, Margaret, and I had been married for four or five years, we went to a conference for pastors where I had been asked to be one of the speakers. Margaret also agreed to do a breakout session for spouses. Speaking is not a passion for her as it is for me. She does a good job, but she doesn't really enjoy it that much. I wanted to support her, so I attended her session. During the Q and A time, a woman stood up and asked, "Does John make you happy?"

I have to say, I was really looking forward to hearing Margaret's answer. I'm an attentive husband, and I love Margaret dearly. What kind of praise would she lavish on me?

"Does John make me happy?" she considered. "No, he doesn't."

I looked to see where the closest exit was. "The first two or three years we were married," she continued, "I thought it was John's job to make me happy. But he didn't. He wasn't mean to me or anything. He's a good husband. But nobody can make another person happy. That was my job."

As a young newlywed in her early twenties, she figured out something some people never learn. Each of us must take responsibility for our own attitude. If you want today to be a good day, you need to take charge of the way you look at it.

DECIDE TO CHANGE YOUR BAD ATTITUDE AREAS

I've read the *Peanuts* comic strip for years, and I've always been a big fan. I recall one strip in which Lucy announces, "Boy, do I feel crabby."

Her little brother Linus, always anxious to relieve tension at home, responds, "Maybe I can be of help. Why don't you just take my place here in front of the TV while I go and fix you a nice snack? Sometimes we all need a little pampering to help us feel better." Then Linus brings her a sandwich, a few chocolate chip cookies, and some milk.

"Now is there anything else I can get you?" he asks. "Is there anything I haven't thought of?"

"Yes, there's one thing you haven't thought of," Lucy answers. And then she suddenly screams, "I don't want to feel better!"

For the many years the late Charles Schulz drew *Peanuts,* that always seemed to be one of Lucy's problems. She didn't *want to* change in the areas where she had a bad attitude—and she had a lot of them!

Many people are like her. I mentioned that there are things in your life you cannot choose, such as your parents, where you were born, or your race. But your attitude is something you can change. And just about everybody has at least a few areas in their thinking that could use some help. If you want to have a better day, then you need to go after those areas.

THINK, ACT, TALK, AND CONDUCT YOURSELF LIKE THE PERSON YOU WANT TO BECOME

If you've been to any kind of class reunion ten or more years after graduation, then you've probably been surprised by the transformation of one of your former classmates—the misfit who became a famous lawyer, the plain Jane who blossomed into a movie star, or the geek who founded a major corporation. How do such transformations occur? Those people changed how they thought of themselves. You saw them as they were (or how you thought they were). They saw themselves as they *could* be. Then they learned to act like and acquire the skills of the people they wanted to be. The transformation usually takes time; often it's barely noticeable to those who see them every day (just as parents don't see changes in babies the way others do). But to someone who hasn't seen them in ten, twenty, or thirty years, the transformation seems miraculous, like a butterfly from a caterpillar.

If you desire to change yourself, then start with your mind. Believe you can improve, that you can change into the person you desire to be. Walt Emerson said, "What lies behind us and what lies before us are tiny matters compared to what lies within us." If your thinking changes, then everything else can follow.

> "What lies behind us and what lies before us are tiny matters compared to what lies within us."
>
> —WALT EMERSON

PLACE A HIGH VALUE ON PEOPLE

One of the secrets of maintaining a good attitude is valuing people. You can't dislike people and have a good attitude at the same time.

Think about it: Have you ever met anyone who always treated people badly but had a positive attitude? Likewise, you cannot have a bad attitude and encourage others at the same time. Encouraging others

> You cannot have a bad attitude and encourage others at the same time.

means helping people, looking for the best in them, and trying to bring out their positive qualities. That process drives negative thoughts right out of your head.

Your interaction with others sets the tone of your day. It's like the music of your life. When your interaction with others is poor, it's like having to listen to cacophonous music. But when you place a high value on people and you treat them well, it's like listening to a sweet melody as you go through your day.

DEVELOP A HIGH APPRECIATION FOR LIFE

Have you ever known people who complain about everything? Their soup's too hot. Their bed's too cold. Their vacation's too short. Their pay's too low. You sit side by side with them at a magnificent banquet, and while you enjoy every morsel, they tell you what's wrong with each and every dish. Such people don't appreciate life no matter how good it gets.

A friend e-mailed to me the story of a very "together" and independent ninety-two-year-old lady who was moving into a nursing home. Since she was legally blind and her husband of seventy years had passed away, the move was her only option. She waited in the lobby of the facility for a long time before finally being told that her room was ready. As she was escorted down the corridor, her attendant described the room, down to the curtains hung on the windows.

"I love it," the elderly lady enthused.

"But you haven't even seen the room yet. Just wait," the attendant responded.

"That doesn't have anything to do with it," she replied. "Happiness is something you decide on ahead of time. Whether I like my room or not doesn't depend on how the furniture is arranged. It's how I arrange my mind."

Appreciation isn't a matter of taste or sophistication. It's a matter of perspective. John Wooden said, "Things turn out best for the people who make the best of the way things turn out." The place to start is with the little things. If you can learn to appreciate them and be grateful for them, you'll appreciate the big things as well as everything in between.

> "Things turn out best for the people who make the best of the way things turn out."
> —JOHN WOODEN

Managing the Disciplines of Attitude

If you want to benefit from the possibilities of a positive attitude, you need to do more than just make the decision to be positive. You also have to manage that decision. For me, in the area of attitude it means one thing: *Every day I will make the adjustments necessary to keep my attitude right.* If this is new territory for you, you may be wondering how to do it. Here are some guidelines to help you on your way:

RECOGNIZE THAT YOUR ATTITUDE NEEDS DAILY ADJUSTMENT

I've discovered that a person's attitude does not naturally or easily stay positive. For example, a lifelong attitude weakness I've had is my impatience with people. It was a problem even back when I was young. In school, when the teacher set aside a day to review before the final exam, I got dirty looks when I asked, "If we got it the first time, do we still have to come for the review?" And I still fight impatience. Every day I ask myself, "Have I been impatient with someone?" When I have, I apologize to the person. I've had to do that more times than I'd like to admit.

Like any discipline, your attitude will not take care of itself. That's why it needs to be attended to daily. The stronger your natural inclination to be pessimistic or critical, the more attention your attitude will need. Begin each day with an attitude check. And watch for red flags signaling that your attitude might be in trouble.

> Like any discipline, your attitude will not take care of itself. You need to attend to it daily.

FIND SOMETHING POSITIVE IN EVERYTHING

Not long ago I came across a prayer that I thought was wonderful. It said,

> Dear Lord,
>
> So far today, I am doing all right. I have not gossiped, lost my temper, been greedy, grumpy, nasty, selfish, or self-indulgent. I have not whined, cursed, or eaten any chocolate.
>
> However, I am going to get out of bed in a few minutes, and I will need a lot more help after that. Amen.

It may not always be easy, but if you try hard enough, you can find something good, even in the midst of difficult situations. In *Laugh Again,* my friend Chuck Swindoll explains that when Mother Teresa was asked the requirements for people assisting in her work with the destitute in Calcutta, she cited two things: the desire to work hard and a joyful attitude. If someone could be expected to be joyful among the dying and the poorest of the poor, then certainly we can do the same in our situation.

FIND SOMEONE POSITIVE IN EVERY SITUATION

Nothing helps a person to remain positive like having an ally. The world is filled with negative people; in fact, they often flock together. But positive people are everywhere too. You'll often find them soaring above the negative people—like eagles. When you do, seek them out. If you're having a hard time, get close and "draft" behind them the way racers do. If they're having difficulty, you be the one to go out front and make things easier. Two positive people are much better at fighting off the blues than someone going it alone.

SAY SOMETHING POSITIVE IN EVERY CONVERSATION

I've tried to make it a habit to include positive comments in every conversation with others. It starts with those closest to me. When my wife looks beautiful (which is *often*!) I tell her so. I compliment my children every time I see them. And I absolutely pour out positive praise every time I see my grandchildren. But I don't stop there. I sincerely compliment, praise, acknowledge, bolster, raise up, and reward people whenever I can. It's wonderful for me as well as for others. I highly recommend it, and I know you can learn to do it too.

REMOVE NEGATIVE WORDS FROM YOUR VOCABULARY

My father retired in his mid-seventies, but he has spent his entire life in public speaking. He came from a modest background, so he was always working hard to learn and grow. When I was a kid, he used to pay my brother, Larry, and me ten cents for every grammar mistake we found him making when he was preaching. It was just one example of how he was constantly trying to improve himself. (I suspect he also did it so that we would learn more about grammar ourselves.)

You can do a similar kind of thing when it comes to your attitude. You—or someone you enlist—can be on the lookout for negative words in your vocabulary so that you can try to eliminate them. Here's a list to get you started:

Eliminate These Words	Say These Instead
I can't	I can
If only	I will
I don't think	I know
I don't have the time	I will make the time
Maybe	Absolutely
I'm afraid	I'm confident
I don't believe	I'm sure

If you continually look for and embrace the positive and eliminate the negative, you'll help yourself to begin *thinking* more positively every day.

EXPRESS GRATITUDE TO OTHERS DAILY

Of all the virtues, gratitude seems to be the least expressed. How often do people go out of their way to thank you? How often do you receive a thank-you note when you give a gift? More important, how often do you extend your thanks to others? In our culture of plenty, we tend to take things for granted.

A few years ago, Oprah Winfrey encouraged her millions of TV viewers to keep a gratitude journal to help them appreciate life. Amy Vanderbilt, journalist and etiquette book author, said, "When we learn to give thanks, we are learning to concentrate not on the bad things, but on the good things in our lives." Thinking about the good things helps us to be grateful. Remaining grateful helps us to have a more positive attitude. And having a positive attitude prompts us to think about the good rather than the bad. It's a positive cycle that helps to fuel itself.

Reflecting on Attitude

When I made the decision at age seventeen to maintain a positive attitude, I did it because it was giving me immediate positive results. And that is what usually prompts us to make decisions. But as you get older and reflect more, you can see things much more clearly.

Looking back, I can see the impact that my attitude has made in my life since 1964:

In my teens . . .   My attitude made me captain of the basketball team.

In my 20s . . .   My attitude helped me convince Margaret to marry me.

In my 30s . . .   My attitude helped me step out of my comfort zone by leaving my organization and taking a new position in California.

In my 40s . . .   My attitude kept me going during eight years of red tape and conflict while trying to build a new campus for my church.

In my 50s . . .   My attitude allowed me to bounce back from a heart attack.

I can honestly say that for forty years, my attitude has been my greatest asset in influencing others. And as I approach my sixties, my attitude has motivated me to lead an effort to train and equip one million leaders internationally. I want to keep making a positive impact until the day I die.

Always Against the Odds

When you make the decision to have a positive attitude and then manage that decision well, there's almost nothing you can't accomplish. Just ask Lance Armstrong. In 1999 he became the second American cyclist to ever win the Tour de France, professional cycling's most prestigious event. (Cyclists pedal over two thousand miles in a grueling three-week race.) When Armstrong won, a journalist asked his mother, Linda, who was waiting for him at the finish line in Paris, whether his victory was against the odds. Her response was emphatic: "Lance's whole life has been against all odds."[7]

Lance Armstrong had several things working against him growing up. His mother was only seventeen when Lance was born, and she spent much of the time raising him as a single parent. They often struggled financially. And Lance often felt like an outsider. In Texas, the big sport is football. Armstrong says he was too uncoordinated for any sport with a ball, so he gravitated to activities that required endurance. In fifth grade, he ran in a distance race and won. Soon afterward, he joined a swim team. In a year, he went from being a "remedial" case to fourth best swimmer in Texas in the 1500-meter freestyle. Every day he would swim 4,000 meters before school and then return in the afternoon to swim an additional 6,000 meters. Soon he began riding his bike to practice— twenty miles round-trip.

At thirteen, he entered a competition called IronKids. It was a junior triathlon, combining swimming, biking, and running. He won it easily. When he was fifteen, he started competing against men. He came in thirty-second in his first race. After the race, he told a reporter, "I think in a few years I'll be right near the top, and within ten years I'll be the best."[8] Armstrong, always seen as a misfit, was mocked by his friends, who laughed and thought he was ridiculously cocky. The next year when he finished fifth in that same race, they stopped laughing. By the time he was sixteen, he was earning $20,000 a year entering and winning triathlons and 10K races around the country. He also got his first taste of bicycle racing. He was so good at it that he quickly jumped to the most competitive category and began training with the best local cyclists.

Over time, Armstrong began to focus entirely on cycling. He experienced success in the United States, but he wanted to ride in Europe, where the best athletes competed. His first professional race, the Clasica San Sebastian, was memorable. It was a bitterly cold day with pouring rain. He finished *dead last*, a full twenty-seven minutes behind the winner—a terrible finish. The Spanish crowd lining the course jeered him. He recalled his humiliation:

> A few hours later, I sat in the Madrid airport, slumped in a chair. I wanted to quit the entire sport. It was the most sobering race of my life; on my way to San Sebastian, I had actually thought I had a chance of winning, and now I wondered if I could compete at all. They had laughed at me. . . . I pulled a sheaf of unused plane tickets out of my pocket. Among them, I had a return portion to the States. I considered using it. *Maybe I should just go home,* I thought, and find something else to do, something I was good at.[9]

What carried him through was natural ability, a fiery competitive nature, and an incredibly positive attitude. The words of his mother were constantly in the back of his mind: "Make an obstacle an opportunity. Make a negative a positive. If you can't give 100 percent, you won't make it. Never quit!"

A Sharp Curve in the Road

In 1996 at age twenty-five, Armstrong was the top-rated cyclist in the world. It looked as though he had finally made it. He was making a good living. He was at the top of his form. And he was winning races against the best in Europe. But then he started experiencing intense pain in his groin and coughing up blood. When he saw a doctor, he found out he had testicular cancer. But the news kept getting worse: The cancer had spread, it was pervasive in his lungs, and his prognosis was grim. Through all that, he kept his positive attitude, his fighting spirit. But then they found cancer in his brain.

"I met a wall," Armstrong says. "Much as I wanted to be positive and unafraid, all I knew was, when people get brain tumors, they don't live."[10]

Armstrong underwent brain surgery and a procedure to remove his cancerous testicle. Then he started the excruciating process of chemotherapy. Doctors told Armstrong he had a 50 percent chance of surviving. After he finished his treatment and his recovery seemed certain, one doctor admitted that his case was the worst the doctor had ever seen, and he had really given Armstrong only a 3 percent chance of living.

Through it all, Armstrong managed his attitude so that he would remain positive. He believes that "hope is the only antidote to fear."[11] When asked if the rigors of cancer treatment had depressed him, Armstrong said no, explaining, "I thought being depressed would be detrimental. . . . I have to say it was a very positive time in my life."[12]

> "Hope is the only antidote to fear."
> —Lance Armstrong

Positive Comeback

Surviving cancer with a positive attitude intact is quite an accomplishment. But Armstrong wanted something more. He wanted to start racing again. He had some difficult moments during his comeback. At one point he actually quit in the middle of a race—something he had never done before. "In the start area, I sat in a car trying to keep warm and thought about how much I didn't want to be there," says Armstrong. "When you start out thinking that way, things can't possibly get any better. Once I got out in the cold, my attitude just deteriorated."[13] But he came back from that setback. And he went on to win not one but *five* consecutive Tour de France races!

Armstrong knows what a great asset a positive attitude is. He commented,

> Without belief, we would be left with nothing but an overwhelming doom, every single day. And it will beat you. I didn't fully see, until the cancer, how we fight every day against the creeping negatives of the world, how we struggle daily against the slow lapping of cynicism. Dispiritedness and disappointment, these were the real perils of life, not some sudden illness or cataclysmic millennium doomsday.[14]

After winning his first Tour de France in 1999, Armstrong spoke to reporters and wanted them to pass along this piece of advice to their readers: "I would just like to say one thing. If you ever get a second chance in life for something, you've got to go all the way."[15] I want to pass that same advice along to you. If your attitude hasn't been good in the past, you've got a second chance. You can change it. You can choose a good attitude and manage it daily. When you do that, a whole new world of possibilities opens up to you.

ATTITUDE APPLICATION AND EXERCISES
CHOOSING AND DISPLAYING THE
RIGHT ATTITUDES DAILY

Your Attitude Decision Today

Where do you stand when it comes to your attitude today? Ask yourself these three questions:

1. *Have I already made the decision to choose and display the right attitude daily?*
2. *If so, when did I make that decision?*
3. *What exactly did I decide? (Write it here.)*

Your Attitude Discipline Every Day

Based on the decision you made concerning attitude, what is the one discipline you must practice *today and every day* in order to be successful? Write it here.

Making Up for Yesterday

If you need some help making the right decision concerning attitude and developing the everyday discipline to live it out, do the following exercises:

1. *Think about all the factors that have contributed to your attitude. Make a list of them here:*

_____

_____

_____

_____

_____

Now forget about them. What happens *to* you is largely outside your control. But what happens *in* you is totally your choice. Your response is what matters. Make a commitment to yourself that you will take *entire* responsibility for your current attitude and that you will *choose* to be positive—no matter what.

2. *Begin working on your bad attitude areas. Make a list of your negative thoughts or habits:*

_____

_____

_____

_____

_____

Now, next to each item, write the positive response or opposite characteristic to that thought. For example, if you wrote that you believe people want to take advantage of you, then write the word "trust" next to it. You can use this list to help you conquer your attitude breakdowns.

3. *Every day, choose one of the positive attitude characteristics from one of your lists (the bad attitude list or the positive qualities list). As you go through your day, make it your objective to exhibit that positive quality. You may even want to give yourself a goal of the*

number of times to do it. Repeat this process until your attitude becomes what you desire it to be.

4. *One of the best ways to remain positive is to express gratitude and appreciation. Find at least one opportunity every day to tell someone how grateful you are.*

5. *Every week, place an attitude quote or a positive saying where you will see it several times a day: on your bathroom mirror, next to your computer at work, in your day planner, etc.*

6. *Set the tone for your day by treating people better than you expect to be treated by them. Be the first to smile. Express your appreciation for them. Expect the best out of them. If you act first, you will set yourself up for success.*

7. *If you find yourself falling back into old negative patterns of thought or action, then make an appointment with yourself midway through the day to check on your attitude. Make an assessment, and if your attitude is not up to par, make an adjustment. The sooner you do it, the better off you'll be.*

Looking Forward to Tomorrow

Spend some time reflecting on how your decision concerning attitude and the daily discipline that comes out of it will positively impact you in the future. What will be the compounding benefits? Write it here.

_____

_____

_____

_____

Keep what you've written as a constant reminder, because . . .
Reflection today motivates your discipline every day, and
Discipline every day maximizes your decision of yesterday.

CHAPTER 4

Today's **PRIORITIES** Give Me Focus

What would you do if you suddenly found yourself independently wealthy and the owner of a successful multimillion-dollar business? That's the question Howard Hughes found himself facing when he was only eighteen years old. Hughes's mother had died during surgery in 1922 when he was sixteen. When his father died of a heart attack less than two years later, the young man inherited the Hughes Tool Company.

Hughes's father, Howard Hughes Sr., had built his company from the ground up. Born in 1869, he worked in the Missouri zinc and lead mining industries in the 1890s. When he heard about the major petroleum discovery near Beaumont, Texas, in 1901, he recognized it as the opening of a new industry offering great opportunities. (In one day of production, the first well had produced half the United States' cumulative oil production.) He soon moved to Texas and started a drilling business with partner Walter B. Sharp.

For seven years they worked successfully. But then they were unable to complete jobs that involved drilling two different wells because they could not drill through especially hard rock. To solve the problem, Hughes Sr. went off and invented (and patented) rotary bits to do the job. The equipment revolutionized the industry. Within five years, his bits were being used in eleven states and thirteen foreign countries. Between 1908 and 1924, he obtained seventy-three patents and became wealthy.[1] He is reported to have said about his drill bits, "We don't have a monopoly. People who want to drill for oil and not use the Hughes bit can always use a pick and shovel."

Who Wants to Be a Millionaire?

When the senior Hughes died, his son became a millionaire. He hired a management company to run the Hughes Tool Company, and then he thought about what he wanted to do with his life. As a boy, he had loved all kinds of machines. He had built a radio and talked to ship captains when he was in his early teens. And he had gotten a barnstormer to give him flying lessons secretly when he was fifteen. He was intelligent, and the whole world was open to him.

He decided to go into the moviemaking business. After marrying a Houston socialite, he promptly moved to Los Angeles. *Biography* writer Michael Sauter says, "The impulsiveness of the move would become typical of Hughes, who repeatedly threw himself into expensively risky ventures like a boy obsessed with a new hobby."[2] Soon Hughes was producing movies and buying theaters in which to show them. His work got little attention until he made an aviation movie called *Hell's Angels,* which he also directed. He later went on to produce *The Front Page* and *Scarface,* both hits. He was in a position to build a major studio and become a force in Hollywood, but by then he had lost his focus. He seemed to be more interested in pursuing glamorous Hollywood actresses than in making movies. His wife divorced him in 1929.

In the late 1920s, he turned his attention to aviation. He received a pilot's license in 1928, and soon he was experimenting with aircraft design. He started his own aircraft company in 1932: Hughes Aviation. He'd buy a plane, strip it down, and redesign it for speed. Then he worked as his own test pilot. For several years he set many of the world's airspeed records. For a decade, he repeated the pattern of redesigning planes and pushing them to the limit from the cockpit.

Then in 1940, when Trans World Airlines was in need of cash, Hughes was invited to invest in the company. He didn't just invest; he bought a controlling interest. At that time he decided he wanted to make air travel more popular, so he engaged Lockheed to build planes for TWA according to his specifications. The next year, he opened a large aircraft manufacturing plant of his own in Los Angeles, which supplied parts in support of the war in Europe. Meanwhile, Hughes continued to dabble in the entertainment business, producing and sometimes directing movies.

In September of 1942, Hughes added another major activity to his agenda. He was awarded a contract from the government to construct prototypes of flying boats. He agreed to deliver the planes in 1944 for a cost of $18 million. For the next several years, he worked on developing the planes. But by 1945, he still had not delivered any planes to the government, despite having spent over $800 million, including the construction of a huge hangar for $175 million.[3] His lack of focus not only prevented him from succeeding in that venture, it also led to a mental breakdown (one of three he experienced).

Anything Goes

Howard Hughes went on to buy RKO Pictures, several small airlines, television stations, and numerous hotels and casinos in Las Vegas. No matter what got his attention, he was able to do it thanks to Hughes Tool Company, which bankrolled his pursuits. But nothing seemed to maintain his attention for long, and nothing seemed to satisfy him. He got married again in 1957, but he and his second wife drifted apart. In 1966, he moved to Las Vegas without informing her, and despite numerous attempts, she was never able to see him again. A few years later, he left the country. By then he was becoming more and more eccentric. The rumor was that he lived like a hermit, was phobic about germs, and had succumbed to drug addiction. In 1976, he died while being flown back to the United States for medical treatment.

There are those who would call Hughes a success because of his wealth; he was the nation's first billionaire and at one time the wealthiest person in the world. But when I read about Hughes, I see a broken life of unfulfilled potential. He was unable to sustain any long-term relationships. His marriages didn't last. He had no children. And the only companies he owned that thrived are the ones he either never ran or eventually relinquished control of. He transferred ownership of Hughes Aircraft to the nonprofit Howard Hughes Medical Institute in 1955, drove RKO Pictures into bankruptcy in 1958, and relinquished control of TWA when it neared collapse in 1960. In 1971, he signed away control of the remainder of his empire. He died alienated and alone.

Why Priorities Matter Today

Business consultant and author Michael LeBoef says, "Devoting a little of yourself to everything means committing a great deal of

> "Devoting a little of yourself to everything means committing a great deal of yourself to nothing."
>
> —MICHAEL LEBOEF

yourself to nothing." That aptly describes the life of Howard Hughes. Focused concentration is one of the keys to success. To have focus, you must understand priorities. Here's why:

TIME IS OUR MOST PRECIOUS COMMODITY

Given the choice, would you rather save time or money? Most people focus on dollars. But how you spend your time is much more important than how you spend your money. Money mistakes can often be corrected, but when you lose time, it's gone forever.

Your priorities determine how you spend your time, and time is precious. The following statements may help you put time in perspective:

To know the value of *one year* . . . ask the student who failed the final exam.

To know the value of *one month* . . . ask the mother of a premature baby.

To know the value of *one week* . . . ask the editor of a weekly newsmagazine.

To know the value of *one day* . . . ask the wage earner who has six children.

To know the value of *one hour* . . . ask the lovers who are waiting to meet.

To know the value of *one minute* . . . ask the person who missed the plane.

To know the value of *one second* . . . ask the person who survived the accident.

To know the value of *one millisecond* . . . ask the Olympic silver medalist.[4]

Your time is priceless. As Ralph Waldo Emerson advised, "Guard well your spare moments. They are like uncut diamonds. Discard them and their value will never be known. Improve them and they will become the brightest gems in a useful life."

WE CANNOT CHANGE TIME, ONLY OUR PRIORITIES

Have you ever found yourself thinking, *I need more time?* Well you're not going to get it! No one gets more time. There are 1,440 minutes in a day. No matter what you do, you won't get more today.

Sales consultant and author Myers Barnes says, "Time management has nothing to do with the clock, but everything to do with organizing and controlling your participation in certain events that coordinate with the clock.

> Since you can't change time, you must instead change your approach to it.

Einstein understood time management is an oxymoron. It cannot be managed. You can't save time, lose time, turn back the hands of time or have more time tomorrow than today. Time is unemotional, uncontrolled, unencumbered. It moves forward regardless of circumstances and, in the game of life, creates a level playing field for everyone."[5] Since you can't change time, you must instead change your approach to it.

WE CANNOT DO EVERYTHING

There was a time in my life when I thought I could do everything, but I was very young, energetic, and naive. Chinese author and philosopher Lin Yutang said, "Besides the noble art of getting things done, there is the noble art of leaving things undone. The wisdom of life consists of the elimination of nonessentials."

You can have anything you want, but you cannot have everything you want. You have to choose. Excellence comes from doing the right things right. You've got to let go of the rest. If you're not sure what the right things are, pretend you have only six months to live. The things you would do in that short time are the right things.

WE CHOOSE OUR LIFE BY HOW WE SPEND TIME

Everything you now do is something you have chosen to do. Some people don't want to believe that. But if you're over age twenty-one, your life is what you're making of it. To change your life, you need to change your priorities.

Jack Welpott, who ran the photography program at San Francisco State University for many years, was once asked how he was able to teach so effectively and create art so prolifically. Here was his answer: "From the day I was hired I began cultivating a reputation within the Art Department of being sort of a flake. I found that after a year or so of losing track of my committee assignments, forgetting to answer memos, and missing departmental meetings— well, after a while they just stopped *asking* me to do all those things." Welpott placed a higher priority on creating art and teaching others to do the same than he did on the politics and bureaucracy of university life. You may not necessarily endorse the way he achieved his priorities, but you have to agree that he knew what they were.

PRIORITIES HELP US TO CHOOSE WISELY

Author Robert J. McKain says, "The reason most goals are not achieved is that we spend our time doing second things first." Let's face it, there are a lot of things vying for your attention. Many people want to put you on their agenda. Thousands of manufacturers want you to spend your money on their products. Even your own desires can be so diverse and your attention so scattered that you often aren't sure what should get your concentration. That's why you need to focus. To be successful, you can't just run on the fast track; run on *your* track. People who

> To be successful, you can't just run on the fast track; run on *your* track.

reach their potential and fulfill their dreams determine and act on their priorities daily.

Making the Decision to Determine and Act on Important Priorities Daily

When I first graduated from college and began my career, I was not working according to my own agenda. Back in the 1960s when I studied for the ministry, the majority of my course work had prepared me to do counseling and administration. So when I began working in 1969, guess what I spent most of my time doing. That's right, counseling and administration. Nothing could have been further from my natural gifts—or my natural inclinations. Despite much hard work, I was neither fulfilled nor effective.

Because I wanted to improve myself and pick up skills I didn't learn in college, in 1971 I began working on a business degree. While reading for one of the courses, I came across a paragraph written about Italian economist Vilfredo Pareto. It contained information about prioritizing called the Pareto Principle. It said that by focusing your attention on the top 20 percent of all your priorities, you would get an 80 percent return on your effort. That was my eureka moment! That's when I made this decision: *I will prioritize my life and give focus and energy to those things that give the highest return.*

I never looked at myself or my work the same again. I realized that I needed to focus 80 percent of my time, energy, and resources on my areas of strength, not on counseling and administration. Those activities were not bad things. They were just bad things for me. From the moment I made that decision, I have been a practitioner of the Pareto Principle, and I have taught it to others for thirty-three years. (If you want to read a more in-depth treatment of the Pareto Principle, read *Developing the Leader Within You.*)

Most of the time this has kept me focused and on track, although when I first began applying it, the results sometimes didn't work out the way I intended. Margaret and I still laugh about the time she asked me to start helping her mow the lawn. "Margaret," I said, having *just* learned Pareto, "I don't want to waste time on something like that. I'm trying to stay focused. We can *pay* somebody to do that."

Margaret looked at me and replied, "Pay with what?" We worked it out, but it was a defining moment for us. From that time on, I have tried to focus on those things that are important and not get sidetracked.

If you want to change the way you look at yourself and what you do by making a decision concerning your priorities, then do the following:

TAKE BACK TODAY

Have you ever noticed that the people who have nothing to do usually want to spend their time with you? Poet Carl Sandburg said, "Time is the most valuable coin in your life. You and you alone will determine how that coin will be spent. Be careful that you do not let other people spend it for you."

Your greatest possession is the twenty-four hours you have directly ahead of you. How will you spend it? Will you give in to pressure or focus on priorities? Will you allow pointless e-mails, unimportant tasks, telemarketers, interruptions, and other distractions to consume your day? Or will you take complete responsibility for how you spend your time, take control of the things you can, and make today yours? If you don't decide how your day will be spent, someone else will.

ASK YOURSELF THREE QUESTIONS

No Daily Dozen issue has added more to my success than the principle of priorities. When I discovered that I needed to change my approach to my day and my career, I started by asking myself three critical questions:

1. **What is *required* of me?** Any realistic assessment of priorities in any area of life must start with a realistic assessment of what a person *must* do. For you to be a good spouse or parent, what is required of you? To satisfy your employer, what must you do? (If you lead others, then the question should be, What must you personally do that cannot be delegated to anyone else?) When ordering priorities, always start with the requirement question and give it careful thought before moving on to the next question.

2. **What gives me the greatest *return*?** As you progress in your career, you begin to discover that some activities yield a much higher return for the effort than others do. (Anyone who hasn't discovered that probably *isn't* progressing in his career!) The next place to focus your attention is on those high-return activities.

3. **What gives me the greatest *reward*?** If you do only what you must and what is effective, you will be highly productive, but you may not be content. I think it's also important to consider what gives you personal satisfaction. However, I find that some people want to start with the *reward* question and go no further than that. No one can be successful who doesn't possess

the discipline to take care of the first two areas before adding the third.

Philosopher William James said, "The art of being wise is the art of knowing what to overlook." If you bring your priorities into focus by answering those three questions, you will have a much better idea of what you should overlook.

> "The art of being wise is the art of knowing what to overlook."
>
> —WILLIAM JAMES

STAY IN YOUR STRENGTH ZONE

People don't pay for average. People don't go looking for a mediocre restaurant and middling movie when they go out at night. Employers don't award the contract to the salesman known as Mr. Average. Nobody says, "Let's give the contract to the company that will do a merely adequate job."

It was a great day in my church when I stopped counseling people and stopped getting bogged down in administrative details. But finding my strength zone took some time and exploration. If you don't already have a good handle on your strengths, then you may want to explore some of these suggestions. They're based on what I did to find mine:

- ◆ **Trial and Error:** Nothing teaches you more than your successes and failures. Any time something seems to be all "trial," and you make a lot of mistakes, it's probably time to move on. But you've got to take the risk of failing to find your successes.
- ◆ **The Counsel of Others:** Asking others to evaluate your effectiveness is not always fun, but it is always helpful. Be sure to choose people who don't have an agenda—other than to help you.

- **Personality Tests:** Evaluations, such as DISC, Florence Littauer's Personality Profile, and Myers-Briggs, can be very helpful. They will help to clarify some of your natural inclinations and help to reveal some strengths and weaknesses you aren't aware of.
- **Personal Experience:** You really get a feel for how well you do something by doing it repeatedly. Just remember this: Experience isn't always the best teacher—evaluated experience is!

British prime minister William Gladstone said, "He is a wise man who wastes no energy on pursuits for which he is not fitted; and he is wiser still who from among the things he can do well, chooses and resolutely follows the best." The more you stay in your strength zone, the greater your productivity and the greater your ability to reach your potential.

> Experience isn't always the best teacher— evaluated experience is!

Managing the Disciplines of Priorities

One of the things I noticed very quickly after making my priorities decision was that priorities shift very easily. For that reason they must be continually evaluated and guarded. My reminder to manage the disciplines of priorities is this: *Every day I will live my life according to my priorities.* What does that mean? Five things:

1. EVALUATE PRIORITIES DAILY

A man went to the Super Bowl and climbed to the top row in the end zone section of the stadium to reach his seat. After the game started, he spotted an empty seat on the fifty-yard line. After working his way down to it, he asked the man in the next seat, "Excuse me, but is anyone sitting here?"

"No," replied the man. "Actually, the seat belongs to me. I was supposed to come with my wife, but she died. This is the first Super Bowl we haven't been to together since we got married in 1967."

"That's very sad. But still, couldn't you find anyone else to take the seat—a relative or close friend?"

"No," replied the man, "they're all at the funeral."

Priorities don't stay put; you have to revisit them every day. Why? Because conditions continually change. So do methods of getting things done. Your values, once defined, are going to be steady. You will be able to rely on them. But how you carry them out needs to be flexible.

2. PLAN YOUR TIME CAREFULLY

I once read that Charles Schwab, president of Bethlehem Steel in the early twentieth century, met with public relations and management consultant Ivy Lee because he wanted to improve his company's productivity. "We know what we should be doing," explained Schwab. "Now, if you can show us a better way of getting it done, I'll listen to you—and pay you anything within reason."

Lee said that he could help him, and that it would take only twenty minutes of his time. He handed Schwab a blank sheet of paper and said, "Write down the six most important things you have to do tomorrow." Schwab complied.

"Now number them in the order of their importance to you and the company." When Schwab had finished, Lee continued, "Now put that paper in your pocket, and first thing tomorrow morning, take it out and look at item number one. Don't look at the others, just number one, and start working on it and stay with it until it's completed. Then take item number two the same way, then number three, and so on until you have to quit for the day. Don't worry if you have finished only one or two. You'll be working on the most important ones. The others you could not have finished with any other method. And without some kind of system, you'd probably take ten times as long to finish them—and might not even have them in the order of their importance.

"Do this every workday," said Lee. "After you're convinced of the value of this system, have your people try it out. Try it as long as you like, and then send me a check for whatever you think the idea is worth."

In a few weeks, Schwab sent Lee a check for $25,000 along with a letter saying that it was the most profitable lesson he had ever learned. Not long after that, Bethlehem Steel became the largest independent steel producer of its day.

According to a survey taken by Day-Timers, Inc., only one-third of American workers plan their daily schedules. And only 9 percent follow through and complete what they planned.[6] If you want to be effective, you must be able to make the transition to planning. I plan my calendar forty days at a time. But when I get ready to approach a day, I have the whole thing laid out. Hour by hour. It's a rare day that I get up in the morning wondering what I will be doing that day—even when on vacation.

3. FOLLOW YOUR PLAN

I don't mean to insult your intelligence by suggesting that you follow your plan, but it needs to be said. According to time management expert Alec Mackenzie, surveys show that most executives don't get to their most important tasks until midafternoon. Why? Most finished off low-priority tasks so that they could have a sense of accomplishment.[7]

German novelist Johann Wolfgang von Goethe said, "Things

that matter most must never be at the mercy of things that matter least." If you prioritize your life and plan your day but don't follow through, your results will be the same as those of someone who didn't prioritize at all.

4. DELEGATE WHENEVER POSSIBLE

I've observed that most people fall into one of two categories when it comes to delegation; they're either clingers or dumpers. Clingers refuse to let go of anything they think is important—whether they are the best person to do it or not. Their goal is perfection. Dumpers are quick to get rid of tasks, yet give little thought to how successful their delegation efforts will be. Their goal is to get things off their desk.

How do you find the right standard for delegation? When is it right to hand something off, and when is it right to hold on to it? Here's the guideline I use: If someone else can do a task I'm doing 80 percent as well as I do, then I hand it off. That's pretty darned good. And if I do a good job of motivating, encouraging, and rewarding them, then they will only get better. I've handed off responsibilities using that standard, and after a while, the person who's taken on the job has gone on to do it much better than I could. When that happens, it's very rewarding.

Today I am surrounded by people on my team who do things much better than I can. They make up the difference in my weak areas, and they exceed my expectations in others. They lift me to a level higher than I could ever attain myself, and they allow me to live out my priorities. The advice of management expert Peter Drucker is true: "No executive has ever suffered because his subordinates were strong and effective."

> "No executive has ever suffered because his subordinates were strong and effective."
> —PETER DRUCKER

5. INVEST IN THE RIGHT PEOPLE DAILY

There's one more area I want to address in the area of priorities, and that's the need to prioritize how we spend time with people. My friend Waylon Moore has observed that often "we spend priority time with problem people when we should be spending it with potential people." I think that's true.

How do you decide whom to spend time with? Certainly, you want to treat everyone with respect and try to have a good, positive relationship with everyone. But you should not spend time with everyone equally. Here's what I use to evaluate where to invest my time:

- Value to the team
- Natural ability
- Responsibility
- Timing
- Potential
- Mentoring fit

The person I currently most enjoy mentoring is Kevin Small, the president of INJOY, one of my companies. His talent is huge. His potential is limitless. No one impacts the team the way he does. He is already one of the finest young executives in the country at age thirty-two. I can't wait to see how he develops over the next decade.

Reflecting on Priorities

I am grateful that I learned to prioritize my life early in my career. No decision I've made has had as great an impact on my life and career. Here's how:

In my 20s . . .   My priorities took away the guilt of not doing everything.

In my 30s . . .   My priorities helped me separate my strengths from my weaknesses.

In my 40s . . .   My priorities gave me a high return on my work.

In my 50s . . .   My priorities allow me to staff according to my weaknesses.

If you want to increase your focus and become effective on a level you've never experienced before, then make a decision to prioritize your life and manage the discipline of priorities every day.

Children Are Her Priority

Any time people reach the highest level in their profession, you can be sure that priorities have been very important to them. That was certainly the case with Betsy Rogers, a teacher in Leeds, Alabama, who became the 2003 National Teacher of the Year. Rogers can't remember a time when she didn't want to be a teacher. It was in her blood—and in her family. Her grandmother taught in rural Alabama beginning when she was only sixteen years old. Both her grandmother's sisters followed her into the profession. And Rogers's mother taught Sunday school for fifty years. So when she went off to college, she naturally studied to become a teacher too.

"I wanted to change the world for them," says Rogers. "It took me several years to realize I could not change the world in which my students lived. But by understanding that school was the best place for some of my children, I became committed to making my classroom a place where students feel safe as well as creating an environment that provides joy to those with unfortunate lives."[8]

Rogers began teaching in 1974, immediately after finishing her degree. She took six years off to take care of her sons until they were school age, but she knew that as soon as they were old enough, she would be back in the classroom. And being connected in the community where she would teach was a priority. So in the early 1980s, she and her husband bought an abandoned farm near her school. Rogers says,

> When my husband and I moved our family from a more affluent neighborhood to Leeds twenty-one years ago, our purpose was to raise our children in an environment with a more diverse population with a rural background. . . . Many of my colleagues do not believe it is beneficial to live in the community where you teach, but I have found this relationship with the Leeds community to be very rewarding and productive. By living and working in Leeds, I truly became a stakeholder in the community.[9]

By making that community connection a priority, she has been better able to help her students. She reaches out to parents, has students over to her house, and attends many of their extracurricular activities. "We should be very proud of our profession," she says, "and we need to be models. We shouldn't lose sight of the fact that we have impact we may never see."[10]

Focused on Improvement

Because Rogers is focused, she is constantly improving and working to reach her potential in her profession. She believes that teachers must model a dedication to lifelong learning. And she doesn't just give lip service to it. When both her sons were in college, she went back to school herself. She has since earned three graduate degrees—in 1998, 2000, and 2002.

As National Teacher of the Year, she will be expected to spend a year visiting schools and serving as an international spokeswoman for education. When she's finished, she could use the recognition she has received as a springboard to a plum teaching job or a higher paying administrative position. But that's not what she's about. According to county superintendent Bob Neighbors, Rogers has inquired about going back to work in a county school on academic alert because of poor test scores.[11] After all, what's the use of improving herself if she can't use what she's learned to help others? Neighbors calls Rogers "one of those extraordinary naturals for whom teaching is not only her vocation, it is her joy, her daily discovery and her avocation."[12] Rogers sums it up this way: "I was taught that we are here on this earth to serve."[13] That's her priority—and she is living it out every day!

PRIORITIES Application and Exercises
Determining and Acting on Important
Priorities Daily

Your Priorities Decision Today

Where do you stand when it comes to priorities today? Ask yourself these three questions:

1. Have I already made the decision to determine and act on important priorities daily?

2. If so, when did I make that decision?

3. What exactly did I decide? (Write it here.)

_____

_____

_____

_____

_____

_____

Your Priorities Discipline Every Day

Based on the decision you made concerning priorities, what is the one discipline you must practice *today and every day* in order to be successful? Write it here.

_____

_____

_____

_____

_____

_____

Making Up for Yesterday

If you need some help making the right decision concerning attitude and developing the everyday discipline to live it out, do the following exercises:

1. *How have you looked at time in the past? Have you seen it as a precious commodity or have you been lackadaisical about it? How has your approach to time shaped your life so far?*

2. *Take a day off from work to really reflect on these questions in the chapter:*

   What is required of you?
   What gives you the highest return?
   What gives you the greatest reward?

   How will your assessment in those three areas prompt you to change your life?

3. *Practice a priority approach to going after a major goal that you currently have on your agenda using the following pattern:*

   ◆ *Prioritize: Know what is important.*
   ◆ *Organize: Decide how will it be done.*
   ◆ *Plan: Decide when you will do it.*
   ◆ *Communicate: Share your priorities with your team.*
   ◆ *Execute: Follow through on your plan.*
   ◆ *Evaluate: Examine yourself and your results in light of your priorities.*

Looking Forward to Tomorrow

Spend some time reflecting on how your decision concerning priorities and the daily discipline that comes out of it will positively impact you in the future. What will be the compounding benefits? Write them here.

Keep what you've written as a constant reminder, because . . .
Reflection today motivates your discipline every day, and
Discipline every day maximizes your decision of yesterday.

CHAPTER 5

Today's **HEALTH** Gives Me Strength

I need to begin this chapter by making a confession. Usually when people pick up a book, especially a book that contains advice, they expect the author to be an expert in every area he writes about. That is not the case with me when it comes to health.

For much of my life, I have dropped the ball in this area. It was really more a matter of neglect than anything else. I've always been as healthy as a horse. The only thing that regularly bothers me is seasonal allergies, and I just work around them. In fact, in thirty years of public speaking, first as a pastor and then as a conference and seminar leader, I have never missed an engagement due to illness. Not one! I just don't get sick, and I've always had lots of energy. Even when I had to burn the candle at both ends, I still had plenty of energy left over.

I have lived a very fast-paced life. For about ten years, I held down two demanding jobs. I led a church of more than 3,000 people with a staff of over 50 and a budget of $5 million a year. At the same time, I led a leadership development organization that required me to travel to speak more than 100 days a year. When I gave up the pastorate to dedicate my time to my organization, I nearly doubled my travel. I also built up the company and increased the number of employees from 18 to 175.

Maintaining a lifestyle at that pace meant that I rarely exercised, I didn't eat well, and I was overweight. But I didn't worry. Every year I took a physical and received an excellent report from my doctor. So I simply took my health for granted.

Party Hearty

All that changed for me on December 18, 1998. That was the night of the annual Christmas party for my employees and their spouses. We had all enjoyed a nice dinner at the 755 Club at Atlanta's Turner Field where the Braves play, and many of us were enjoying music and doing some dancing. At the end of the party, I didn't feel well. One of my employees gave me a good-bye hug and felt cold sweat on the back of my neck. Then suddenly I felt an excruciating pain in my chest that brought me to my knees. I had never experienced anything like it. As I lay on the floor awaiting the paramedics, it felt like an elephant was sitting on my chest. I was grateful that Margaret, our children, and many of my closest friends were there with me at the party, because I thought I wasn't going to make it.

When I got to the hospital, I was told I was having a serious heart attack. As I lay in the emergency room for the next few hours with doctors trying different treatments, none of which seemed to be working, my assistant, Linda Eggers, made a phone call. Six months earlier a cardiologist from Nashville named John

Bright Cage had met me for lunch and shared his concern for my health. At the end of our conversation, he said that if I ever needed his help, I could call him, day or night, and he included his home phone number. So even though it was 2:00 a.m., Linda called him. Less than an hour later, in walked Dr. Jeff Marshall and some of his colleagues, announcing, "The A-team is here." Dr. Cage had called one of the finest cardiologists in Atlanta and asked him to help me.

In the wee hours of the morning, Dr. Marshall performed a procedure to remove a clot that had made its way into my heart. He saved my life. Afterward, he explained that he had used a new procedure that had only recently been developed. If I'd had my heart attack a year or two earlier, nothing could have been done. It would have killed me!

Why Health Matters Today

It almost seems too obvious to mention that your health matters today, yet I believe I must say it, because many people treat their bodies the way I did for more than fifty years. So here's a reminder of what's at stake when it comes to health:

YOUR HEALTH IMPACTS YOU EMOTIONALLY, INTELLECTUALLY, AND SPIRITUALLY

You can escape from a lot of things that might hurt you. You can quit a hazardous job. You can move from one climate to another. You can stay away from someone who wants to harm you. But you can't get away from your body. For as long as you live, you're stuck with it. If you make choices that cause you to be continually hurting or unhealthy, it will affect every aspect of your life—your heart, mind, and spirit. Think about how hard it is to be positive, concentrate, or pray when you have a toothache. More serious conditions can be even more distracting.

HEALTH OFTEN DETERMINES QUALITY AS WELL AS QUANTITY OF LIFE

My friend Zig Ziglar asks the question, "If you had a million-dollar racehorse, would you allow it to smoke cigarettes, drink whiskey, and stay out all night? How about a thousand-dollar dog?" Of course you wouldn't. A thoroughbred horse that was not taken care of would never be capable of winning a race. A dog whose health ran down would not work effectively or show well. The real question is, If you wouldn't allow your animals to do such things, then why would you allow yourself to?

Have you ever known people who used excessive amounts of alcohol, drugs or tobacco? Such abuses sometimes cause early death. Others become old before their time and suffer serious health problems.

IT'S EASIER TO MAINTAIN GOOD HEALTH THAN TO REGAIN IT

People are funny. When they are young, they will spend their health to get wealth. Later, they will gladly pay all they have trying to get their health back. I fell into a similar trap, even though I wasn't trying to accumulate wealth. I was driven by a sense of mission and the desire to achieve. That caused me to make a number of costly mistakes:

- ◆ I was arrogant about my health.
- ◆ I thought because I felt good, I was healthy.
- ◆ I worked too hard.
- ◆ I did not exercise enough.

◆ I didn't listen to loving friends who tried to warn me about my lifestyle.

It's always easier to maintain good health than to regain it. (Remember what it felt like trying to get back in shape to play a sport after an off-season of inactivity?) Unfortunately, some lapses in health are permanent, and you can't get back what you've lost.

> People are funny. When they are young, they will spend their health to get wealth. Later, they will gladly pay all they have trying to get their health back.

Making the Decision to Know and Follow Healthy Guidelines Daily

As I recovered from my heart attack in the hospital, I felt very fortunate to be alive. Cardiovascular diseases are the number one cause of death in the United States and Europe.[1] But I didn't discover how blessed I was until Dr. Marshall told me that I had sustained no damage to my heart. That meant I had the potential to make a full recovery.

Dr. Marshall told me that men who survive an early heart attack (and learn from it) often live longer and healthier lives than those who never suffer a heart attack. The key to my future health would be whether I was willing to make the decision to change the way I lived and stick with it. More specifically, he asked me to eat low-fat foods and exercise every day. I had of course tried to put myself on diets before. But they often worked out something like this:

Breakfast
1/2 grapefruit
1 slice plain whole wheat toast
8 oz. skim milk

Lunch
4 oz. broiled skinless chicken breast
1 cup steamed broccoli
1 Oreo cookie
Unsweetened tea

Midafternoon Snack
The rest of the package of Oreos
1 qt. Rocky Road ice cream
1 jar of fudge

Dinner
2 loaves garlic bread
Large pepperoni pizza
Pitcher of Coke
3 Milky Way candy bars
Entire frozen cheesecake eaten at the freezer

No more! At the age of fifty-one, I made this health decision: *I will take good care of myself by exercising and eating right.*

If you know the value of good health, yet you've had a hard time making the commitment to know and follow healthy guidelines, here are some suggestions to help you turn your attention to the subject and tackle it:

HAVE A PURPOSE WORTH LIVING FOR

Nothing is better than perspective for helping a person want to do the right thing. When you have something to live for, not only does it make you desire a long life, but it also helps you to see the importance of the steps along the way. Seeing the big picture enables us to put up with little irritations.

It's hard to find motivation in the moment when there is no

hope in the future. A sense of purpose helps a person to make a decision to change and then to follow through with the discipline required to make that change permanent. I found that to be true after my heart attack. A friend

> It's hard to find motivation in the moment when there is no hope in the future.

who spent a lot of time with me during my recovery saw me pass on desserts time after time—something that was not characteristic of me—and finally he asked, "Have you lost your craving for desserts?"

"No," I answered, "but my craving for life is greater."

DO WORK YOU ENJOY

One of the greatest causes of debilitating stress in people's lives is doing jobs they don't enjoy. It's like comedienne Lily Tomlin said, "The problem with the rat race is that even if you win, you're still a rat." I believe two major frustrations contribute to that stress. The first is doing work you don't think is important. If you do work that you believe adds no value to yourself or to others, you quickly become demoralized. If you work in that state for a long time, it begins to wear you down. To remain healthy, your work must be in alignment with your values.

Another reason some people don't like their work is because they do jobs that keep them in an area of weakness. Nobody can do that long and succeed. For example, most people hate the thought of public speaking. How would you like to get up in front of an audience and speak to them every day? That's some people's number one fear. But for me, that's my greatest joy. After speaking to people for six or seven hours at a conference, I'm not tired. I'm fired up! Speaking to an audience energizes me.

One of the ways you can tell you're working in an area of strength is that it actually gives you energy. Even if you are in the early stages of your career or are starting out on a new venture and you're not very good at something you're doing, you can still tell it's an area of strength by paying attention to how you respond to your failures. Mistakes that challenge you show your areas of strength. Mistakes that threaten you show your areas of weakness.

FIND YOUR PACE

Mickey Mantle reportedly said, "If I had known I was going to live this long, I would have taken better care of myself." I think that statement could apply to many people as they age. Part of taking care of yourself includes finding and maintaining the pace that's right for you. If you take life more slowly than your energy level is capable of, you can become lazy. If you continually run at a pace faster than you are capable, you can burn out. You need to find your balance.

> Mickey Mantle reportedly said, "If I had known I was going to live this long, I would have taken better care of myself."

As I mentioned previously, I've always been a high-energy person, and I always thought there was nothing I couldn't do. But in 1995, when I was forty-seven years old, I was so tired of leading my church and my own organization that I was worn out. I loved both, but doing them at the same time for over a decade was finally taking its toll on me.

One day I told Margaret, "I can't keep doing this. I've got to give up one or the other." Margaret had been advising me for years to cut back my busy schedule, but she was shocked by my statement.

"John," she said, "in all the years I've known you, that's the first time I've ever heard you say you are exhausted."

Even today, at age fifty-seven, I still have a tendency to take on too much and go at a faster pace than is really good for me. There are so many opportunities I want to pursue, books I want to write, and people I want to help. I'm constantly trying to strike a balance between my desire to maintain a healthy pace of life and my drive to accomplish all I can during my lifetime.

ACCEPT YOUR PERSONAL WORTH

During the weeks and months after the terrorist attack on New York's World Trade Center, the song "God Bless America" regained popularity and was performed repeatedly at ball games and other events. The song was written by Irving Berlin, creator of innumerable popular and Broadway hits such as "White Christmas," "Easter Parade," "Puttin' on the Ritz," and "There's No Business Like Show Business." Back when I lived in San Diego, I remember reading an interview with Berlin in the *Union Tribune* in which Don Freeman asked the songwriter whether there was a question he wished someone would have asked him. Berlin replied, "Yes, there is one. 'What do you think of the many songs you've written that didn't become hits?' My reply would be that I *still* think they are wonderful!"

Berlin had a good sense of self-worth and confidence in his work, regardless of whether it was accepted by others. That's certainly not true of everyone. In fact, a poor or distorted self-image is the cause of many health-threatening conditions and activities, from drug use and alcoholism to eating disorders and obesity.

Psychologist Joyce Brothers says, "An individual's self-concept affects every aspect of human behavior. The ability to learn . . . the capacity to grow and change . . . the choice of friends, mates, and careers. It is no exaggeration to say that a strong

> "It is no exaggeration to say that a strong positive self-image is the best possible preparation for success in life."
>
> —DR. JOYCE BROTHERS

positive self-image is the best possible preparation for success in life." If your self-image is driving you to do things that negatively impact your health, seek help.

LAUGH

Physician Bernie S. Siegel wrote in *Peace, Love and Healing*, "I've done the research and I hate to tell you, but everybody dies— lovers, joggers, vegetarians and non-smokers. I'm telling you this so that some of you who jog at 5 a.m. and eat vegetables will occasionally sleep late and have an ice cream cone."[2]

We should never take life or ourselves too seriously. Each of us has idiosyncrasies that can cause us to despair or to laugh. For example, when it comes to anything related to tools or technology, I'm clueless. I'm not Mr. Handyman—I'm Mr. Hopeless. I don't let that bother me at all. If you can laugh at yourself loudly and often, you will find it liberating. There's no better way to prevent stress from becoming distress.

Managing the Disciplines of Health

For some people, the disciplines of health appear to be easy. My friend Bill Hybels seems to manage them well. He eats well, runs regularly, and keeps his weight down. For years before I had my heart attack, he used to challenge me to take better care of myself. He used to joke to friends that while he was eating birdseed, I was eating steaks and rich desserts. He was right about it catching up with me. Although much of my problem was hereditary, my lifestyle made things worse.

After meeting with Dr. Marshall following my heart attack, I had a new discipline to manage: *Every day I will eat low-fat foods and exercise for at least thirty-five minutes.* He told me that 85 percent of all heart patients quit their healthy regimen within six months. Even though I had not succeeded in this area my first fifty years, I was determined to succeed in it the rest of my life.

Margaret and I learned everything we could about heart issues, low-fat diets, and exercise. I became a model of discipline. And in May of 2001 when I visited Dr. Marshall, he congratulated me. "John," he said, "you're doing all the right things. You don't need to consider yourself a heart patient anymore."

I wish I had never heard those words. You see, I love food, and I possess a "foodaholic" bent. Because of the good news I received from Dr. Marshall, I gave myself permission to cheat on my diet once in a while—something I had not done even once in two and a half years. A few weeks later, Margaret and I went on vacation to London with some friends, and I ate food that I had not touched in all that time. I loved every bit of it, especially the fish and chips.

The problem was that I quit managing my life according to the decision I had made. I had relaxed my discipline. Once my commitment was less than 100 percent, I got into trouble. I need to exercise and stay on my diet *every day.* But I began to slide: from every day, to most days, to some days. I ignored my own teaching that **today matters.** Neglect enough todays, and you'll experience the "someday" you've wanted to avoid!

> Neglect enough todays, and you'll experience the "someday" you've wanted to avoid!

The good news is that I'm no longer "off the wagon." I'm recommitted to my daily discipline. The bad news is that I'm doing only 80 percent of what I was doing before. Dr. Marshall is trying to help me. He's a good doctor and a good friend, and he knows that sometimes the best medicine is a good kick in the butt. The area of health is still a battle, but it's one I'm determined to win. As I fight the good fight, I hope you'll join me by doing the following things daily:

EAT RIGHT

One day an old couple died in a car crash. They had been married for sixty years, and they were in excellent health due to the wife's insistence that they exercise and adhere to a healthy diet. In heaven, St. Peter met them at the gate and ushered them to their mansion. It was equipped with a massive kitchen, an elegant master suite, and a Jacuzzi.

"This is wonderful," said the man. "But how much is it going to cost us?"

"Nothing, of course," answered St. Peter. "This is heaven." He then ushered the couple outside and showed them that their house was on the eighteenth fairway of a golf course exactly like that at Augusta.

"You can play as much golf as you like," said St. Peter. "This week it's Augusta. Next week it's Pebble Beach, then St. Andrews—you can check out the schedule in the pro shop."

"This is unbelievable!" said the man. "What are the greens fees?"

"There are no greens fees in heaven. It's free," answered St. Peter.

Next they visited the clubhouse where there was a buffet unlike anything they'd ever seen. It had steamed lobsters, caviar, prime rib, exotic fowl, every kind of vegetable prepared to perfection, fresh-baked breads, mounds of sweet butter, and a dessert table that took their breath away.

"What do we have to pay to eat?" asked the old man.

"Don't you understand?" said St. Peter, exasperated. "This is heaven! The food is free. *Everything* is free!"

"Okay," replied the man, "but where are the low-cal and low-fat food tables?"

"That's the best part," said St. Peter. "You can eat as much as you like, and you'll never get fat or sick."

The old man went ballistic. He threw down his hat, stomped on it, and tore around the room screaming. When St. Peter and the man's wife finally calmed him down enough to speak, he looked at his wife and said, "This is all your fault! If it weren't for your blasted bran muffins, we could have been here ten years ago!"

It was Mark Twain who observed that "the only way to keep your health is to eat what you don't want, drink what you don't like, and do what you'd rather not." Twain was being cynical, but there's a lot of truth to what he said. If we could write our own rules for healthy eating, I think they would look something like this:

1. If no one sees you eat it, then it has no calories.
2. If you drink a diet soft drink with a candy bar, the calories are canceled out.
3. If you eat with a friend and you eat the same amount, the calories don't count for either of you.
4. Foods used for medicinal purposes never count; examples include chocolate, brandy, and Sara Lee cheesecakes.
5. The secret of looking thinner is getting the people around you to gain weight.

The key to healthy eating is moderation and managing what you eat every day. Don't rely on crash diets. Don't worry about what you ate yesterday. Don't put off good eating until tomorrow. Just try to eat what's best for you in the moment. Focus on now.

> "The only way to keep your health is to eat what you don't want, drink what you don't like, and do what you'd rather not."
> —MARK TWAIN

If you're not sure how you're doing or what you should (and

shouldn't) be eating, get a physical. Your doctor will let you know how you're doing and how to change your diet.

EXERCISE

Most people I know either love exercise and do it excessively or they hate it and avoid it completely; yet consistent exercise is one of the keys to good health. Dr. Ralph S. Paffenberger Jr., a research epidemiologist and physician at the University of California at Berkeley, performed pioneering studies that revealed the impact of exercise on health. Paffenberger states,

> We know that being physically fit is a way of protecting yourself against coronary heart disease, hypertension and stroke, plus adult-onset diabetes, obesity, osteoporosis, probably colon cancer and maybe other cancers, and probably clinical depression. Exercise has an enormous impact on the quality of life.[3]

Paffenberger, who ran 151 marathons, asserts that exercise is beneficial for people of all ages.

One of the tough things about exercising is that the immediate payoff seems so small. You weigh yourself after exercising. Nothing. You exercise the next day. Nothing. And the next day and the next. Still nothing. Then after the fifth day of exercise, maybe you see that you've lost half a pound. It's easy to get discouraged, especially when you don't see results most of the time. But your four days of discipline make the progress you see on the fifth day possible.

The key to success in this area is consistency. I exercise a minimum of five days a week by walking on a treadmill for at least thirty-five minutes a day. That's what my doctor has recommended. If you don't already practice the daily habit of exercise, then find a way to get started. It doesn't really matter what you do as long as you do it. Talk to your doctor. Hire a trainer. Do whatever it takes to begin a regimen that's right for you.

HANDLE STRESS EFFECTIVELY

A hundred years ago, most causes of illness were related to infectious disease. Today, they are related to stress. I once read a list of questions produced by the United Kingdom-based National Association for Mental Health to help a person gauge whether stress was becoming a problem. Here's what it asked:

- ◆ Do minor problems and disappointments bother you more than they should?
- ◆ Are you finding it hard to get along with people (and them with you)?
- ◆ Have you found that you're not getting a kick out of things you used to enjoy?
- ◆ Do your anxieties haunt you?
- ◆ Are you afraid of situations or people that didn't bother you before?
- ◆ Have you become suspicious of people, even your friends?
- ◆ Do you ever feel that you are trapped?
- ◆ Do you feel inadequate?

If you answer yes to many of these questions, stress may be a problem for you. Everybody faces problems and feels pressure at times. Whether or not that pressure becomes stress depends on how you handle it. Here's how I handle issues to keep them from becoming stressful to me:

- ◆ Family Problems: communication, unconditional love, time together

◆ Limited Options: creative thinking, advice from others, tenacity
◆ Staff Productivity Problems: immediate confrontation with the person and addressing the issue
◆ Staff Leaders with Bad Attitudes: removal

I've found that the worst thing I can do when it comes to any kind of potential pressure situation is to put off dealing with it. If you address problems with people as quickly as possible and don't let issues build up, you greatly reduce the chances of being stressed out.

Reflecting on Health

Successful people make the major decisions in their life early and manage them daily. In the other chapters of this book, I try to show you how the decisions I've made and the disciplines I've practiced have created a positive compounding effect in my life. I'm sorry to say that I can't do that when it comes to health. Instead, I'll tell you how poor decisions have had a different kind of effect:

In my teens . . . I developed many bad eating habits.

In my 20s . . . Food became a stress reliever when I worked especially hard.

In my 30s . . . I finally started to exercise, but it was usually last on my agenda.

In my 40s . . . I realized I needed to attend to my health and made a decision to change, but I failed to add the necessary daily discipline.

In my 50s . . . I finally made the decision to know and follow healthy guidelines daily, a commitment I am working hard to keep.

Perhaps you have fallen short in one or more of the areas discussed in this book. Maybe you don't feel good about it either and you want to improve, as I do. Please don't be discouraged. And don't give up! The following words were written for you and me at times like this:

> Successful people make the major decisions in their life early and manage them daily.

Though you cannot go back and make a brand-new start, my friend,
You can start now, and make a brand-new end.

Age Doesn't Matter

Any time I'm tempted to be discouraged because of my late start in the area of health, I think about someone who never allowed age to overcome his desire to know and follow healthy guidelines daily. Take a look at some of the feats he's accomplished during the second half of his life:

- At age 41—Swam from Alcatraz to Fisherman's Wharf in San Francisco in handcuffs.
- At age 45—Did 1,000 push-ups and 1,000 chin-ups in one hour twenty-two minutes.
- At age 61—Swam the length of the Golden Gate Bridge underwater (with air tanks) while handcuffed, shackled, and towing a one-ton boat behind him.
- At age 70—Towed seventy boats with seventy passengers one and a half miles in Long Beach Harbor while handcuffed and shackled.[4]

The man I'm describing is eighty-eight-year-old fitness expert Jack LaLanne, whose exercise program was on television from

1951 to 1985. If you're my age, you probably remember him. I began seeing him on television in the fifties.

LaLanne is someone who made his health decision when he was just fifteen. That's when he heard a lecture about healthy foods and exercise. He changed his eating habits and began working out using weights he discovered at the Berkeley YMCA. "I turned myself into an athlete," says LaLanne. "I was a skinny, awkward kid who became captain of the high school football team."[5]

LaLanne studied premed, intending to become a doctor, but he decided that he wanted to focus on prevention for people's health. (He later graduated from chiropractic college.) Instead, he opened a gym. LaLanne explains, "I took a lot of criticism from doctors who thought weight training was dangerous and that I was a charlatan. I've always said I'd be six-foot-two instead of five-foot-four if the health experts hadn't spent so many years beating me down. Now the medical community is on my side."[6]

That was in Oakland, California, back in 1936 when he was only twenty-one years old. LaLanne went on to develop many of the weight machines used in gyms today. And he became a bodybuilder. But his emphasis has always been on helping people. Even today as he approaches ninety, he travels the United States and around the world lecturing on health and fitness. And of course he still takes care of his health every day. He works out for two hours a day seven days a week. But he calls himself a workout nut and doesn't recommend that kind of routine for everyone. He says, "For average folks . . . you don't need more than twenty, thirty minutes . . . three or four times a week is plenty, but make it vigorous. And start out slowly, and if you're going to start working out, get a physical."[7]

LaLanne believes that anyone at any age in any health situation can become more healthy. His advice is straightforward:

If they're overweight, normalize that weight. Quit exceeding the feed limit. And exercise is number one! I don't care what you have wrong with you, you can do something—right? Maybe there are ten exercises you can't do, but there are a hundred you can do.[8]

LaLanne is still going strong. And he says he has one more feat he'd like to accomplish: He wants to swim from Catalina Island to Los Angeles—twenty-six miles—underwater. "I never think of age," he says, "I think about *today;* I don't think about tomorrow. I think about this moment and what I am going to do."[9] That's advice each of us should take.

HEALTH Application and Exercises
Knowing and Following Healthy
Guidelines Daily

Your Health Decision Today

Where do you stand when it comes to health today? Ask yourself these three questions:

1. *Have I already made the decision to know and follow healthy guidelines daily?*
2. *If so, when did I make that decision?*
3. *What exactly did I decide? (Write it here.)*

Your Health Discipline Every Day

Based on the decision you made concerning your health, what discipline must you practice *today and every day* in order to be successful? Write it here.

Making Up for Yesterday

If you need some help making the decision to commit to good health and developing the everyday discipline to live it out, do the following exercises:

1. *Take some time to write a list of all the things (and people) you have to live for. Then write the benefits that will come from having a long and healthy life.*

2. *Assess your work situation. Are you doing work you love? Does your career make the best use of your natural abilities, skills, and interests? Is your work aligned with your life purpose? The older you are, the greater the degree of alignment should be. If you're over forty and you are still waiting to get "on track" or still trying to figure out what you want, you need to make some changes.*

3. *Take the most basic steps to achieving better health through following the ten guidelines suggested by the surgeon general of the United States, Dr. Richard Carmona:*

   1. *Don't smoke.*
   2. *Eat a balanced diet.*
   3. *Get exercise.*
   4. *If you drink alcohol, do so in moderation, and never, ever drink and drive.*
   5. *Don't put off checkups and screenings.*
   6. *Don't abuse drugs.*

7. *Use protective gear (seat belts, protective goggles, batting helmets, etc.).*
8. *Talk about what you're feeling.*
9. *Know your family health history.*
10. *Relax.*[10]

4. *Make an appointment with your doctor to discuss your overall health and physical condition. Ask him or her to give you a plan for adopting a healthy lifestyle. (Note: Compared to women, men are only half as likely to visit a doctor once a year and much less likely to schedule regular checkups or to see a doctor when they exhibit symptoms.[11] So we need to be especially diligent and push ourselves to follow through with this step.)*

Looking Forward to Tomorrow

Spend some time reflecting on how your decision concerning health and the daily discipline that comes out of it will positively impact you in the future. What will be the compounding benefits? Write them here.

_____

_____

_____

_____

_____

_____

Keep what you've written as a constant reminder, because . . .
Reflection today motivates your discipline every day, and
Discipline every day maximizes your decision of yesterday.

CHAPTER 6

Today's **FAMILY** Gives Me Stability

What difference does family make? How does it impact an individual's life? That's a question Richard L. Dugdale ended up asking himself in 1874. As a member of the executive committee of the Prison Association of New York, he was chosen to inspect thirteen county jails in the state. When he got to one particular county, he was surprised to discover that six people related by blood were in the same jail. They were being held on a variety of offenses including burglary, attempted rape, and assault with intent to kill. When Dugdale talked to the county sheriff and an eighty-four-year-old local physician, he discovered that the family had been in the area since the settling of New York State and they were notorious for their criminal behavior.

Dugdale was intrigued, and he decided to study the family and publish what he found, using the fictitious name "Jukes" to describe them. He traced their line back to a man he called Max, born sometime between 1720 and 1740. He had six daughters and two sons. Some of his children were born out of wedlock. He was a heavy drinker and wasn't known to be particularly fond of work.

Dugdale estimated the family probably comprised about 1,200 people, but he was able to study only 709 members of the family. In 1877, he published his findings in *The Jukes: A Study in Crime, Pauperism, Disease and Heredity*. What he found was that they exhibited a pattern of criminality, harlotry, and pauperism that defied statistical averages:

- ◆ 180 were paupers (25 percent).
- ◆ 140 were criminals (20 percent).
- ◆ 60 were habitual thieves (8.5 percent).
- ◆ 50 were common prostitutes (7 percent).

The family's reputation was so bad, according to Dugdale, "Their family name had come to be used generically as a term of reproach." And the owner of a factory in the area used to keep a list of Jukes family members' names in his office to make sure none of them got hired.[1]

Dugdale and many subsequent researchers desired to establish the role heredity played in the behavior of the Jukes family. Today, scientists agree that there is no "criminal" gene to explain behavior. But one thing is certain: Being in the Jukes family had a negative, destabilizing effect on the lives of many people.

Another Kind of Family

Were there people in the Jukes family who escaped the cycle of destruction exhibited by its worst members? Certainly. But the negative pattern is easy to see. If you look at another family that lived in the same general region at the same time, you can see a very different kind of pattern.

The family is that of Jonathan Edwards, the theologian, pastor, and president of Princeton, who was born in 1703 and lived in Connecticut, New York, Massachusetts, and New Jersey. Edwards was a devoted family man. He and his wife, Sarah, had eleven children—three sons and eight daughters. They remained married for thirty-one years until he died of fever following a smallpox inoculation.

In 1900, A. E. Winship studied 1,400 descendants of Jonathan and Sarah Edwards. Among them Winship found:

- 13 college presidents
- 65 professors
- 100 lawyers, including a law school dean
- 30 judges
- 66 physicians, including a medical school dean
- 80 holders of public office, including 3 U.S. senators, 3 mayors of large cities, 3 governors, a controller of the U.S. Treasury, and a U.S. vice president[2]

The contrast couldn't be greater. Were all of Edwards's descendants high achievers? Certainly not. But again, the pattern is clear: A good family is an incredible advantage in life.

Why Family Matters Today

You may be thinking, That's all well and good. But my family isn't like the Edwardses. Where does that leave me? Let's face it. Some people's families don't build them up; they tear them down. The great American novelist Mark Twain said that he spent a large sum of money to trace his family tree and then spent twice as much trying to keep his ancestry secret! He was like the family that reportedly wanted its history written up so they hired a professional biographer to do it, but they were worried about how the document would handle the family's black sheep. Uncle George had been executed in the electric chair for murder. "No problem," said the biographer. "I'll say that Uncle George occupied a chair of applied electronics at an important government institution. He was attached to his position by the strongest of ties, and his death came as a real shock."

It's true that you can't do anything to change your ancestry or upbringing. You have no control over what your parents or grandparents did or how they treated you. But while you can't do much about your ancestors, you can influence your descendants greatly. You determine how *you* treat *your* family. You're the one who decides whether you will stay and work things out or leave your family

> While you can't do much about your ancestors, you can influence your descendants greatly.

when the going gets rough—as it always does. You're the one who decides how much time you spend with relatives who build you up versus those who try to knock you down. (Even the most dysfunctional or destructive families have some good solid people in them. That was true of the Jukeses.) You determine how you treat others.

The way you approach family life has a profound impact on how you live (and on the legacy you leave *your* descendants). If you're willing to work at it—and I know that for people with especially difficult families, it can be an incredible amount of work—your family can become a source of stability and strength. A healthy, supportive family is like . . .

A SAFE HAVEN IN A STORM

People have to deal with a lot of pressure these days. The workplace is demanding. Schools are often hostile environments. The pace of life is out of control. Even driving from place to place is stressful in most large cities. Where can a person find shelter in such a climate? If it's not at home, then it probably isn't anywhere.

A reporter once asked President Theodore Roosevelt with whom he most enjoyed spending his time. He responded that he would rather spend time with his family than with any of the world's notables. For him—and for his family—home was a safe haven in the midst of a storm.

A Photo Album of Memories

A newlywed couple returned from their honeymoon and set up house. On the first morning in their new home together, the wife decided to make her husband breakfast as a special treat. She fried up some eggs, made toast, and poured him a big cup of coffee. She hadn't done much cooking in her life, and she hoped he would be pleased by her effort, but after taking a few bites, he said, "It's just not like Mom used to make."

She tried not to let his comment hurt her feelings, and since she wanted their life together to start on a positive note, she determined to get up the next morning and try again. Once again, she got up early, prepared a meal, and put it in front of her husband. And again, his response was, "It's just not like Mom used to make."

Two more times she made him breakfast, and two more times she got the same response. Finally, she was fed up. The next morning, she cooked two eggs until they were as hard as rubber. She incinerated some bacon. She kept putting the bread back in the toaster until it turned black. And she cooked the coffee until it was like mud.

When her husband came to the table, she put his food in front of him, and she waited. The man sniffed the coffee, took one look at his plate, and said, "Hey! It's just like Mom used to make!"

Even people with less than perfect childhoods have fond memories of home and family. Think back to your own childhood. What are your favorite memories? What positive images still make you smile? If you have children, which of their memories do you think are their favorites? (You may want to ask them.) The more positive and loving the environment you strive to create at home, the more good memories they will have to keep them grounded.

A CRUCIBLE OF CHARACTER

More than any other single factor in a person's formative years, family life forges character. Perry F. Webb says, "The home . . . is the lens through which we get our first look at marriage and all civic duties; it is the clinic where, by conversation and attitude, impressions are created with respect to sobriety and reverence; it is the school where lessons of truth or falsehood, honesty or deceit are learned; it is the mold which ultimately determines the structure of society."[3]

Your family life not only helps to form the character of any children living at home, but it also continues to mold your character as an adult. Your character is little more than the collection of choices you make and habits you cultivate every day. Since your family creates your primary environment, it influences those choices and habits. Strong, healthy families encourage people to make constructive choices, to develop positive disciplines, and to pay the price today for success tomorrow.

A MIRROR REVEALING TRUTH

To grow, you have to know yourself. You must know your weaknesses and strengths. You must be able to be yourself and look at yourself realistically and know where you need to change. Where is one of the best places to learn that ability? At home. If you can create a secure environment at home where it's safe to tell the truth about yourself and others, it becomes a strong learning environment.

That kind of home is one filled with unconditional love. It allows family members to be open about their mistakes and shortcomings. It's a safe place to fail. And it creates a listening environment filled with understanding and empathy. I was privileged to grow up in that kind of home. Although I was disciplined whenever I did something wrong, my parents always verbally and physically expressed their love for me. That made me a very secure person who learned a lot about himself.

A Treasure Chest of Most Important Relationships

Harvard psychologist Samuel Osherson studied family relationships in his practice and did additional research with 370 Harvard graduates over a twenty-year period. His conclusion is that if you don't come to terms with past relationships, particularly with your parents, you will probably find yourself repeating those patterns. You may become the parent you swore you would never be.[4]

> If you don't come to terms with past relationships, particularly with your parents, you will probably find yourself repeating those patterns.

There's no doubt that the relationships you have with members of your immediate family and with your spouse are the most important ones in your life. The people closest to you form you—and are formed by you. That should be reason enough to value them.

When Mother Teresa received the Nobel peace prize, she was asked, "What can we do to promote world peace?" Her answer:

"Go home and love your family." If you want to make a positive impact, no matter how far-reaching, start at home. Treat your family members like treasures.

Years ago I cut out a quote by Nick Stinnet that summarized the importance of family. It reads, "When you have a strong family life, you receive the message that you are loved, cared for, and important. The positive intake of love, affection and respect . . . gives you inner resources to deal with life more successfully."[5] In other words, family gives you stability.

Making the Decision to Communicate with and Care for My Family Daily

In 1986, when I was thirty-nine years old, I began to notice a terrible trend. The marriages of some of my colleagues, college buddies, and friends were falling apart and ending in divorce. That really got my attention because even some of the relationships that Margaret and I had considered to be strong had fallen by the wayside. We didn't think our relationship was in any kind of danger, but I also discovered that prior to their breakdowns, some of the couples had thought nothing like that could ever happen to them.

This all occurred about the same time my career was really taking off. I still wanted to be successful, but I didn't want to lose my family in the process. That prompted me to make one of my key life decisions, and I would do so by rewriting my definition of success. From that moment, *Success meant having those closest to me love and respect me the most.*

That decision put my wife, Margaret, and my children, Elizabeth and Joel, right in the middle of my definition of success. Success would be impossible if I achieved outwardly but failed to take my family with me on the journey. The applause of others would never replace the appreciation of my family. Respect from others meant little if I did not have the respect of my loved ones. I would make caring for and communicating with my family one of my life's priorities.

I don't know where you stand with your family now; everyone's situation is unique. You may have a great family life. Or you may have made some serious mistakes from which you fear you will never recover. You may be single with no children, so that all you have is extended family. But I can tell you this: No matter what your situation is, you can benefit from the stability that comes from communicating with and caring for your family daily. Here's how to get started:

DETERMINE YOUR PRIORITIES

There's a Russian proverb that gives this advice:

> Before going to War—pray once.
> Before going to Sea—pray twice.
> Before getting Married—pray three times.

In other words, anytime you're going to engage in a great (and potentially risky!) endeavor, give it serious consideration first. How else are you going to know where it ranks in priority in your life?

I began learning this lesson the hard way. In the space of one month in 1969, I graduated from college, got married to Margaret, and started my first job. As soon as we got back from our honeymoon, we moved to a new town and I started working. I was the senior pastor of a small country church, and I was determined to be successful. I threw myself into the job, giving it everything I had. And when I say everything, I mean *everything*. I worked all day at the church, and every evening I set appointments to meet with people in the community. I worked a six-day workweek, but I cheated by working on my day off too. Meanwhile, Margaret worked a couple of jobs to keep us going financially because my salary was so low. The problem was that I was neglecting her and our marriage.

Margaret and I have known each other since high school, and we dated for six years before we got married, so we had a lot of history together, especially for a couple so young. Back then I believed our history was going to carry us through while I devoted myself to my career. But a marriage can't survive forever on leftovers. It needs to be fed continually, or it will eventually starve.

> A marriage can't survive forever on leftovers.

A lot of people are allowing their families to "starve." According to psychologist Ronald L. Klinger, president of the Center for Successful Fathering, parents spend 40 percent less time with children than parents of previous generations.[6] Families are breaking up at a terrible rate. Within five years, 20 percent of all first marriages end in divorce. Within ten years, that number rises to 33 percent.[7] More than a fourth of all families in the United States (28 percent in 2000) are headed by single parents.[8] And nearly three-fourths of children in single-parent families will experience poverty by the time they reach age eleven.[9] Every year, $20 to $30 billion in taxpayers' money goes to support children whose noncustodial parents neglect them financially.[10]

Building a solid family doesn't just happen on its own. You have to work at it. After I got the message that I was neglecting Margaret, I changed my approach to my career. I carved out time for her. I protected my day off. And we dedicated money in our budget to facilitate special times together. I still wanted to be successful, but not at the cost of my family! And I'm still working on making my family a priority. Anyone who neglects or abandons his family for fame, status, or financial gain isn't really successful.

DECIDE ON YOUR PHILOSOPHY

Once you've determined to make your family a priority, you have to decide what you want your family to stand for. That should be based on your values. In the first decade of our marriage, Margaret and I decided on our personal philosophy of family. First, we tried to live it out as a couple. Then when we had children, we worked to make it the foundation of our choices as parents. For us, the bottom line on family was for us to cultivate and maintain . . .

- ◆ **Commitment to God:** Our faith came first in our lives. If we neglected or compromised that, nothing else would be of value.
- ◆ **Continual Growth:** Reaching our personal potential and helping our children do the same is one of our highest values. When we come to the end of our lives, we want to look back knowing we lived life to the fullest.
- ◆ **Common Experiences:** The greatest bonds between people come as the result of their experiences together, both good and bad. We create as many positive experiences as we can, and we weather the negative ones together.
- ◆ **Confidence—in God, Ourselves, and Others:** Your belief determines *how* you will live life, and it also impacts the outcome of everything you do.
- ◆ **Contributions to Life:** People should try to leave the world a better place than they found it. We want to add value not only to the people in our family, but also to every other life we touch.

As I said, this is our list. I'm not suggesting that you adopt our philosophy regarding family. I know you will want to create your own. Here's my suggestion: Keep it simple. If you come up with a list of seventeen things you want to live out, you won't be able to do it. You may not even be able to remember it! Whittle the list down to the nonnegotiables.

DEVELOP YOUR PROBLEM-SOLVING STRATEGY

I think a lot of people go into marriage expecting it to be easy. Maybe they've seen too many movies. Marriage isn't easy. Family isn't easy. Life isn't easy. Expect problems, stay committed, and develop a strategy for getting through the rough times. Some people call family meetings to discuss issues. Others create systems or rules.

My friends Kevin and Marcia Myers developed a system of fair fight rules after they had been married a few years. Kevin is very outgoing, energetic, and verbal, where Marcia is more quiet and reserved. Early in their marriage, he used to bulldoze right over her verbally. And they would get into marathon arguments. So they decided on a set of rules to follow any time they got into a disagreement. One rule was that they would set an appointment to talk about an issue rather than picking at each other. Another was that Marcia *always* got to talk first. They've been married over twenty years, and their system has worked great for them.

Think about how you could improve your problem solving at home. Talk to your family members about it (during a calm time, not in the middle of a conflict). Use whatever kind of problem-solving strategy works for you. Just be sure that it fosters and promotes three things: (1) better understanding; (2) positive change; and (3) growing relationships.

Managing the Disciplines of Family

The desire to make your family a priority is one thing; actually living it out is something else. I found that it's often easier to get the approval of strangers and colleagues than it is to get respect from those who know you best. So I practice this discipline: ***Every day I work hard on gaining the love and respect of those closest to me.***

Years ago, when something exciting happened during the day or I heard a bit of interesting news, I'd share it with colleagues and friends. By the time I got home, I had little enthusiasm for sharing it with Margaret. So I purposely began keeping things to myself until I could share them with Margaret first. That way she never got the leftovers. I've found that the best way to place my family first is to give them some of my best energy and attention.

If you desire to strengthen your family life and make it a source of stability, then try practicing some of these disciplines:

PUT YOUR FAMILY ON YOUR CALENDAR FIRST

I have found that my work will gobble up every bit of my time if I let it. Before I made the decision to make my family a priority, I didn't give them the time I should have. I think that's true of most people who enjoy their careers. Other people have hobbies or interests that can be very time consuming. If you don't create boundaries for how you spend your time, your family will always get the leftovers. Even today, if I let my guard down, I'm liable to let work take over my schedule.

I battle that trend by putting my family on my calendar first. I block out weeks for family vacations. (That may sound too obvious to you, but I mention it because for the first several years I was married, we determined where we would vacation based on meeting people and going places that would benefit my work.) I schedule time with Margaret not only for us to go do things, like see a movie or a show, but also for us to simply be together. I devote time to our grandchildren. And when our children were young, I set aside time to attend ball games, recitals, and other activities.

Someone once said you should never let yourself feel that you ought to be at work when you're with your family, and you should never feel that you ought to be with your family when you're at work. That's a great perspective. If you and your family can figure out and agree on how much time you should spend together and you protect those times, you should be able to adopt that mind-set.

CREATE AND MAINTAIN FAMILY TRADITIONS

I want you to try an experiment. Get out a piece of paper and write down all the Christmas and birthday gifts you received when you were a kid up until you moved away from home. Take as much time as you need.

How many are you able to remember? There may be a handful that really stand out, but if you're like most people, you have a hard time recalling most of them. Now try this: List all the vacations you took with your family during those same years. Again, take as much time as you'd like.

I'd be willing to bet that if you took vacations every year, you were able to remember more of them than the presents you received. Why? Because what makes families happy isn't receiving things. It's doing things together. That's why I recommend establishing family traditions.

Traditions give your family a shared history and a strong sense of identity. Don't you remember how your family celebrated Thanksgiving as a child? How about Christmas? (And didn't you think yours was the *right* way when you got married and your spouse wanted to do something else?) The traditions your family kept helped you define who you were and who your family was.

Give thought to how you want to enjoy holidays, mark milestones, and celebrate rites of passage in your family. Start by basing traditions on your values. Add others you enjoyed from your childhood. If you're married, include those of your spouse as well. Mix in cultural elements if you want. Build some around your children's interests. Give traditions meaning and make them your own.

FIND WAYS TO SPEND TIME TOGETHER

For a while, the family buzzwords were "quality time." But the truth is, no substitute exists for quantity of time. As psychiatrist Armand Nicholi says, "Time is like oxygen—there's a minimum amount that's necessary for survival. And it

> "Time is like oxygen—there's a minimum amount that's necessary for survival. And it takes quantity as well as quality to develop warm and caring relationships."
> —ARMAND NICHOLI

takes quantity as well as quality to develop warm and caring relationships."

Since busy, single-parent households are so common, and in the majority of two-parent families both parents work, you have to figure out ways to spend time together. For about six years when my children were teenagers, I gave up golf so that I would have more time available. And Margaret and I always worked especially hard to find time for certain things, such as . . .

◆ **Significant Events:** We made birthdays, ball games, recitals, etc., important.

- ◆ **Significant Needs:** You can't put a family member in crisis on hold.
- ◆ **Fun Time:** We found that everybody relaxed and talked more when we were having fun.
- ◆ **One-on-One Time:** Nothing lets another person know you care more than your undivided attention.

Come up with your own list of ways to spend time with your family.

KEEP YOUR MARRIAGE HEALTHY FIRST

The relational foundation of any family is a couple's marriage. It sets the tone for the household, and it is the model relationship that children learn from more than any other. That's why former Notre Dame president Theodore Hesburgh asserted, "The most important thing a father can do for his children is love their mother."

> "The most important thing a father can do for his children is love their mother."
> —THEODORE HESBURGH

No marriage is easy to keep going. It's been said that a successful marriage is one that can go from crisis to crisis with a growth in commitment. That's what it's really all about: commitment. Commitment is what carries you through. People who use their feelings as a barometer for the health of their marriage are destined for a breakup. If you intend to stay married only as long as you *feel* the love, you might as well give up. Just like anything else worth fighting for, marriage requires daily discipline and commitment.

EXPRESS APPRECIATION FOR EACH OTHER

Psychologist William James said, "In every person from the cradle to the grave, there is a deep craving to be appreciated." If people don't receive affirmation and appreciation at home, there's a good chance they won't get it because, in general, the world does not fulfill that desire. One of the most positive things you can do for your spouse and children is really get to know them and love them simply because they are yours—not based on performance.

RESOLVE CONFLICT AS QUICKLY AS POSSIBLE

I've already mentioned how important it is to develop a strategy for resolving conflict, but it's such an important point that I want to remind you of it again. Every family has conflict, but not all families resolve it positively. A family's response to problems will either promote bonding or be destructive. Do it quickly and effectively, and you bring healing. Neglect conflict, and you may find yourself agreeing with novelist F. Scott Fitzgerald, who said, "Family quarrels are bitter things. They don't go according to any rules. They're not like aches or wounds, they're more like splits in the skin that won't heal because there's not enough material." It doesn't have to be that way.

Reflecting on Family

As I reflect on my family decision, I look back with intense gratitude to Margaret and my children. And I realize that . . .

In my 30s . . .	My family decision gave me protection from making the life-shattering mistakes of many of my friends.
In my 40s . . .	My family decision helped me place my family first.
In my 50s . . .	My family decision has allowed me to see the positive outcome of the success of my grown children.

For eighteen years, my family and I have benefited from my decision to live by a different definition of success. I can't imagine what life would have been like without the stability provided by my family.

Top of the World

Communicating with and caring for your family often isn't easy. It usually requires sacrifice. Have you ever thought about what you would be willing to give up for your family? Almost certainly you'd put your life on the line if, for example, your house was on fire and your children were inside. You would go in to get them. But what about something less dramatic—like your dream job? Karen Hughes searched herself and found out that for her, the answer to that question was yes.

Karen Hughes has been called the most powerful woman in America.[11] *BusinessWeek* pointed out that she "became the highest-ranking woman in the White House—indeed in any administration in American history."[12] The day before the inauguration, George W. Bush pointed to her and said, "I don't want any important decision made without her in the room."[13] She regularly performed tasks that are normally the domain of vice presidents and secretaries of state. And President Bush regularly delegated twenty of his one hundred daily decisions to her. Andrew Card, Bush's chief of staff, marveled, "It's really odd for the most trusted old hand from back home to also be just about the most naturally talented, forceful, brilliant person in the whole building. . . . It's a fluke! It's amazing."[14]

Karen Hughes had arrived. She had served her party in Texas since the mid-1980s and had served George W. Bush beginning in 1994 when he began his run for governor. She was instrumental in his campaign for president. For a former television journalist who had never held elected office, there could be no greater position of power than the one she possessed. She was influencing the man who influenced the world. The only step up would be winning elected office herself at the national level.

But in 2002, Karen Hughes left her powerful office in the White House's west wing because she had other priorities. True, she remained a counselor to the president, but she was giving up the power and influence of being the "right hand" of the leader of the free world on a daily basis.

In a press conference, she explained, "My husband and I have made a difficult, but we think, right decision to move our family home to Texas. As you know, our roots are there. I have a daughter and granddaughter in Austin. My son is going into his final three years of high school before he goes off to college, and we want him to have his roots in Texas, as well."[15]

Not long after she made her decision, President Bush was meeting in the Oval Office with King Mohammed VI of Morocco. When he was asked about Hughes, Bush explained to the monarch that she was leaving "because her husband and son will be happier in Texas, and she had put her family ahead of her service to my government. And I am extremely grateful for that approach and that priority."[16]

The position Karen Hughes held was a once-in-a-lifetime kind of job. The window of opportunity for someone like her is really very small. It's either four or eight years. Because of her unusual connection to Bush, she probably won't get another chance. The window for her son, Robert, to go to high school is also small. He won't get a second chance at that either. She chose her family over her career. Not many people in her position would do that.

Doug Fletcher, the Austin senior pastor of the church where Karen Hughes is an elder, explained how Hughes could do such a thing: "Karen never enjoyed the perks of power. [Her husband] Jerry didn't either. Karen served to be faithful and steadfast . . . and now she is being faithful to herself and her family."[17] That's something we should all aspire to do. For Karen Hughes, today's family gives her stability.

FAMILY APPLICATION AND EXERCISES
COMMUNICATING WITH AND CARING FOR
FAMILY DAILY

Your Family Decision Today

Where do you stand when it comes to family today? Ask yourself these three questions:

1. Have I already made the decision to communicate with and care for my family?
2. If so, when did I make that decision?
3. What exactly did I decide? (Write it here.)

_____

_____

_____

_____

_____

Your Family Discipline Every Day

Based on the decision you made concerning family, what is the one discipline you must practice *today and every day* in order to be successful? Write it here.

_____

_____

_____

_____

_____

_____

Making Up for Yesterday

If you need some help making the right decision concerning family and developing the everyday discipline to live it out, do the following exercises:

1. *What percentage of your waking hours do you give to family? Is it usually "prime time" or leftovers? Write down your estimates.*

   _____

   _____

   Now talk to members of your family about it. Ask them to give you their honest assessment. If you've been terrible about it, you need to ask their forgiveness.

2. *Dedicate some time to articulating your philosophy of family life. If you're married, try to arrange some getaway time with your spouse to do it. Don't expect to have a final polished philosophy after spending a few hours or a weekend on it. It will evolve over time, and it may take you a few years to finalize your philosophy.*

3. *If you're married, create some fair fight rules based on your personalities, values, and history together.*

4. *Learn to manage your calendar effectively in order to spend time with your family. Set aside a few hours to look over the coming thirty days. Mark the important events in your family's life on it. And look for creative ways to spend time together. (For example, you might be able to take your spouse or child with you on a business trip, you can invite them to participate in your hobby, or you can tag along on one of their activities.) Once you've set things on your calendar, manage your other responsibilities in such a way that you guard your family days. While you're reviewing, look for holidays and other special days that might offer an opportunity to start a fun or meaningful family tradition.*

5. *If you're married, when was the last time you and your spouse got to spend some significant time alone? If it's been more than six months—or you can't remember when it was—plan something.*

6. *Find a time in your day when you can think about something you're grateful for about each family member. (Every phase of your chil-*

dren's lives has both positives and negatives. Focus on the good things.) Now find a way to express that thought to at least one of them today.

Looking Forward to Tomorrow

Spend some time reflecting on how your decision concerning family and the daily discipline that comes out of it will positively impact you in the future. What will be the compounding benefits? Write it here.

_____

_____

_____

_____

_____

_____

Keep what you've written as a constant reminder, because . . .
Reflection today motivates your discipline every day, and
Discipline every day maximizes your decision of yesterday.

CHAPTER 7

Today's **THINKING** Gives Me an Advantage

I'm continually reading books on leadership and communication. Every month I try to read one excellent book in its entirety and skim a second one that may not have as much content. In 2001, one of the outstanding books I read was *Good to Great* by business expert Jim Collins. It contains an interesting story about the A&P grocery company that is a superb example of what can happen when people fail to make the decision to practice and develop their good thinking daily.

The company certainly started out well. In 1859, George Huntington Hartford convinced his employer, George P. Gilman, the owner of a hide and leather company in New York City, to go into the tea business. The Great American Tea Company was born. The idea was to buy tea in bulk—a whole clippership load at a time—and sell it directly to the public, thus cutting out the middleman. It was good thinking. Their product was priced at a third of their competitors', and they were well on their way. Four years later, they had expanded from one shop to six, and they began selling groceries as well as tea.

Innovation and Expansion

In 1869, Gilman sold his shares to Hartford and retired. That same year, Hartford changed the name of the company in order to capitalize on the opening of the transcontinental railway. From then on, it was known as the Great Atlantic and Pacific Tea Company— A&P for short. Hartford also decided to create his own brand of coffee, which he called Eight O'Clock Breakfast Coffee. It was very popular and profits soared. Hartford's good thinking and strong business sense were making the company succeed. By 1880, the company had more than ninety-five stores, as far east as Boston and as far west as Milwaukee.

As good a thinker as George Huntington Hartford was, his sons George and John were even better. The younger George figured out that the company could keep costs down and increase profits by manufacturing its own products. Meanwhile, John looked more closely at the needs of customers. At the time, most grocers delivered their wares to customers and allowed people to buy on account. John wanted to try something new and innovative. He convinced his father and brother to open a cash-and-carry "economy" store. It opened in 1912, and in only six months, it drove a nearby traditional A&P out of business. In two years, the company opened 1,600 of the new kind of stores. In 1916, the elder Hartford handed the business over to his sons. By then their sales had doubled from $31 million to $76 million. Nine years later, the company owned 13,961 stores that produced annual sales of $437 million.[1] Plus, by 1929, A&P was the world's largest coffee retailer.[2]

In the early 1930s, the grocery industry was on the verge of another major change. Competitors were introducing "super" markets. The Hartford brothers changed their thinking and met the challenge. They began closing their economy stores and opening supermarkets. Even though they closed nearly six old stores for every new one they opened, they prospered. Sales volume was high—and so were profits. By 1950, A&P's annual sales topped $3.2 billion. It was the largest privately owned company and the largest retail organization in the world. The only company in the world with a greater sales volume was General Motors.[3]

Another Change in the Wind

In the 1960s and 1970s, the customers' wants changed rapidly once again. Value was no longer as important as choices. People no longer wanted supermarkets; they wanted superstores. They were looking for large clean stores with more choices, not only of products but also of brands. And they wanted to make fewer stops for their shopping needs. Instead of visiting a drugstore for medicine, a bakery for fresh-baked goods, a health-food store for vitamins, a photo shop to drop off film, a florist for flowers, and a bank to cash a check, they wanted to do it all right there in the grocery store. It was a shift no larger than the one the younger John Hartford saw and took the company through in the 1930s. The only problem was that Hartford no longer ran A&P. His successor was Ralph Burger, who became president of A&P in 1950 and was named chairman of the board in 1958.

According to Collins, Burger was not up to the challenge.

Where Hartford had used his thinking to create an advantage in the industry, Burger "sought to preserve two things: cash dividends for the [Hartford] family foundation and the past glory of the Hartford brothers."[4] Collins quotes an A&P director who said that Burger "tried to carry out, against all opposition, what he thought Mr. John [Hartford] would have liked." Collins goes on to say, "Burger instilled a 'what would Mr. Hartford do?' approach to decisions, living by the motto 'You can't argue with a hundred years of success.' "[5]

You may not be able to argue with it, but you sure can run it into the ground. No one knows what a great leader would have done given a new set of circumstances. There is no tried-and-true formula for success that can be handed down through the generations. To succeed, we must do our own thinking. Burger worked to repeat Hartford's past actions rather than trying to approach problems using Hartford's innovative style of thinking.

A Key Unused

The worst example of poor thinking that Collins offers about A&P was their experiment with a new store called the Golden Key to find out why they were quickly losing market share. It was to be run independently and given the freedom to try out new and innovative departments. Customers liked it, and it started to evolve into a modern superstore. All the data indicated that A&P needed to shut down their traditional stores and create new superstores. What was their response? Because they didn't like the answers they were getting from the Golden Key, they closed it.

Instead, they kept thinking old strategies would solve their problems. They pursued the latest fads. They fired CEOs. They even tried a radical price-cutting strategy, but that led to cost cutting, and the stores they had became more run down and the service became poorer. As A&P shrank, they went into acquisitions mode. They acquired numerous regional food store chains, but that failed to return them to their past glory. (Collins did an acquisitions analysis of the great companies and the companies he compared them to in his book. The highest possible score was +3 and the lowest −3, based on financial and qualitative analysis. A&P tied with three other companies with the lowest score of −3.[6])

Today, A&P operates 667 stores in 12 states, the District of Columbia, and Ontario, Canada, under the following trade names: A&P, Waldbaum's, Food Emporium, Super Foodmart, Super Fresh, Farmer Jack, Kohl's, Sav-A-Center, Dominion, Barn Markets, Food Basics, and Ultra Food & Drug.[7] Financial analysts aren't enthusiastic about the company, and Standard & Poor's Rating Services announced on August 1, 2003, that the company was being downgraded from "B+" to "B." It seems unlikely that the company will ever regain the status or profitability it once possessed.

Why Thinking Matters Today

Claude M. Bristol, author of *The Magic of Believing,* said, "Thought is the original source of all wealth, all success, all material gain, all great discoveries and inventions, and all achievement."[8] That's a bold statement! What kind of value do you put on good thinking? Has it been a priority in your life? I'm guessing that you do think it's important, or you wouldn't be reading

> "Thought is the original source of all wealth, all success, all material gain, all great discoveries and inventions, and all achievement."
>
> —CLAUDE M. BRISTOL

a book to improve your mind right now. But have you considered thinking to be a decision and discipline to be practiced daily? Here are some reasons to make thinking a priority in your life every day:

GOOD THINKING PRECEDES GOOD RESULTS

A friend sent me some interesting questions that show the funny way people sometimes think. Here are a few of them:

- Should a person engage a plastic surgeon if his office is filled with Picasso portraits?
- How much deeper would the oceans be if sponges didn't live in them?
- If FedEx and UPS were to merge, would the company be called Fed UP?
- When elderly people spend more time reading the Bible, is it because they're cramming for their finals?[9]
- If a bus station is where the bus stops and a train station is where the train stops, what should happen at my workstation?

Obviously the questions aren't serious, but they do show a thinking mind at work. It doesn't matter what profession a person pursues, thinking precedes achievement. Success doesn't come by accident. People don't repeatedly stumble into achievement and then figure it out afterward. Whether you're a doctor, a businessperson, a carpenter, a teacher, or a parent, your level of success will increase dramatically if you place high value on thinking. The greater your thinking, the greater your potential. As playwright Victor Hugo said, "A small man is made up of small thoughts."

GOOD THINKING INCREASES YOUR VALUE

Who has the greatest value in any organization? The answer is: the person with the ideas. Industrialist Harvey Firestone said, "Capital isn't so important in business. Experience isn't so important. You can get both these things. What is important is ideas. If you have ideas, you have the main asset you need, and there

> "What is important is ideas. If you have ideas, you have the main asset you need, and there isn't any limit to what you can do with your business and your life."
> —HARVEY FIRESTONE

isn't any limit to what you can do with your business and your life."

Ideas are what our country was founded on. Ideas have helped to create great companies and to drive our economy, the largest in the world. Ideas are the foundation for everything we build, every advance we make. When a person is a good thinker and has lots of ideas, he or she becomes very valuable. If you're a good thinker, you have a great advantage. Gerald Nadler, author of *Breakthrough Thinking,* says, "Only 10 percent to 12 percent of all managers are effective enough to make and stay on the fast track."[10] The reason? Most don't stay in the game mentally.

POOR THINKERS ARE SLAVES TO THEIR SURROUNDINGS

People who do not develop and practice good thinking often find themselves at the mercy of their circumstances. They are unable to solve problems, and they find themselves facing the same obstacles over and over again. And because they don't think ahead, they are habitually in reaction mode. An old

> A German proverb says, "Better an empty purse than an empty head."

German proverb says, "Better an empty purse than an empty head." Good thinkers can always overcome difficulties, including lack of resources. And poor thinkers are also frequently at the mercy of good thinkers.

Making the Decision to Practice and Develop Good Thinking Daily

I was very fortunate. I learned about the power of good thinking very early in life. My father required all three of his children to read for thirty minutes every day. Sometimes we chose what we read, but often he selected the reading material for us. Two of the books he asked me to read made a profound impression on me. The first was *The Power of Positive Thinking* by Norman Vincent Peale, which I read in the seventh grade.[11] That year, my father also took me to Veterans Memorial Auditorium in Columbus, Ohio, to hear and meet Dr. Peale. It shaped my life.

Even more impacting than meeting Dr. Peale was reading *As a Man Thinketh* by James Allen.[12] I read the book in 1961 when I was fourteen years old, and it made such an impression on me that I was prompted to make one of my Daily Dozen decisions. I still have the book. On page 49, Allen wrote, "All that a man achieves or fails to achieve is the direct result of his thoughts." The entire book made an impression on me, but that statement made me realize that my thinking would make or break me. So I decided, *I will think on things that will add value to myself and others.*

If you desire to make good thinking a daily part of your life, consider this:

UNDERSTAND THAT GREAT THINKING COMES FROM GOOD THINKING

One night at dinner, a friend of John Kilcullen's described something he overheard in a bookstore. A customer asked the clerk,

"Do you have any simple books on Microsoft DOS—something like DOS for dummies?" It was only a passing comment, meant as a joke. But it stuck with Kilcullen. And he did something with it. He launched the "Dummies" books.

Some unknown consumer had a good idea, and it went nowhere. In fact, he probably didn't even know his idea was a good one. But in the hands of a thinker, that good idea became a great idea. Then it became a bunch of great ideas. The "Dummies" books now encompass a product line of 370 titles in 31 languages with sales of more than 60 million copies.[13]

If you want to become a great thinker, you first need to become a good thinker. Before becoming a good thinker, you need to become a thinker. In order to become a thinker, you need to be willing to first produce a bunch of mediocre and downright bad ideas. Only by practicing and developing your thinking daily will your ideas get better. Your thinking ability is determined not by your desire to think, but by your past thinking. To become a good thinker, do more thinking. Once the ideas start flowing, they get better. Once they get better, they keep improving.

RECOGNIZE THERE ARE MANY KINDS OF THINKING

Up to now I've referred to thinking as if it were a single skill. But the truth is that it's really a collection of skills. It's like a mental decathlon, the track-and-field contest where athletes compete in ten events: 100-meter dash, 400-meter dash, long jump, shot put, high jump, 110-meter hurdles, discus throw, pole vault, javelin throw, and 1500-meter run. Thinking is multifaceted.

I believe eleven different thinking skills come into play when it comes to good thinking. I wrote about them in detail in *Thinking for a Change*. Here is an overview of the skills:

1. **Big Picture Thinking:** the ability to think beyond yourself and your world in order to process ideas with a holistic perspective.
2. **Focused Thinking:** the ability to think with clarity on issues by removing distractions and mental clutter from your mind.
3. **Creative Thinking:** the ability to break out of your "box" of limitations and explore ideas and options to experience a breakthrough.
4. **Realistic Thinking:** the ability to build a solid foundation on facts to think with certainty.
5. **Strategic Thinking:** the ability to implement plans that give direction for today and increase your potential for tomorrow.
6. **Possibility Thinking:** the ability to unleash your enthusiasm and hope to find solutions for even seemingly impossible situations.
7. **Reflective Thinking:** the ability to revisit the past in order to gain a true perspective and think with understanding.
8. **Questioning Popular Thinking:** the ability to reject the limitations of common thinking and accomplish uncommon results.
9. **Shared Thinking:** the ability to include the heads of others to help you think "over your head" and achieve compounding results.
10. **Unselfish Thinking:** the ability to consider others and their journey to think with collaboration.
11. **Bottom-Line Thinking:** the ability to focus on results and maximum return to reap the full potential of your thinking.[14]

It's a real mistake to believe there is only one kind of thinking. That's a very narrow view. It can cause a person to value only the kind of thinking in which he excels and to dismiss all other types of thinking. I'm sorry to say that some academicians fall into this trap.

MAXIMIZE YOUR STRENGTHS AND STAFF YOUR WEAKNESSES

Most people are naturally good at a few thinking skills and weak at others. Just as it's rare to find an athlete who is good enough in all ten events to compete in the decathlon, it's a rare thinker who has skill in all eleven thinking areas. So if you recognize that there are many different kinds of thinking, what should you do? Should you try to master all of them? No, I believe that's a mistake.

Let's say, for example, that you are a very good creative thinker, but you're weak in bottom-line thinking, yet you want to *master* both kinds of thinking. How would you get started? Where would you focus your attention? You could probably work on bottom-line thinking to get it up to average, but that would require a tremendous amount of time, energy, and resources. And what would it take to advance to merely good? It would take even more effort. The higher you try to climb, the more energy it takes to make less progress. No matter how hard you try, you might not ever make bottom-line thinking a strength.

What if you gave that time to improving your creative thinking instead? Since you are already good, a moderate amount of time and energy could make you excellent. If you really gave it your all, perhaps you could become a world-class creative thinker. That would enable you to generate ideas and make contributions few others could. That would make you much more valuable and give you a real advantage in your life and career.

So what do you do about your weaknesses? Gather people around you who are strong in those areas. That's what I've done for years. In my current season of life, I can hire staff who possess strengths in my areas of weakness. But even before I was "the boss," I practiced this principle. For thirty-five years my wife, Margaret, and I have worked as a team to compensate for one another's weaknesses. I've often relied on my brother, Larry, to help me in the area of realistic thinking. And I've made it a practice to partner with friends who think better than I do in a particular area while I do the same for them. Not having to rely entirely on myself when it comes to thinking has been a real advantage for me.

Managing the Discipline of Thinking

It's easy to allow situations and other people to influence your thinking negatively as well as positively. One of the tricky things about seeking ideas and perspective from others is that some people have an agenda other than helping you. That's why it's important to take responsibility for your own thinking. When I was in my twenties, I began to practice this discipline: *Every day I will set aside a time to think, and I will determine to think on the right things.* If you desire to do the same thing, then do this:

FIND A PLACE TO THINK

Beginning with my first job in 1969, I've always found a place to be my daily thinking spot. During those early years in Hillham, Indiana, it was beside a spring outside our home. In Lancaster, Ohio, I used to sit on a big rock. In San Diego, it was an isolated room upstairs at the church. In Atlanta, it's a particular chair in my office. The only time I sit in it is when I need thinking time.

Those certainly haven't been the only places I've done my thinking, but they are the ones I've designated for the task. But I can make almost any place a good thinking place as long as I don't have to deal with interruptions. Right now as I write this, I'm sitting in a chair on the balcony of a cruise ship. My family is scattered all over the ship doing different things, and I sneaked away for a few minutes by myself to think about this book and write down some ideas.

I want to encourage you to find a thinking place. When it comes to what works, everybody's different. Some people like to be connected to nature. Others want to be in the midst of—but removed from—activity. My friend Andy Stanley likes to sit alone in a restaurant to think—he says he needs a little distraction. J. K. Rowling, author of the "Harry Potter" books, wrote her early books while sitting in a café. Where you go doesn't matter as long as it stimulates your thinking.

Set Aside Think Time Every Day

As important as finding the right place to think is carving out the time. I do nearly all my best thinking early in the morning—except for reflective thinking. I usually do that in the evenings before I go to bed. That's when I review my day and try to measure how I did with my Daily Dozen. But all the other kinds of thinking come best to me in the morning. I often wake up in the wee hours and spend time just jotting ideas on a legal pad while sitting in my thinking chair. I recommend that you try to discover the time of day when your thinking is the sharpest. Then set aside a block of time every day just to think. I believe you'll find that you're much more productive and focused as a result.

Find a Process That Works for You

Everybody has a different way of approaching the process of thinking. Poet Rudyard Kipling had to have pure black ink for his pen before he could write. Philosopher Immanuel Kant used to stare out his window at a stone tower to think; when trees grew up threatening to block his view, he chopped them down. Composer Ludwig van Beethoven poured cold water over his head to refresh himself and stimulate his thinking. Poet Friedrich von Schiller's thinking was stimulated by the smell of rotting apples, which he kept on his desk. Critic and lexicographer Samuel Johnson said that he needed a purring cat, an orange peel, and a cup of tea in order to write. Composer Gioacchino Rossini felt that he worked best in bed under the covers.

I don't need anything specific to trigger my thinking. Some people need music. Some think best while at a computer. Some must write in longhand. Do whatever works for you.

Capture Your Thoughts

If you don't write down your ideas, there is a great danger you will lose them. In *Bird by Bird,* Anne Lamott explains how she keeps from losing her best ideas:

> I have index cards and pens all over the house—by the bed, in the bathroom, in the kitchen, by the phones, and I have them in the glove compartment of my car. I carry one with me in my back pocket when I take my dog for a walk. . . . I used to think that if something was important enough, I'd remember it until I got home, where I could simply write it down in my note-book. . . . But then I wouldn't. . . . [Writing down your ideas right away is] not cheating. It doesn't say anything about your character.[15]

I always write down my ideas. When I'm in my thinking spot, I use a legal pad. The rest of the day, I keep a small leather-bound notebook with me. I even have something to write with next to my bed at night: a small pad with a light attached that illuminates when you remove the pen. That way, I can write a note while still in bed without disturbing Margaret by turning on a light. Have a system and use it.

PUT YOUR THOUGHTS INTO ACTION QUICKLY

When you have a great idea but don't do anything with it, then you don't reap the advantage it brings. Dave Goetz, founder of CustomZines.com, says, "For me, when an idea hits me, it strikes fire, almost like God speaking. I know that sounds heretical, but there it is. The more time that passes after the idea strikes, the less heat it gives off. I forget parts of it, it doesn't seem as great. Ideas have a short half-life."[16]

Have you ever had an idea for a product or service and a few months or years later seen someone else with the same idea take it to market? Author Alfred Montapert said, "Every time a person puts an idea across, he finds ten peo-

> "Every time a person puts an idea across, he finds ten people who thought about it *before* he did—but they only *thought* about it."
>
> —ALFRED MONTAPERT

ple who thought about it *before* he did—but they only *thought* about it." Ideas, put into action, give an advantage.

TRY TO IMPROVE YOUR THINKING EVERY DAY

It's true that the more thinking you do, the better you become at it. But you can quickly improve your thinking if you do the following on a daily basis:

- ◆ **Focus on the Positive:** Thinking alone won't guarantee success. You need to think about the right things. Negative thinking and worry actually hinder the thinking process rather than improve it. I believe in this so wholeheartedly that the first book I wrote was a collection of short uplifting and instructive chapters. I called it *Think on These Things,* based on a Bible passage that always inspired me:

"Whatever is true, whatever is honorable, whatever is just, whatever is pure, whatever is pleasing, whatever is commendable, if there is any excellence and if there is anything worthy of praise, think about these things."[17] Focus on the positive, and your thinking will move in a positive direction.

- **Gather Good Input:** I've always been a collector of ideas. I do a lot of reading, and I continually file the ideas and quotes I find. (I'll tell you more about that in the chapter on growth.) I've found that the more good ideas I'm exposed to, the more my thinking improves.

- **Spend Time with Good Thinkers:** If you were to interview a group of top executives in any profession, you would find that well over half had the benefit of being mentored at some time in their careers. And I believe that the greatest benefit anyone receives in that kind of relationship is learning how the mentor thinks. If you spend time with good thinkers, you will find that the exposure sharpens your thinking.

I believe that many people take thinking for granted. They see it as a natural function of life. But the truth is that *intentional* thinking isn't commonplace. What you do every day in the area of thinking really matters because it sets the stage for all your actions, and it will bring you either adversity or advantage.

Reflecting on Thinking

When I was young and highly energetic, I was all for action. But the longer I live, the more I cherish my thinking time. Perhaps that's because I have begun to realize the value it has brought to me:

In my teens . . .	My thinking began to be focused on that which was positive.
In my 20s . . .	My thinking separated me from many of my peers.
In my 30s . . .	My thinking gave me an audience and a following.
In my 40s . . .	My thinking took *my work* to a much higher level.
In my 50s . . .	My thinking has taken *me* to a much higher level.

And the best part is that I'm not done yet. I'm fifty-seven years old, and I believe my best thinking is still ahead of me. I'm always trying to increase the quantity and quality of my thinking, because few things give as great a return as good ideas. When a person's thinking is good, a lot of other things in life take care of themselves.

A Boy in Bondage

I mentioned previously that people who don't practice good thinking become slaves to their surroundings. Recently I saw a movie that illustrated that truth—and also showed how when people change their thinking, they can be freed from that bondage and change their lives. The movie was called *Antwone Fisher,* and it was based on the life of the real Antwone Fisher, who was also the film's screenwriter.

Unlike most movies based on a true story, *Antwone Fisher* very closely followed the life of its protagonist. Fisher was born in an Ohio correctional facility while his mother was incarcerated. By then his father had already been dead for two months. As a result, he grew up a ward of the state in foster care. For over thirteen years, he lived with a couple who abused him horribly. Daily he was beaten down—physically, verbally, and psychologically. He never received a Christmas gift or a dime of allowance from his foster parents. For years he was the victim of sexual abuse. And he was often tied to a post in the basement and beaten. His foster mother used to brag that she had once beaten him until he was unconscious. When an interviewer asked him whether the movie portrayal of his foster parents had been accurate, Fisher answered, "I was kind to them in the movie and the book. . . . They are worse."[18]

In the movie, Fisher's life doesn't really change for the better until he's been in the U.S. Navy for many years. That's when a psychiatrist (portrayed by Denzel Washington) takes an interest in him and helps him work through the pain of his past. In real life, Fisher did encounter a navy psychiatrist who helped him, but long before that, another person sowed the seeds of hope in his life.

By the time Fisher entered the third grade, he had lost any natural love for learning. In addition, the constant admonition from his foster mother that he was the worst child in the world had convinced him that he couldn't learn and had no future. He failed fourth grade and was scheduled to repeat it. But then something wonderful happened. His foster family moved, which put him in a new school district. His new teacher was Mrs. Profit. "If there is such a thing as human beings who act as angels in our lives, Brenda Profit was that for me."[19]

Under Mrs. Profit's care, Fisher began to change his thinking about himself. He says, "If self-esteem was what you used to fill up like a tank of gas, the Picketts [his foster family] had siphoned mine out to nothing. Mrs. Profit helped change all that."[20] Despite his gains, his academic progress was still meager by the end of the year. He was in danger of once again failing fourth grade. But then Fisher got another break. It was decided that Mrs. Profit would stay with her class of students and continue teaching them in fifth and sixth grades. Knowing that, she passed Fisher into the fifth grade. And it was then an event occurred that would change his thinking forever.

It happened one day during reading. Fisher, a terribly shy child who sometimes stuttered, was asked to read aloud, and instead of panicking, he read well, including successfully sounding out a difficult word. Then Mrs. Profit praised him, saying, "I'm proud of you. I want you to know that I really struggled over promoting you, and I'm so glad that I did. You are doing very well this year." That's when something clicked in Fisher's head. He writes,

> Her honest, careful words are the equivalent of lightning bolts and thunderclaps. Outside I shyly accept her praise, but inside I'm flying with the birth of a revelation. It's the first time I've ever realized that there is something I can do to make things different for myself. Not just me, but anyone. That no matter how often someone says you can't do something, by simply working harder and trying, you can prove them wrong and actually change your circumstance. This lesson is a piece of gold I'll keep tucked in my back pocket for the rest of my life.[21]

In that moment, Fisher changed his thinking—and it changed his life. He had plenty of ups and downs after that, but he knew that he wasn't hopeless and a better future was possible for him. He didn't follow the path of his older foster brother and friends into a life of drugs and crime.

Today, Antwone Fisher thinks for a living. He is a successful screenwriter in Hollywood. He learned his craft by writing forty-one drafts of the screenplay that tells his own story. And he has become the kind of responsible citizen and family man he always desired to be, with a wife and young daughter. When asked what message he wants his story to convey, his answer is, "That there is hope even when you have the hardest beginnings, and there are good people in the world."[22]

I don't know what kind of background you have. I don't know what type of circumstances you currently face. But I do know there's hope. No matter what kind of goals you have or obstacles you need to overcome, thinking can give you an advantage. And that advantage has the potential to change your life for the better, just as it did for Antwone Fisher.

THINKING Application and Exercises
Practicing and Developing Good
Thinking Daily

Your Thinking Decision Today

Where do you stand when it comes to thinking today? Ask yourself these three questions:

1. *Have I already made the decision to practice and develop good thinking daily?*
2. *If so, when did I make that decision?*
3. *What exactly did I decide? (Write it here.)*

_____

_____

_____

_____

_____

_____

Your Thinking Discipline Every Day

Based on the decision you made concerning thinking, what is the one discipline you must practice *today and every day* in order to be successful? Write it here.

_____

_____

_____

_____

_____

_____

Making Up for Yesterday

If you need some help making a commitment to become a better thinker, do the following exercises:

1. Begin by assessing yourself in each of the eleven thinking skills outlined in the chapter. On a scale of 1 to 10 (with 10 being complete mastery), rate your ability using the questions below:

____ **Acquire the Wisdom of Big Picture Thinking:** Am I thinking beyond myself and my world so that I process ideas with a holistic perspective?

____ **Unleash the Potential of Focused Thinking:** Am I dedicated to removing distractions and mental clutter so that I can concentrate with clarity on the real issue?

____ **Discover the Joy of Creative Thinking:** Am I working to break out of my "box" of limitations so that I explore ideas and options to experience creative breakthroughs?

____ **Recognize the Importance of Realistic Thinking:** Am I building a solid mental foundation on facts so that I can think with certainty?

____ **Release the Power of Strategic Thinking:** Am I implementing strategic plans that give me direction for today and increase my potential for tomorrow?

____ **Feel the Energy of Possibility Thinking:** Am I unleashing the enthusiasm of possibility thinking to find solutions for even seemingly impossible situations?

____ **Embrace the Lesson of Reflective Thinking:** Am I regularly revisiting the past to gain a true perspective and think with understanding?

____ **Question the Acceptance of Popular Thinking:** Am I consciously rejecting the limitations of common thinking in order to accomplish uncommon results?

____ **Encourage the Participation of Shared Thinking:** Am I consistently including the heads of others to think "over my head" and achieve compounding results?

___ **Experience the Satisfaction of Unselfish Thinking:** Am I continually considering others and their journey in order to think with collaboration?

___ **Enjoy the Return of Bottom-line Thinking:** Am I staying focused on results in order to gain the maximum return and reap the full potential of my thinking?

The two or three skills you rated the highest are probably your thinking strengths. Confirm those findings with friends, colleagues, your spouse, or your boss. Then focus on developing yourself in those areas. The group of skills you rated the lowest are the ones for which you need to enlist help. Bring friends, colleagues, or staff members around to help you balance out in those areas.

2. *During the next two or three weeks, try out different spots in which to do your thinking. Experiment with a variety of places. After you've tried out at least a half dozen, go back to the ones you liked best to give yourself more thinking time there. When you figure out which place is best for you, plan to use it on a regular basis.*

3. *Once you've found the best spot, find the best time to think. Experiment with the time of day. Ideally, you would do your thinking when you're the sharpest. However, it's most important to carve out a time that works in your schedule on a daily basis.*

4. *Try different processes and practices to stimulate your thinking. Play music. Do something physical like taking a walk or exercising. Do something that requires right-brain thinking, such as putting together a puzzle, drawing, or putting a golf ball. You want to clear your mind and stimulate thinking at the same time. That will bring clarity to your thinking. Jazz musician Charles Mingus said, "Making the simple complicated is commonplace; making the complicated simple, awesomely simple, that's creativity." That's what you're going for.*

Looking Forward to Tomorrow

Spend some time reflecting on how your decision concerning thinking and the daily discipline that comes out of it will positively impact you in the future. What compounding benefits do you expect to receive? Write them here.

_____

_____

_____

_____

_____

_____

Keep what you've written as a constant reminder, because . . .
Reflection today motivates your discipline every day, and
Discipline every day maximizes your decision of yesterday.

CHAPTER 8

Today's **COMMITMENT** Gives Me Tenacity

He may have been the most naturally gifted baseball player of all time. In the June 18, 1956, edition of *Sports Illustrated,* writer Robert W. Creamer called him the "new Ruth." When he began his baseball career, he was probably the fastest man in the game. He was clocked making it to first base in 2.9 seconds on a left-handed drag bunt. And he could run the bases in an incredible 13 seconds.[1]

But his speed was nothing compared to the power of his hitting. People speculate that he got his strength from working as a "screen ape" during the summers at the lead mine near Commerce, Oklahoma. The job was to smash large rocks with a sledgehammer. Working with a partner, one man would smash rocks until he couldn't hold the sledgehammer any longer, then the other would take a turn. It's said that there were home run hitters, and then there was this man—in a league of his own. The *Guinness Book of World Records* credits him with the longest home run ever measured, at 643 feet. Many believe he hit the longest ball in baseball history in a 1951 exhibition game at USC (656 feet). And he could smack the ball out of the park with equal ease from either side of the plate.

Born to Play Baseball

The player I'm describing is, of course, Mickey Mantle of the New York Yankees. Growing up in Ohio, I was a Cincinnati Reds fan, but I saw and heard a lot about Mantle—especially in 1961 when the Reds finally made it to the World Series but lost to the Yankees four games to one.

Mantle's prowess on the baseball field was legendary. He seemed to be born for baseball. His father, a former semi-pro ballplayer, and his grandfather began teaching him to hit when he was four years old. They would pitch balls to him after work every day. And since his father was right-handed and his grandfather a lefty, the boy learned to hit from both sides of the plate.

By age sixteen, Mantle was playing semipro ball. In 1948, a scout for the Yankees, Tom Greenwade, went to Oklahoma to see Mantle's teammate, third baseman Billy Johnson, play. Mantle hit two long home runs that day—one right-handed, one left-handed. Greenwade said Mantle was the best prospect he'd ever seen and was ready to sign him on the spot—until he discovered that he was only sixteen and still in high school. Greenwade promised to come back when the kid graduated. And he did: Mantle signed with the Yankees on graduation day in 1949.

What a Record!

That summer, Mickey Mantle played class D ball in the Yankees organization. The next year, he was sent to play for the class C team in Joplin, Missouri. In 1951, he was invited to the Yankees' spring training camp, and he was so good that he jumped straight from class C to the Yankees—the first time that had ever happened in the organization's history. He was nineteen. He went to the World Series that rookie year and came home with a championship. During his career, his team won the American League pennant and went on to the World Series twelve times, winning it seven times.

Mantle had an incredible career before he retired in 1969. He played in more games as a Yankee than any other player (2,401), including Lou Gehrig. He was picked as the American League MVP three times (1956, 1957, 1962). And in 1956, he won what's called baseball's triple crown: He finished the season with the league's best batting average (.353), most home runs (52), and most runs batted in (130). And, remarkably, more than thirty years later he still holds the World Series records for home runs (18), runs scored (42), runs batted in (40), and bases on ball (43).

Despite a one-of-a-kind career, experts believe he never reached his potential. Most people blame it on injuries. Mantle suffered some horrible ones, often to his knees, throughout his career, and he continually played in pain. Before each game he had to carefully wrap each knee in bandages. Sportswriter Lewis Early wrote, "One of the questions baseball scholars ponder is the great 'What if?' What would Mickey have accomplished if he had been healthy during his career?"[2] It's true he suffered injuries that would, as one writer said, "keep a clerk in bed."[3] But that wasn't the root of the problem. What most people didn't know was that Mantle was a raging alcoholic.

Another Kind of Record

The people close to Mantle knew about his problem, but the public didn't until he told his story in *Sports Illustrated* in 1994, a few months after he had gone to the Betty Ford Clinic to become sober. Mantle had begun drinking during his second season with the Yankees after his father died of Hodgkin's disease at age thirty-nine. As he was setting records on the baseball field, he seemed to be trying to set records for drinking with his buddies. He said that early in his career he would quit drinking during spring training, get into shape, and then begin drinking again once the season started. And he never even thought about baseball during the off-season.

After Mantle retired, his drinking became worse. He often started drinking early in the day and continued until he was incoherent in the evenings. Somehow, he managed to keep his professional commitments. Mantle said,

> I always took pride in my dependability when I was doing public relations work, endorsements and personal appearances. I always wanted to do my best. It was when I had no commitments, nothing to do or nowhere to be that I lapsed into those long drinking sessions.[4]

He often did and said things he couldn't remember the next day. Many times he was horrified when someone told him about his previous night's behavior. Fans would ask him about his playing days and what kind of pitch he liked to hit, and he couldn't remember.

Finally, at age sixty-two, Mantle hit rock bottom. He had made a mess of his family. His health was wrecked. And he wanted to sober up. That's when he checked into the Betty Ford Clinic. He said that was the first time he had thought seriously about anything in his life. From the perspective of sobriety, Mantle assessed himself and his career:

> My last four or five years with the Yankees, I didn't realize I was ruining myself with all the drinking. I just thought, This is fun. . . . Today I can admit that all the drinking shortened my career. When I retired in the spring of '69, I was 37. Casey [Stengel, the Yankees' manager] had said when I came up, "This guy's going to be better than Joe DiMaggio and Babe Ruth." It didn't happen. I never fulfilled what my dad had wanted [to be the greatest player who ever lived], and I should have. God gave me a great body to play with, and I didn't take care of it. And I blame a lot of it on alcohol.
>
> Everybody tries to make the excuse that injuries shortened my career. Truth is, after I'd had a knee operation, the doctors would give me rehab work to do, but I wouldn't do it. I'd be out drinking. . . . I thought, Hey, I'll be all right. I hurt my knees again through the years, and I just thought they'd naturally come back. Everything has always come natural to me. I didn't work hard at it.[5]

It's a tragedy anytime someone neglects his potential and misses many of the possibilities life has to offer. Sportswriter Tom Swift speculates that without the alcoholism, Mantle might have hit eight hundred home runs.[6] Despite his great natural talent, Mickey Mantle never gave the commitment off the field that he displayed on it.

The Man in the Mirror

Only after giving up drinking and taking an honest look at his life did Mantle develop the kind of commitment that would have served him well during the previous decades. After being sober for three months, he said, "I'd rather put a gun to my head than have another drink."[7] But by the time Mantle was ready to change, it was too late. His liver was ruined from a life of alcoholism. He received a liver transplant, but doctors soon discovered that Mantle had inoperable cancer.

In the last months of his life, Mantle relied on his faith, fought the good fight, and regained some of the dignity he had lost during his drinking days. He died on June 8, 1995. On August 15, a group came together to honor Mantle. One of the eulogists was sportscaster Bob Costas. He said, "All of America watched [Mantle] in admiration. His doctors said he was, in many ways, the most remarkable patient they'd ever seen. His bravery, so stark and real, that even those used to seeing people in dire circumstances were moved by his example."[8] And Costas also described a cartoon that had appeared in the *Dallas Morning News* that day: Saint Peter is at the gates of heaven with his arm around Mickey Mantle's shoulders, and he says, "Kid, that was the most courageous ninth inning I've ever seen." During his last year of life—at age sixty-three—his commitment carried him through.

Why Commitment Matters Today

What were *you* born to do? What do you think your future holds? Do you believe you have a purpose or a destiny? If so, will you fulfill it? To become the person you have the potential to be, you will need great tenacity. That quality comes from commitment. Take a look at these truths concerning commitment:

COMMITMENT CAN CHANGE YOUR LIFE

In *Choices,* Frederic F. Flach writes, "Most people can look back over the years and identify a time and place at which their lives changed significantly. Whether by accident or design, these are the moments when, because of a readiness within us and a collaboration with events occurring around us, we are forced to seriously reappraise ourselves and the conditions under which we live and to make certain choices that will affect the rest of our lives."9

Think about a time in your life when you made a real commitment to do something differently. Didn't your life change as a result? It may not have turned out exactly as you expected, but it undoubtedly set you on a new course. If you want to change, you must embrace commitment.

COMMITMENT HELPS YOU OVERCOME MANY OF LIFE'S OBSTACLES

You've got problems, I've got problems, all God's children have got problems. The question is, How are you going to deal with them? Clergyman and author Maltbie D. Babcock said,

> One of the most common mistakes and one of the costliest, is thinking that success is due to some genius, some magic something or other which we do not possess. Success is generally due to holding on and failure to let go. You decide to learn a language, study music, take a course in reading, train yourself physically. Will it be a success or failure? It depends upon how much pluck and perseverance that word "decide" contains. The decision that nothing will overrule, the grip that nothing can detatch will bring success.

When Mickey Mantle was confronted with the problem of his father's death, instead of making a commitment to face the loss and deal with it, he turned to alcohol. And that started him on the road to ruin.

YOUR COMMITMENT WILL BE TESTED EVERY DAY

I think many people see commitment as an event, something that is done in a moment. They say "I do" in a wedding ceremony.

They shake hands to close a business deal. They buy a treadmill in order to ex-

> Any time you make a commitment to something, it will be tested.

ercise. But the commitment doesn't end with that decision; it's just getting started. And you better believe that any time you make a commitment to something, it will be tested. That happens in any number of ways:

- **Experiencing Failure:** Perhaps the greatest challenge to commitment is failure. Olympic gold medalist Mary Lou Retton says, "Achieving that goal is a good feeling, but to get there you have to also get through the failures. You've got to be able to pick yourself up and continue."
- **Having to Stand Alone:** When you want to accomplish something, people will try to distract you. They will challenge you. They may even try to get you to compromise your values. It may be unintentional. It may be because they're worried that if you grow, they will feel left behind. In those moments, you need to ask yourself, "Who am I trying to please?" If you desire to please yourself by following through on your commitments to yourself, there will be times you need to stand alone.
- **Facing Deep Disappointment:** Let's be honest, a lot of things can go wrong in life. How are you going to react in the face of those disappointments? Sportscaster Harry Kalas once introduced Philadelphia Phillies outfielder Garry Maddox by saying, "Garry has turned his life around. He used to be depressed and miserable. Now he's miserable and depressed." That's not how you want to end up.

When things go wrong, when life gets rough, when the pain becomes great, will you be able to keep going? If you determine to make and keep proper commitments daily, you greatly improve

> "Always bear in mind that your own resolution to success is more important than any other thing."
>
> —ABRAHAM LINCOLN

your chances of being able to carry on. As Abraham Lincoln said, "Always bear in mind that your own resolution to success is more important than any other thing."

Making the Decision to Make and Keep Proper Commitments Daily

I don't think I really understood the true value of commitment until 1976. I was the senior pastor of one of the fastest-growing churches in Ohio. And the success we were seeing necessitated a $1 million expansion of our facilities. But there was a problem: I was only twenty-nine years old, and I had never led a major building program. Frankly, the task seemed impossible. But at the same time, the future of the church absolutely depended on its success. That's when I made a life decision concerning commitment: *If something is worth doing, I will commit myself to carrying it through.* I decided that come what may, I would lead my congregation through the building program.

Little did I realize how much that commitment would be tested. Each time we made a decision, more problems arose. Here are just a few:

1. To accommodate the growth, I needed to improve my staff. That meant terminating some people who were very popular.
2. More than 200 people in the church (nearly 15 percent) left the church because they did not agree with the vision.
3. Our bank agreed to lend us the money only if we first raised $300,000 from among the congregation, but I had never led

a large financial campaign, and the most I had ever raised for a project was $25,000.

4. The church board's decision not to give the bid for the building contract to a member of our congregation who owned a construction company caused him to leave the church, and he had been the church's most generous giver.

5. Our architect was careless with disbursements to contractors, which made the project cost over $125,000 more than it should have.

You've heard the old saying that motion causes friction? During the entire process, there was enough friction to cause a five-alarm fire. I felt like I was in the hot seat every day. If I hadn't made the commitment early in the process, I never would have made it through.

If you desire to have greater tenacity to accomplish the things you desire, then make the decision to embrace commitment wholeheartedly in your life. Begin by doing the following:

COUNT THE COST

After the Nazis drove the British army from the European continent at Dunkirk and obtained France's surrender in June of 1940, the Germans were certain that victory in Europe was at hand and that Great Britain would seek a peace agreement. France also believed that was true. French General Maxime Weygand told Charles de Gaulle, who was a colonel at the time, "When I've been beaten here, England won't wait a week before negotiating with the Reich."[10]

But the Germans and the French underestimated the commitment of Winston Churchill, who had become England's prime minister in May, and of the British people. Churchill knew what was at stake in the conflict, as evidenced by his remarks at the time:

What General Weygand called the Battle of France is over. I expect that the battle of Britain is about to begin. Upon this battle depends the survival of Christian civilisation. Upon it depends our own British life. . . . Hitler knows that he will have to break us in this island or lose the war. If we can stand up to him, all Europe may be free. . . . But if we fail, then the whole world, including the United States, including all that we have known and cared for, will sink into the abyss of a new dark age. . . . Let us therefore brace ourselves to our duties, and so bear ourselves that, if the British Empire and its Commonwealth last for a thousand years, men will still say, "This was their finest hour."[11]

The war that England fought was long and bloody. They suffered terrible bombing from the Nazis, and for a long time they stood alone. But they stood. Their commitment was unwavering. And because they stood, the Allies won the war. I believe their resolve was strong not only because they knew what was at stake, but they also had a sense of what price they were being asked to pay. It can be very difficult to stand by a commitment naively made. The commitment becomes much stronger when you have already counted the cost.

DETERMINE TO PAY THE PRICE

Once you count the cost, then you have to decide whether you are really willing to do what it takes to follow through. U.S. Senator Sam Nunn said, "You have to pay the price. You will find that everything in life exacts a price, and you will have to decide whether the price is worth the prize."

> "You have to pay the price. You will find that everything in life exacts a price, and you will have to decide whether the price is worth the prize."
>
> —SAM NUNN

When I went off to college, I was determined to stay committed and focused on preparing for the ministry. But I knew there would be a price. Many of my college friends got married while still in school, and some even had children; Margaret and I waited, despite our shared desire to begin our married life. It was a difficult journey. And to this day, I don't recommend engagements as long as ours. But our commitment paid off. A few weeks after we graduated, we got married. And we waited several years before having children. As a result, I was prepared when I entered the ministry, and I could focus on establishing my career during those important early years.

ALWAYS STRIVE FOR EXCELLENCE

Howard W. Newton said, "People forget how fast you did a job— but they remember how well you did it." Few things fire up a person's commitment like dedication to excellence. The desire for excellence carried Michelangelo through to the comple-

> "People forget how fast you did a job—but they remember how well you did it."
>
> —HOWARD W. NEWTON

tion of his work on the Sistine chapel. Excellence drove Edison to keep trying until he figured out how to make a lightbulb that worked. Excellence drives the companies Jim Collins wrote about in *Built to Last* and *Good to Great.*

Anyone who desires to achieve and become successful must be like a fine craftsman: committed to excellence. A great craftsman wants you to inspect his work, to look closely at its finest details. In contrast, sloppy people hide their work. And if anyone finds fault with it, shoddy workers find fault with their tools. Which are you most like? Excellence means doing your very best in everything, in every way. That kind of commitment will take you where half-hearted people will never go.

Managing the Discipline of Commitment

After I made the decision to commit myself to the building program at my church, I knew that I would need to find a way to keep myself on track. So I determined to live out this discipline: *Every day I will renew my commitment and think about the benefits that come from it.* To do that, I carried a laminated card with me every day for eighteen months. Here's what was written on it:

> The moment one definitely commits oneself, then Providence moves too. All sorts of things occur to help one that would never otherwise have occurred. A whole stream of events issue from the decision, raising in one's favor all manner of unforeseen incidents and meetings and material assistance which no man could have dreamed would come his way.　　—William H. Murray

I read that card every day as we were going through the project. On especially difficult days when I felt like throwing in the towel, I read it two or three times. It helped me to stay focused and feel encouraged. I thought, If I stay committed and do all I can, and then I ask God to make up the difference, we can achieve this. And we did!

When you accomplish something that you once believed was impossible, it makes you a new person. It changes the way you see yourself and the world. My thinking went to a new level, and the vision for my leadership expanded. I never would have gotten there without commitment. My personal commitment—and that of many others—was the key to our success.

As you strive to keep your commitments daily, keep the following in mind:

EXPECT COMMITMENT TO BE A STRUGGLE

When our children were young and living at home, Margaret and I decided one summer we wanted to take them on a vacation that focused on how the United States was built as a nation. We started out in New York City. We went to Ellis Island, the longtime gateway into the country, and got a feel for the millions of immigrants who came to America with the dream of building a better life. We visited Philadelphia. We saw the room where our country became a nation with the signing of the Declaration of Independence. We viewed the Liberty Bell. And we visited the graves of the brave men who signed the Declaration of Independence.

After that, we traveled south to Williamsburg, Virginia, the home of Patrick Henry, who declared, "Give me liberty or give me death!" And we ended the trip in Washington, D.C. As we looked up at the towering Washington Monument, we were reminded of the United States' struggle to become a nation. As we gazed at the huge statue of Lincoln at his memorial, we recalled the struggle we have endured to *remain* a nation.

Everywhere we went, we were confronted with the commitment of the men and women who founded and preserved our country. We learned about the risks they took, the battles they fought, the sacrifices they made. The greatest honors were reserved for those who endured the greatest struggles. The stakes were high, but so were the rewards. We still enjoy the freedom they won for us.

That trip taught a great lesson to our family. Anything worth having is going to be a struggle. Commitment doesn't come easy, but when you're fighting for something you believe in, the struggle is worth it.

DON'T RELY ON TALENT ALONE

When you read about someone like Mickey Mantle, you realize that *too much* talent can actually work against someone. If Mantle's commitment to taking care of himself, working during the off-season, and improving his game had matched his natural talent, the results would have been radically different.

If you want to reach your potential, you need to add a strong work ethic to your talent. Poet Henry Wadsworth Longfellow shared much insight when he wrote:

> The heights by great men reached and kept
> Were not attained by sudden flight,
> But they, while their companions slept,
> Were toiling upward in the night.[12]

> If you want something out of your day, you must put something in it.

If you want something out of your day, you must put something in it. Your talent is what God put in before you were born. Your skills are what you put in yesterday. Commitment is what you must put in today in order to make today your masterpiece and make tomorrow a success.

FOCUS ON CHOICES, NOT CONDITIONS

In general, people approach daily commitment in one of two ways. They focus on the external or the internal. Those who focus on the external expect conditions to determine whether they keep their commitments. Because conditions are so transitory, their commitment level changes like the wind.

In contrast, people who base their actions on the internal usually focus on their choices. Each choice is a crossroad, one that will either confirm or compromise their commitments.

When you come to a crossroad, you can recognize it because . . .

♦ A personal decision is required.
♦ The decision will cost you something.
♦ Others will likely be influenced by it.

Your choices are the only thing you truly control. You cannot control your circumstances, nor can you control others. By focusing on your choices, and then making them with integrity, you control your commitment. And that is what often separates success from failure.

BE SINGLE-MINDED

Nothing stokes commitment like single-minded effort that results in achievement. A great example of that truth can be found in the story of English minister William Carey. Although he had only an elementary education, by the time Carey was in his teens, he could read the Bible in six languages. Because of his talent for languages, when he was in his early thirties he was chosen to be a missionary to India. Six years later in 1799, he founded the Serampore mission. A few years after that, he became professor of Oriental languages at Fort William College in Calcutta. He also used his talent with languages in becoming a publisher. His press at Serampore printed Bibles in forty languages and dialects for more than three hundred million people.

To what did Carey attribute his success? How was he able to accomplish what he did? He said it was because he was a "plodder." Describing himself, Carey said, "Anything beyond this will be too much. I can plod. That is my only genius. I can persevere in any definite pursuit. To this I owe everything."[13]

DO WHAT'S RIGHT EVEN WHEN YOU DON'T FEEL LIKE IT

Thomas A. Buckner said, "To bring one's self to a frame of mind and to the proper energy to accomplish things that require plain hard work continuously is the one big battle that everyone has. When this battle is won for all time, then everything is easy." One

> "To bring one's self to a frame of mind and to the proper energy to accomplish things that require plain hard work continuously is the one big battle that everyone has. When this battle is won for all time, then everything is easy."
>
> —THOMAS A. BUCKNER

of the things I admire about great athletes is their understanding of this truth. That's one of the reasons I enjoy watching the Olympics. When the Olympic athletes come into the stadium during the opening ceremonies and prepare to participate in the games, one of the things they do is recite the following:

I have prepared.
I have followed the rules.
I will not quit.

Anyone who can say that with integrity can be proud of him- or herself, no matter what happens afterward. As Arthur Gordon,

> "Nothing is easier than saying words. Nothing is harder than living them, day after day."
>
> —ARTHUR GORDON

author of *A Touch of Wonder,* said, "Nothing is easier than saying words. Nothing is harder than living them, day after day. What you promise today must be renewed and redecided tomorrow and each day that stretches out before you."[14]

If you do what you should only when you *really* feel like it, you won't keep your commitments consistently. My friend Ken Blanchard says, "When you're interested in something, you do it only when it's convenient. When you're committed to something, you accept no excuses, only results." If you refuse to give in to excuses, no matter how good they may sound or how good they will make you feel in the moment, you have the potential to go far.

Reflecting on Commitment

I believe my commitment continues to be a key to life. That's true in my marriage, my career, my spiritual life—there's not an area it doesn't touch. Twenty-eight years after settling the commitment issue in my life, I look back and realize the importance of that decision:

In my 20s . . . My commitment made up for my inexperience.

In my 30s . . . My commitment motivated many to follow my leadership.

In my 40s . . . My commitment kept me going during my most difficult leadership years.

In my 50s . . . My commitment has pushed me out of my comfort zone and into my productivity zone.

When you have commitment, there's almost nothing you can't do.

Horrible Circumstances

Recently I read a story that exemplifies commitment. In 1999, the *New York Times* began awarding college scholarships in a program open to New York high school seniors. The stated goal was "to support the aspirations of students who hope to build on their achievements in college and to make significant contributions to society." The administrators of the program wanted especially to help students who had succeeded despite the odds. Their materials said, "Candidates must have demonstrated academic achievement, community service and a commitment to learning especially in the face of financial and other obstacles."[15]

When the names and stories of the first recipients were announced, there were many great success stories. But one in particular stood out: the story of Liz Murray. To say that she had demonstrated commitment in the face of obstacles would be putting it mildly.

Liz grew up in the Bronx, a notoriously rough part of New York City, the child of two parents who were alcoholics and IV drug users. She says her parents always loved her, but they neglected her because of their preoccupation with drugs. Once she woke up to find they had sold her sister's winter coat to get money for a fix. So to keep herself and her sister fed, she worked from the time she was nine years old. She offered to pump gas at self-service gas stations and bagged groceries at stores for tips.

It wasn't until Liz was in junior high school that she realized most kids didn't have parents who shot up cocaine in the living room. That was around the same time her mother's AIDS, which had been diagnosed a few years earlier, became acute. Liz wasn't going to school much by then. A lot of her time she tried to take care of her mother, who was also schizophrenic. A lot of her time she spent on the street and with friends. When Liz was fifteen, her mother died. And Liz became homeless.

The First Great Commitment

Ironically, that experience had a positive impact on her. When she saw her mother buried in a pauper's grave, Liz had a realization. And that brought her to a decision. She says, "I connected the lifestyles that I had witnessed every day with how my mother ended up. And if there was anything that I could do about it, that would not happen to me. So I wanted to get back into school. But, mind you, I was homeless."[16] Her circumstances were dire, but she committed herself to the task.

First, she found a summer job. (Her employer and coworkers

never knew she was homeless.) Her pay was based entirely on commission—and she excelled. That helped her scrape together enough money to survive. Then she got herself accepted at Humanities Preparatory Academy, a public high school in Manhattan. To make up for lost time, she did four years of course work in two years by taking ten classes at a time. By day, she went to school; by night, she studied in stairwells and often rode subway trains until morning.

She set her sights high. She had visited Harvard on a school trip. She decided to apply there and to apply for the *New York Times* scholarship. Since her mother's death, she had gained tenacity and focus: "Her death showed me how short life is," says Liz. "Something I remind myself of dozens of times a day. Thinking of this, it's easy to prioritize in any difficult situation. It's always the people I care about that matter and also working to bring out all the potential inside of me is a way of loving the people close to me the best I can."[17]

Her determination was tested daily in school and out. The interviews for Harvard and the scholarship fell on the same day. On that day she also had an appointment at the welfare office to keep her meager benefits coming. As she waited in line, she saw her opportunity to get to the interviews ticking away. In frustration, she asked if she could be bumped to the front of the line because of her interview with Harvard. She was told, "Right, and the lady in front of you has an interview with Yale. Sit down." She walked away from her benefits and chose to go to the interviews.

Harvard Bound

In the end, she made her interviews—and her grades. She was awarded a yearly $12,000 scholarship, and she was accepted at Harvard. Randy Kennedy of the *New York Times* observed, "It is no small feat to earn a 95 average at the Humanities Preparatory Academy in Greenwich Village and to graduate at the top of a class of 158. It is almost unheard of to pull it off in two years."[18]

Murray has since transferred to Columbia. She says it's a better fit for her and she can be closer to her father. Her story has been picked up by news programs, Lifetime made it into a movie, and she's currently writing it in book format. She inspires everyone she meets. Her father, who is HIV positive and currently living drug-free, says that she is his hero. But Murray takes it all in stride. She simply sees it as part of her journey. She hopes someday to become a documentary filmmaker.

When asked about her philosophy, Murray summed it up this way: "There's always a way through things if you work hard enough and look close. It all depends on your level of determination."[19] Hard work and determination. That sounds like a good description of commitment.

> "There's always a way through things if you work hard enough and look close. It all depends on your level of determination."
> —LIZ MURRAY

COMMITMENT APPLICATION AND EXERCISES
MAKING AND KEEPING PROPER
COMMITMENTS DAILY

Your Commitment Decision Today

Where do you stand when it comes to commitment today? Ask yourself these three questions:

1. *Have I already made the decision to make and keep proper commitments daily?*
2. *If so, when did I make that decision?*
3. *What exactly did I decide? (Write it here.)*

_____

_____

_____

_____

_____

_____

Your Commitment Discipline Every Day

Based on the decision you made concerning commitment, what is the one discipline you must practice *today and every day* in order to be successful? Write it here.

Making Up for Yesterday

If you need some help making a commitment decision and developing the everyday discipline to live it out, do the following exercises:

1. *How would others describe you? Would they say that overall you are a casual or a committed person? How about when it comes to the things that are important to you? If there are no people or beliefs in your life to which you are completely committed, then you need to figure out why.*

   Is the issue your values? Do you know what you believe in? It's difficult to develop commitment if you don't. If that's your situation, you may want to skip ahead to the chapter on values. Is the issue the price you must pay to be committed? If so, realize that there is also a price to be paid for lack of commitment. Think about Mickey Mantle. If you fail to develop proper commitment, what will you forfeit? On the other hand, if you pay the price, what benefit will you gain?

   If these issues are unclear to you, write down some of your major life goals and figure out what the cost will be for each. Then weigh one against the other. For anything that's worth the price, make the commitment to follow through.

2. *Make excellence your standard. Bring a high standard to everything you do. Begin by thinking about a job, project, or task you've committed to doing. How have you been approaching it? Are you committing the kind of time, attention, and resources to it that will allow you to accomplish it with a high degree of excellence? Reevaluate your approach to it. Then use that experience to examine how you approach the rest of your life.*

3. *Commitment is always a struggle. What is your strategy for winning the battle to stay committed—in your work, important relationships, faith, etc.? Do you need inspiration, as I did while going through the building program? Do you need accountability? Do you need a reminder to stay focused? Use whatever tools you need.*

4. *Commitment is a matter of taking total responsibility for yourself. Choose to grow beyond your natural talent. Choose to make good*

choices. Choose not to blame your circumstances for the outcome of your life. Choose to be responsible for the person you are becoming.

Looking Forward to Tomorrow

Spend some time reflecting on how your decision concerning commitment and the daily discipline that comes out of it will positively impact you in the future. What compounding benefits do you expect to receive? Write them here.

_____

_____

_____

_____

_____

_____

Keep what you've written as a constant reminder, because . . .

Reflection today motivates your discipline every day, and

Discipline every day maximizes your decision of yesterday.

CHAPTER 9

Today's **FINANCES** Give Me Options

What are the two greatest causes of stress in most working people's lives? According to Karen Olson of Xylo Inc. in Bellevue, Washington, they are issues related to time management and money.[1] That's not surprising, considering how people are doing financially these days. In 2002, consumer bankruptcy filings set a record: 1.5 million, up 6 percent from the previous year.[2] And many more people who have not filed are on the brink of financial ruin. SMR Research asserts that 43.7 million households in the United States have less than $1,000 in liquid assets. And 16.3 million households have a net worth of zero or less.[3]

How do people react to such situations? They borrow more money. Consumer debt has risen to $1.7 trillion.[4] And it continues to rise. Stuart Feldstein, president of SMR Research, says, "The amount of borrowing has been rising faster than incomes."[5] In

1981, the debt-to-income ratio for consumers in the United States was 1.14. In 2000, it was 1.63.[6] People are taking on more debt than they can handle. Mortgage delinquencies are also rising. According to the Mortgage Bankers Association of America, foreclosures are at their highest rate in thirty years.[7]

In a recent study, 27 percent of the people surveyed by the *Los Angeles Times* described their personal finances as "shaky." And 40 percent said they had trouble paying insurance premiums, car payments, and other installments on monthly loans.[8] Financial pressure takes a huge toll on people. It even hurts their productivity on the job. A survey conducted by the Consumer Credit Counseling Service found that employees experiencing financial stress waste 13 percent of their workday dealing with money matters on the job.[9] That's more than an hour a day—and 250 hours a year!

Why Finances Matter Today

O. Donald Olson quips that "the average American is busy buying things he doesn't want with money he doesn't have to impress people he doesn't like." There isn't an aspect of life that financial matters don't touch. And when people don't handle finances well day to day, it causes huge problems.

> "The average American is busy buying things he doesn't want with money he doesn't have to impress people he doesn't like."
> —O. DONALD OLSON

Take a look at three simple truths about finances:

1. MONEY *WON'T* MAKE YOU HAPPY

Even though most people would say they agree with the saying "Money won't buy happiness," they sometimes act as if they think it's true. Why else would they make money such a high priority or compromise their values to get it? Several years ago, James Patterson and Peter Kim published the results of a national survey on morals in *The Day America Told the Truth.* They shared some of the things people said they would do for money. Here are some of the things people said they would be willing to do for $10 million (along with the percentage of people who would do it). They would . . .

- Abandon their entire family (25 percent)
- Become prostitutes for a week or more (23 percent)
- Give up their American citizenship (16 percent)
- Leave their spouse (16 percent)
- Withhold testimony, letting a murderer go free (10 percent)
- Kill a stranger (7 percent)
- Put their children up for adoption (3 percent)[10]

If those findings don't show that some people *believe* money will bring them happiness, nothing does!

Journalist Bill Vaughan joked that money won't buy happiness, but it will pay the salaries of a huge research staff to study the problem. That's truer than he might have thought. Studies have shown that having more money really doesn't bring happiness. According to *Fast Company* magazine, "Between 1970 and 1999, the average American family received a 16% raise (adjusted for inflation), while the percentage of people who described themselves as 'very happy' fell from 36% to 29%. We are better paid, better fed, and better educated than ever. Yet the divorce rate has doubled, the teen-suicide rate has tripled, and depression has soared in the past 30 years."[11] Modern research simply confirms something said nearly two thousand years ago by the Roman philosopher Seneca: "Money has yet to make anyone rich."

As a young man, I may have suspected that people with money were happier than people without it. But as I began counseling people with incomes above average, I found that they had no advantage over people with low incomes. Automaker Henry Ford said, "Money doesn't change men, it merely un-

> "Money doesn't change men, it merely unmasks them. If a man is naturally selfish, or arrogant, or greedy, the money brings it out; that's all."
>
> —HENRY FORD

masks them. If a man is naturally selfish, or arrogant, or greedy, the money brings it out; that's all." You are what you are—no matter how much or how little money you have.

2. DEBT *WILL* MAKE YOU UNHAPPY

Having money may not make people happy, but *owing* money is sure to make them miserable. I once saw a piece by Rose Sands that categorized debt this way:

If you owe $1,000, you're a piker.
If you owe $100,000, you're a businessman.
If you owe $1 million, you're a tycoon.
If you owe $1 billion, you're a magnate.
If you owe $100 billion, you're the government.

Novelist Samuel Butler, who satirized Victorian life in England, wrote, "All progress is based upon a universal innate desire on the part of every living or-

> "All progress is based upon a universal innate desire on the part of every living organism to live beyond its income."
>
> —SAMUEL BUTLER

ganism to live beyond its income." Yet the truth is that if your outgo exceeds your income, then your upkeep will be your downfall.

Solomon of ancient Israel summed up the condition of anyone in debt when he said, "The rich rules over the poor, and the borrower becomes the lender's slave."[12] Who wants to be a slave, controlled by someone else?

3. HAVING A FINANCIAL MARGIN GIVES YOU OPTIONS

The bottom line is that money is nothing but a tool. It is good for helping one achieve goals, but the goal of getting money for its own sake is ultimately hollow. If you have very little money, you have fewer choices. If you want to live where it's most convenient to your job, you may not be able to if you lack money. You may not be able to send your children to the school you want. You may not be able to afford a reliable car. You may not be able to take off time from work to see your children's ball games or recitals. You may not be able to switch careers to something you love. You may live every month from paycheck to paycheck. And you may not be able to stop working when you're sixty-five, seventy, or even older.

Making the Decision to Earn and Properly Manage Finances Daily

When I was growing up, it was obvious very early that my brother, Larry, and I had very different attitudes toward money. We were complete opposites. As a kid, all Larry wanted to do was work and make money. All I wanted to do was play with my friends. He spent his summers working. I spent my summers shooting hoops. He saved his money. I had nothing to save. When Larry was sixteen years old, he bought himself a nice car with his own money: a four-year-old Ford. I didn't have a car until I graduated from college. It was an old beat-up Ford Falcon—and guess from whom I borrowed the money to buy it? From Larry—and from my younger sister, Trish.

When I was studying for the ministry, I realized I was choosing a profession where I would not make a lot of money. I didn't mind that because I was doing what I believed I was called to do and what would be personally fulfilling. But I also recognized that when a person has no money, he has few options. In 1985, Margaret and I made a decision: *We will sacrifice today so that we can have options tomorrow.* From then on, we've determined to live by this financial formula:

- ◆ 10 percent to church/charity
- ◆ 10 percent to investments
- ◆ 80 percent to living expenses

Around that same time, our friend Tom Phillippe offered us a wonderful opportunity to invest in one of his retirement centers. We gladly accepted. For several years, we've not only continued to put 10 percent of our income into investments, but when those investments have made money, instead of spending it, we have rolled it over into other investments. Over time our money has been building. And the older Margaret and I get, the more options we have as a result.

If you desire to have options, yet you have not done a good job of earning and properly managing your finances daily, then put yourself in position to make a good decision concerning finances by doing the following:

PUT THE VALUE OF THINGS INTO PERSPECTIVE

A husband and wife attended a county fair where a man in an old biplane was giving rides for $50. The couple wanted to ride, but they thought the pilot's price was too high. They tried negotiating to get him to lower the price, offering $50 for them both, but he wouldn't budge. Finally, the pilot made them an offer.

"You pay me the whole $100, and I'll take you up," he said. "And if you don't say a single word during the flight, I'll give you back all your money."

They agreed, and the couple got into the plane. Up they went, and the pilot proceeded to do every aerial maneuver he knew: diving, looping, rolling, and flying upside down. When the plane landed, the pilot said to the husband, "Congratulations! Here's your $100. You didn't say a word."

"Nope," answered the husband, "but I almost did when my wife fell out."

It's a hokey story, but it directs us to a truth about our culture. People tend to value money and things over what's really important in life: other people. French historian and political scientist Alexis de Tocqueville remarked about the United States that he knew of "no other country where love of money has such a grip on men's hearts." Remarkably, he wrote that more than one hundred years ago! I wonder what he would say if he were alive today.

To know whether your attitude about money and possessions is what it should be, ask yourself the following five questions:

1. Am I preoccupied with things?
2. Am I envious of others?
3. Do I find my personal value in possessions?
4. Do I believe that money will make me happy?
5. Do I continually want more?

If you answered yes to one or more of these questions, you need to do some soul-searching. Billy Graham rightly points out, "If a person gets his attitude toward money straight, it will help straighten out almost every other area of his life." Materialism is a mind-set. There's nothing wrong with possessing money or nice things. Likewise, there's nothing wrong with living mod-

> "If a person gets his attitude toward money straight, it will help straighten out almost every other area of his life."
>
> —BILLY GRAHAM

estly. Materialism is not about possession—it's an obsession. I've known materialistic people with no money and nonmaterialistic people who possess lots of money. Haven't you?

RECOGNIZE YOUR SEASON OF LIFE

Every phase of life isn't the same, nor should we try to make it that way. Ideally, a person's life should follow a pattern where the main focus goes from learning to earning to returning. Here's what I mean about each phase:

◆ **Learn:** When you're young, your focus should be on exploring your talents, discovering your purpose, and learning your trade. For many people, this phase occurs during their teens and twenties—although a few trailblazers do it earlier and some late bloomers don't have things worked out until well into their thirties (or later). The exact timing isn't important. What matters is that you accept that there is a phase of life where learning is your primary objective and that you shouldn't take shortcuts to financial gain and miss the big picture of your life.

◆ **Earn:** If you're on track with your purpose, you've learned your trade well, and you practice it with excellence, the hope is that you will be able to earn a good living. Obviously, your choice of profession impacts your earning power greatly. For many people, the season when their earning is most effective occurs during their thirties, forties, and fifties. During this phase of life, you should strive to take care of your family and prepare for your future.

◆ **Return:** We should always try to be generous, no matter our age. But if you've worked hard and planned well, you may enter a phase of life that is most rewarding, where you can focus on giving back to others. Most often, that occurs when people are in their fifties, sixties, seventies, and beyond. Margaret and I are planning how we hope to do that in the coming years.

Obviously these phases are generalizations, but they present a pattern for which to strive. If you are young, then you may be eager to leave the learning phase. Be patient, because the more diligently you go after phase one, the greater your potential to maximize the other phases. If you're older and you didn't lay a good foundation for yourself, don't despair. Keep learning and growing. You still have a chance to finish well. But if you give up, you'll never go up.

REDUCE YOUR DEBT

Michael Kidwell and Steve Rhode, authors of *Get Out of Debt: Smart Solutions to Your Money Problems,* believe, "Every person in debt is suffering from some type of depression. Debt is one of the leading causes of divorce, lack of sleep, and poor work performance. It is truly one of the deep dark secrets that people have. It robs them of their self-worth and keeps them from achieving dreams."[13]

Going into debt for things that appreciate in value can be a good idea. Purchasing a house, securing transportation so you can work, improving your education, and investing in a business are good things—as long as you can manage them well. But many people incur debt for frivolous things. When you're still paying for something you no longer use or even have, it means trouble.

Kidwell and Rhode suggest five steps to reduce debt:

1. Stop incurring debt.
2. Track your cash.
3. Plan for the future.
4. Don't expect instant miracles.
5. Seek professional help.[14]

Don't let your possessions or your lifestyle possess you. If you're a slave to debt, find a way to free yourself.

PUT YOUR FINANCIAL FORMULA INTO PLACE

Someone once observed that the difference between the rich and the poor is that the rich invest their money and spend what's left, while the poor spend their money and invest what's left. If you haven't decided to plan your finances, you're headed for trouble. Put yourself on a budget. Create a financial formula that works for you. You may want to try the 10-10-80 approach that we use. But do something! The old saying is corny but true: Failing to plan is like planning to fail.

> The difference between the rich and the poor is that the rich invest their money and spend what's left, while the poor spend their money and invest what's left.

Managing the Disciplines of Finances

I have to admit that money has never been my number one motivation in life. Truthfully, finances were so low on my list of priorities that for a time I neglected them, which is probably why I didn't make my good life decision concerning finances until I was in my late thirties. But we've all seen what lack of good financial management can do to people in their twilight years. Recently my son-in-law, Steve, and I went to eat at a restaurant when we were down in Florida, and a lovely lady in her mid-seventies waited on us. Now, you never know another person's situation; some people work into their eighties simply for the joy of work or to be with people. But I know that the majority of people who keep working in physically demanding jobs during that season of life do it because they have no other choice. My friend financial expert Ron Blue says that the average annual income for people over age sixty-five is $6,300.[15] In the case of our waitress, I sensed that she worked because she had no other options. So Steve and I left her a great tip. The next time you find yourself being waited on by senior citizens, you might want to do something for them.

I'm still growing in the discipline of finances. I settled my personal financial issue years ago with 10-10-80, but it's been only in the last decade that I've learned to be better at finances in business. I used to focus on the vision for the organization, hire the best leaders I could find to join me in achieving it, and then lead to the best of my ability. I pretty much left the financial aspects of the business to others. But my brother, Larry, took me to task for that attitude. He told me that I had no right to neglect business finances just because it wasn't an area of strength or passion for me. So now, at home and in business, I maintain this discipline: *Every day I will focus on my financial game plan so that each day I will have more, not fewer, options.* The earlier you make the decision and practice the discipline of sound financial management, the more options you will have.

To help you approach your finances every day with the right attitude, do the following:

BECOME A GOOD EARNER

To become a good financial manager, you must first have something to manage. That's why I believe the first discipline of finances is to maximize your earning potential. By that I don't mean to neglect the other important areas of life in order to make a buck. Nor am I suggesting that your focus should always be on money. Just maintain a strong work ethic, and learn how to make and manage money. Develop relationships with people who are successful in this area and learn from them. There are also plenty of good books about personal and business finances.

Work ethic, on the other hand, is more about desire than knowledge. It comes from within. Anything can fuel that desire: the passion to serve others, the promise of escaping the circumstances of our birth, a vision for progress, or a personal passion. What often puts out the fire of desire is the belief that the work is too great for the return.

If you find yourself thinking that you have it especially hard in your job or career, you might need to put things into perspective. Take a look at the rules that employees at Mt. Corry Carriage and Iron Works were asked to follow in 1872:

1. Employees will daily sweep the floors, dust the furniture, shelves, and showcases.
2. Each day fill lamps, clean chimneys and trim wicks, wash win dows once a week.
3. Each clerk will bring a bucket of water and a scuttle of coal for the day's business.
4. Make your pens carefully. You may whittle nibs to individual taste.
5. This office will open at 7 a.m. and close at 8 p.m. daily except on the Sabbath.

6. Men employees will be given an evening off each week for courting purposes, or two evenings if they go regularly to church.
7. Every employee should lay aside from each pay a goodly sum of his earnings for his benefit during his declining years so that he will not become a burden upon the charity of his betters.
8. Any employee who smokes Spanish cigars, uses liquor in any form, gets shaved at a barber shop, or frequents public halls will give good reason to suspect his worth, intentions, integrity, and honesty.
9. The employee who has performed his labors faithfully and without fault for a period of five years in my service and who has been thrifty and attentive to his religious duties and is looked upon by his fellowman as a substantial and law-abiding citizen will be given an increase of 5 cents per day in his pay, providing that just returns in profits from the business permit.

We enjoy a lot of advantages today that people didn't have in previous generations. One of them is that we don't have to fulfill the same expectations of those in previous centuries. With the right attitude and a willingness to pay the price, almost anyone can pursue nearly any opportunity and achieve it.

BE GRATEFUL EVERY DAY

One of the most important things you can do for yourself is keep your perspective and be thankful for whatever you have. Poet Rudyard Kipling once told his audience while speaking at a graduation ceremony, "Do not pay too much attention to fame, power, or money. Some day you will meet a person who cares for *none* of these, and then you will know how poor you are." If you work hard and maintain an attitude of gratitude, you'll find it easier to manage your finances every day.

DON'T COMPARE YOURSELF TO OTHERS

Whenever people start comparing themselves to others, they get into trouble. Comparisons of money and possessions can be especially detrimental. Wanting to keep up with neighbors or appear well-off gets many people into horrible debt. *New Yorker* financial writer James Surowiecki says, "Americans have always been stricken by the disease that some have called 'luxury fever' or 'affluenza.' Even if we aren't rich yet, we'd like to look as if we were."[16]

If you see your neighbors buying new furnishings for their home, taking elaborate vacations, and driving a new vehicle every year, does something stir inside you to do the same? Just because someone *appears* to be in similar circumstances to you doesn't mean anything. Your neighbors might earn twice as much as you do. Or they may be in debt up to their eyeballs and three-fourths of the way to bankruptcy court. Don't make assumptions, and don't try to be like someone else.

GIVE AS MUCH AS YOU CAN

Author Bruce Larson says, "Money is another pair of hands to heal and feed and bless the desperate families of the earth. . . . In other words, money is my other self. Money can go where I do not have time to go, where I do not have a passport to go. My money can go in my place and heal and bless and feed

> "Money is another pair of hands to heal and feed and bless the desperate families of the earth. . . . A man's money is an extension of himself."
>
> —BRUCE LARSON

and help. A man's money is an extension of himself." That's true of your money only if you're willing to part with it. Or to put it a more colorful way as Hanna Andersson Clothing company founder

Gun Denhart did: "Money is like manure. If you let it pile up, it just smells. But if you spread it around, you can encourage things to grow."

My brother, Larry, recently gave me this quote from Blaise Pascal: "I love poverty because Jesus loved it. I love wealth because it affords me the means of helping the needy. I keep faith with everyone." I've mentioned "options" a lot in this chapter. That may seem like a selfish word to you. But I have to tell you, for me having options is about service. Philanthropist Andrew Carnegie said his goal was to spend the first half of his life accumulating wealth and the second half giving it away. What a great idea! My desire is to spend my future years giving to others. I won't be able to give on the scale that Carnegie did, but that's not important. What matters is that I do what I can by practicing financial discipline.

Reflecting on Finances

As I look back at my life in light of finances, I realize that my thinking has changed over the years as I've gotten more mature and more realistic:

In my 20s . . .	I realized that life consisted of more than money.
In my 30s . . .	I realized that money would give me options.
In my 40s . . .	I realized that I needed to pay now in order to play later.
In my 50s . . .	I realize that the greatest joy in making money is the privilege of giving it away.

Perhaps the best financial guidance I've ever read came from clergyman John Wesley. His advice was, "Earn all you can, save all

you can, give all you can."
That's a philosophy you
can embrace no matter
what phase of life you're
in or how much money you make.

> "Earn all you can, save all you can, give all you can."
>
> —JOHN WESLEY

Discovering Her Dream

If you keep track of the *New York Times* best-seller lists, you know her name. If you watch PBS or Oprah, then you've probably seen her. And if you study sales, you know that she personally sold ten thousand books in twelve minutes on QVC and had to be yanked off the air because they sold out of books so quickly.[17] I'm talking about Suze Orman, the financial guru who wrote the bestselling books *The 9 Steps to Financial Freedom* and *The Laws of Money, the Lessons of Life*. What you may not know is that she wasn't born rich, she doesn't have an MBA, and she used to be a financial wreck.

Orman was born into a Chicago working-class family in 1951. Her father ran a small struggling restaurant. When the family experienced financial difficulties, her mother worked as a legal secretary. Suze worked in the family restaurant while growing up. When she went to college, she studied social work, getting her degree in 1973. After graduating, she promptly moved to Berkeley, California, and got a job as a waitress at the Buttercup Bakery. She stayed there seven years, but she had dreams of doing something bigger. She wanted to open her own restaurant. When a regular patron at the Buttercup Bakery loaned her $50,000 as seed money to start her own restaurant, she knew it wasn't enough. So she decided to invest it. Since she knew little about money, she handed her funds over to a broker. In four months it was gone.

Taken!

Orman says that her broker was dishonest and swindled her.[18] But she was broke just the same. That's when she made a financial decision that would change her life. She decided to learn about finances and become a broker herself. It didn't take her long to become highly successful. One of her mentors, Clif Citrano, a former Merrill Lynch broker, says, "I've met much better investors in my time, but no one could market to investors better."[19]

In 1987, she started her own firm, and she began making even more money. But then she got into trouble. Orman says, "Soon after my firm was established, I was nearly destroyed by one of the most devastating things that ever happened to me."[20] An employee stole from her and tried to ruin her professionally. Although Orman eventually took the employee to court and won the case against her, the experience had other negative effects on her. Though she stopped seeing her clients and put her business on hold, she didn't stop living the high life. She wasn't earning or properly managing her finances, and it just about ruined her financially.

Comeback

What finally brought Suze Orman back to her senses was a traffic ticket received on the Bay Bridge between Oakland and San Francisco. Orman recalls her thinking in the moments after she received it:

> I remember that the ticket was for only $40. But I did not have $40—I didn't have $20, or even $10, unless I was to take another cash advance on one of my credit cards. As I drove away from the bridge in my high-end leased car, wearing my $8,000 credit-card-charged watch and my $2,000 department-store-

charged leather jacket, the magnitude of my lies [I was telling myself] became real to me for the first time. I was speeding down the highway to financial ruin.[21]

After that, Orman determined to change. She faced up to the truth of her situation. She got herself back together financially, and she began working hard again. She also decided she wanted to help others do what she had done: make the decision to change the way they approach finances.

Since then she has sold millions of books. But finances are not her motivation. "I don't do this for the money anymore," she says. "The money doesn't fascinate me. Everybody probably thinks money's my whole life. My apartment is 900 square feet. I could have bought a $10 million place on Park Avenue, but what for?"[22]

Orman has her critics. Some say her approach to money is too simplistic. Others don't care for some of her off-the-wall opinions. But one thing is for sure. She has settled the financial issue in her life. She earns and properly manages her finances daily. It doesn't really matter how much money she has. She lives modestly. She drives an older car. And when she's not in New York, she lives in a tiny modest house in Oakland that she bought before she became a household name. But she has many options. And that's a good measure of success when it comes to finances.

FINANCIAL Application and Exercises
Earning and Properly Managing
Finances Daily

Your Financial Decision Today

Where do you stand when it comes to finances today? Ask yourself
these three questions:

1. *Have I already made the decision to earn and properly manage my
   finances daily?*
2. *If so, when did I make that decision?*
3. *What exactly did I decide? (Write it here.)*

_____

_____

_____

_____

_____

_____

Your Financial Discipline Every Day

Based on the decision you made concerning finances, what is the
one discipline you must practice *today and every day* in order to be
successful? Write it here.

_____

_____

_____

_____

_____

_____

Making Up for Yesterday

If you need some help making the right decision concerning finances and developing the everyday discipline to live it out, do the
following exercises:

1. *Boxer Joe Louis once said, "I don't like money, actually, but it quiets my nerves." What is your philosophy concerning money? What do you expect money to do for you? What won't it do? Where does earning come into play? How will you maximize your earning potential and still maintain the right attitude toward money? Commit those thoughts to paper.*

———————————————————————————

———————————————————————————

———————————————————————————

———————————————————————————

———————————————————————————

———————————————————————————

2. *What season of life are you currently in: learning, earning, or returning? What must you do to maximize the phase you're in? (If you're learning, maybe you should return to school, begin a personal growth program, or find a mentor. If you're earning, you should figure out how to leverage your talents, skills, and experience. If you're returning, you should build wealth while connecting with worthy causes to support.) It may help you to look ahead to the next phase and figure out what you could do better now to prepare for the future.*

3. *If you don't have a handle on the day-to-day management of your finances, you need to make a change immediately. Figure out what you're spending and where you're spending it. Then put yourself on some kind of budget.*

4. *If you're deep in debt, dig yourself out. Eliminate your consumer debt. Depending on your past, it may take you a while. But the payoff is huge. Getting out of debt and getting your finances under control will not only benefit you financially, but it will also help you emotionally and even spiritually.*

Looking Forward to Tomorrow

Spend some time reflecting on how your decision concerning finances and the daily discipline that comes out of it will positively impact you in the future. What compounding benefits do you expect to receive? Write them here.

_____

_____

_____

_____

_____

_____

Keep what you've written as a constant reminder, because . . .

Reflection today motivates your discipline every day, and

Discipline every day maximizes your decision of yesterday.

CHAPTER 10

Today's **FAITH** Gives Me Peace

Nearly thirty years ago when I first began speaking at conferences and hosting leadership seminars, my entire audience was made up of pastors. But over the years, more and more businesspeople have discovered that the leadership principles I teach work equally well for them. Today, about 70 percent of the people I teach are business leaders. And in the last seven or eight years, the number of invitations I have received to speak to large corporations, entrepreneurial businesses, and leadership-intensive institutions has exploded. (One of the highlights of 2003 was accepting the invitation to speak on leadership to cadets and faculty members at the United States Military Academy at West Point.)

When I speak to businesspeople, I often share with them my pastoral background. My faith is the most important thing in my life, but I'm very sensitive to the fact that others may have a very different point of view from mine, and I never push my faith on anyone. In fact, recently when I was speaking to a group of corporate executives, one of the people asked me, "Where did you learn your leadership principles?"

"I don't think you want to know," I told him.

"Sure I do," he said.

"You may not like the answer," I said.

"Try me."

"Okay," I responded. "Everything I know about leadership I learned from the Bible." He was surprised but very respectful.

I know some people who read this book will have ambivalent feelings about my opinions regarding faith. And some may be offended. If that is true for you, I apologize. (Please feel free to simply skip this chapter if that is the case.) However, knowing my background, you're probably not surprised that faith is one of my Daily Dozen. My reasons

> I sincerely believe that faith holds the key to life's meaning.

for including a chapter on the subject in *Today Matters* is twofold. First, for the sake of my integrity, I must include it in the book. All my life I have been trying to increase my faith and encourage others to develop theirs. Second, I want to be sensitive to your views concerning faith. Therefore, I will share with you my personal spiritual journey with the hope that it will encourage you to explore this aspect of your own life. I sincerely believe that faith holds the key to life's meaning.

Skeptical of Faith

It's interesting to see how people react when someone brings up the subject of faith. Over the years, I've found that faith usually gets one of the six following responses. People . . .

1. **Ignore It:** What do people do when something doesn't apply to them? Generally, they ignore it. Some people don't see the relevance of faith. It seems "quaint" or out of date—something for another age.

2. **Misunderstand It:** Others believe that acquiring faith is like trying to get your hand around smoke. They figure it's too mystical and elusive, and they'll never get a handle on it.

3. **Discount It:** There are people who think faith is better suited for somebody else, not for them. Perhaps it's an alien concept. If their family didn't embrace faith and none of their closest friends do, then they assume it couldn't be right for them either.

4. **Fight It:** Have you ever had someone argue with you about your faith? That's what some people do. Because they don't value it, they argue against its value for anyone else.

5. **Delay It:** Some people instinctively believe that faith is important, but they don't want to deal with it now. (I suspect that some are worried they'll have to give up what's important to them if they look into it.) Instead, they say that they'll think about it someday when they're old.

6. **Explore It:** There is one other way people react to faith issues. They are willing to give it a chance. Hopefully, this will be your response.

Why Faith Matters Today

Johann Wolfgang von Goethe said, "I am fully convinced that the soul is indestructible, and that its activity will continue through eternity." Even skeptics will admit that people have a spiritual aspect. As philosopher Teilhard de Chardin said, "We are not human beings having a spiritual experience. We are spiritual beings having

"We are not human beings having a spiritual experience. We are spiritual beings having a human experience."

—TEILHARD DE CHARDIN

a human experience." There are longings of the soul that can be satisfied only with spiritual experiences, though people try and fail to meet them in material ways.

Take a look at just a few of the things faith does:

FAITH GIVES ME A DIVINE PERSPECTIVE TODAY

There are a lot of things in life that are difficult to understand. Faith allows the soul to go beyond what the eyes can see. Or to put it another way, as author Phillip Yancey says, "Faith is trusting in advance what will only make sense in reverse."

If you're a parent, then you already understand how this works. When children are small, they ask a lot of questions. Most of the time we can give them pretty specific answers that satisfy them. But sometimes we tell them something, and their life experience doesn't provide them with what they need to grasp it. It's like trying to explain to a three-year-old that if he falls into a swimming pool when no one is around, he'll drown.

"But why?" he asks. "How do you know?" You try to explain, but at some point, all you can say is, "You just have to trust me on this."

Perhaps the most difficult questions any person faces relate to death. I recently attended the funeral of Jane Chapman, the wife of my good friend Tom Chapman. During the service a poem was read that captures the power of faith and the perspective it brings. It said,

I am standing on the seashore.
A ship appears
and spreads her white sails
to the morning breeze

and starts for the ocean.
She is an object of beauty
and I stand watching her
till at last she fades away on the horizon,
and someone at my side quietly says,
"She is gone." Gone where?
Gone from my vision, that is all;
she is just as large as when I saw her last.

The diminished size
and the total loss of sight
is in me, not in her;
and just at the moment
when someone at my side says,
"She is gone,"
there are others who are watching
her coming and other voices
take up a joyful shout,
"There she comes!"[1]

People of faith understand that when you seek to broaden your perspective and try to see life from a heavenly vantage point, everything makes a lot more sense. Being willing to make that jump may not be easy, especially if you're a natural skeptic. But I believe that if you're willing to sincerely try to seek perspective from God, you will be rewarded.

FAITH GIVES ME HEALTH TODAY

Years ago, I read about a study from Purdue University that found people who practice their religion regularly develop only half as many medical problems as nonbelievers. The researchers concluded that religion kept people's stress down and their sense of well-being up because their faith added meaning and perspective, as well as valuable social networks.[2] Recently a group of physicians recon-firmed these findings. They wrote,

> We have recently completed a systematic review of over 1200 studies on the religion health relationship. These studies have been conducted by different investigators, working at different institutions, studying different clinical and community popula-tions located in different parts of the United States and world over the span of a century. The vast majority of these studies show a relationship between greater religious involvement and better mental health, better physical health, or lower use of health services.[3]

If you desire to improve your physical well-being and your emotional outlook, increasing your faith can help you.

FAITH GIVES ME STRENGTH FOR TODAY

A strong faith of any kind gives a person strength. Few things can help a person overcome adversity the way faith can. S. G. Holland, former prime minister of New Zealand, asserted that "faith draws the poison from every grief, takes the sting from every loss, and quenches the fire of every pain; and only faith can do it." Faith gives a person power.

The opposite is also true. Faithlessness is de-energizing. Where there is no faith in the future, there is no power in the present. Years ago, a hydroelectric dam was planned in Maine that would create a lake whose waters would cover up a small town there. Quite a bit of time elapsed after the plans for the dam were an-nounced before the citizens of the town would have to relocate.

As the flood date ap-proached, the people in the town stopped doing

> Where there is no faith in the future, there is no power in the present.

every kind of maintenance. They didn't paint or repair buildings. Sidewalks went untended. Roads deteriorated. The town got so shabby that it looked abandoned long before the inhabitants moved away.

FAITH GIVES ME RESILIENCE TODAY

Not only does faith give a person strength, it also makes them more resilient. Soon after actor Christopher Reeve fell from his horse and broke his neck, he was almost ready to give up. But he found the strength to bounce back because his wife, Dana, had faith in him. Now he is known for his determination and faith, which he believes is part of how Americans are wired. Reeve says,

> America has a tradition that many nations probably envy. We frequently achieve the impossible. But that's part of our national character. That's what got us from one coast to another. That's what got us the largest economy in the world. That's what got us to the moon. Now, in my room while I was in rehab, there was a picture of the space shuttle blasting off. It was autographed by every astronaut down at NASA. On the top of that picture it says, "We found nothing is impossible." Now, that should be our motto. . . . So many of our dreams, so many dreams at first seem impossible, and then they seem improbable. And then when we summon the will, they soon become inevitable. So if we can conquer outer space, we should be able to conquer inner space, too. And that's the frontier of the brain, the central nervous system and all the afflictions of the body that destroy so many lives and rob our country of so much potential.[4]

When you believe in something, you have something to live for. And that keeps you going, even under extremely difficult circumstances. Perhaps Mother

> "Faith keeps the person who keeps the faith."
>
> —MOTHER TERESA

Teresa summed it up best when she said, "Faith keeps the person who keeps the faith."

Making the Decision to Deepen and Live Out My Faith Daily

I grew up in a household filled with faith. My father, Melvin, became a pastor as a young man and remains in ministry to this day at age eighty-three. I heard words of faith from him and my mother, Laura, every day growing up. But you can't live on someone else's faith. There are no spiritual grandchildren. Each person must make his own decision and act on it with integrity. At age seventeen, I made my faith decision: *I will accept God's gift of his Son, Jesus Christ, as my Savior.*

That decision, more than any other, has shaped my life. It has forged my worldview. Recognition of God's love for everyone has influenced how I view others. The Golden Rule has taught me how to treat people. God's love for me has given me great self-worth. And the Bible has taught me how to lead people. Whenever I am asked to sign a copy of the *Maxwell Leadership Bible,* the edition that contains leadership notes from my thirty years of studying leadership in Scripture, I write, "Everything I know about leadership I learned from this Book."

It is my privilege to be a national board member of the Center for Faith Walk Leadership. The organization, founded by my friend Ken Blanchard, encourages leading in the workplace according to the highest standard. Here's what Ken says that means:

> It doesn't mean the bottom line, or looking good to Wall Street, or being praised by your peers. It's not about getting the credit, or the promotions, or the raises. It's about working with those you lead to get results in a way that honors God. It's about peo-

ple, service, and results. It's a new way of leading based on the teachings of Jesus, the greatest leader of all time. He gave his followers a vision of something greater than themselves. He consistently reminded them of the long-term effects of their work. He allowed those around him to fail, but held them accountable. He redirected them. He forgave them, and he inspired the best in others. And the result? He started a movement that continues to thrive more than 2,000 years later.

True leadership starts with the heart—with character. The underlying message from God is not to act differently, but to become different. Not to act honestly, but to become an honest person. Then honesty will be at the core of

> True leadership starts with the heart—with character.

your leadership style. It will be at the core of your life. My faith has not only given me peace; it has given me a wonderful model for leadership and life.

If you desire to make an honest exploration of faith, then know this:

WE ALREADY HAVE FAITH . . . THE IMPORTANT CHOICE IS WHERE WE PLACE IT

Author John Bisagno observed, "Faith is at the heart of life. You go to a doctor whose name you cannot pronounce. He gives you a prescription you cannot read. You take it to a pharmacist you have never seen. He gives you a medicine you do not understand and yet you take it."

We all have faith. Every day we act on beliefs that have little or no evidence to back them up. That is also true in a spiritual sense. Just as one person has faith that God is real, an atheist has faith that there is no God. Both people hold strong beliefs, and neither person can produce evidence to absolutely prove his point of view.

Right now, you already have faith in something. Your goal should be to align your beliefs with the truth. Seek the truth, and I believe you will find it.

UNDERSTAND THAT FAITH IS OFTEN BIRTHED OUT OF DIFFICULTIES

I've already shared that some skeptical people see faith as a negative thing, almost as a sign of weakness. If faith is new to you and you are uncertain how to approach it, then I would advise you to view it as an opportunity for a course correction in the journey of life. In a play by T. S. Eliot, one of the most influential poets of the twentieth century, one character expresses it in those kinds of terms. He describes a faith that comes after extreme disappointment. He calls it the "kind of faith that arises after despair. The destination cannot be described; you will know very little until you get there; you will journey blind. But the way leads toward possession of what you have sought for in the wrong place."

If you are experiencing difficulties, allow yourself to explore faith in response to it. Henri Nouwen said this "is the great conversation in our life: to recognize and believe that the many unexpected events are not just disturbing interruptions of our projects, but the way in which God molds our hearts and prepares us." Faith not only can help you through a crisis, it can help you to approach life after the hard times with a whole new perspective. It can help you adopt an outlook of hope and courage through faith to face reality.

> "[This] is the great conversation in our life: to recognize and believe that the many unexpected events are not just disturbing interruptions of our projects, but the way in which God molds our hearts and prepares us."
>
> —HENRI NOUWEN

A FAITH THAT HASN'T BEEN TESTED CAN'T BE TRUSTED

You may have noticed that the heading for this section of the chapter is titled "Making the Decision to Deepen and Live Out My Faith Daily." It's not enough to simply make a faith decision. If you want to live it out, then you have to work at deepening it. Faith gives you peace and strength only if it's not superficial. The deeper the faith, the greater its potential to carry you through the rough times. As Rabbi Abraham Heschel said, "Faith like Job's cannot be shaken because it is the result of having been shaken."

Perhaps nothing in recent history tested the faith of so many people as severely as the Holocaust. Viennese psychiatrist Victor Frankl was one of the survivors of the Nazi's atrocities. He spent 1942 to 1945 in the concentration camps of Auschwitz and Dachau. Frankl once said, "A weak faith is weakened by predicaments and catastrophes whereas a strong faith is strengthened by them." Despite the horrors he witnessed and the treatment he suffered, his faith didn't weaken—it deepened.

Managing the Disciplines of Faith

Thousands of books have been written on how to live out the disciplines of faith. Perhaps that is so because it is such a difficult thing to do. For me, the discipline can be captured in one simple phrase: *Every day to live and lead like Jesus.* While the words are simple, following through is not. Living out the discipline of faith is the greatest challenge of my Daily Dozen. The problem is that instead of being like Jesus, I often want to be like John Maxwell. I fall short of the mark. But with God as my helper, I keep growing. And when I *do* follow in his footsteps and live his principles, people are helped and I am fulfilled.

Following are four suggestions for managing your discipline of faith:

1. EMBRACE THE VALUE OF FAITH

I've already given a number of reasons why I think faith is beneficial. But let me add to that list. There are some things in life you will arrive at only through faith. In the past, many people hoped that science would provide all the answers to life's questions. But science cannot do that. Ironically, what is embraced as scientific fact changes from generation to generation. Just look at the way scientists have viewed our solar system. Ptolemy believed the earth was at its center. Copernicus asserted that the sun was at its center and the planets moved in circular orbits around it. Kepler proved that the orbits were elliptical. Today, scientists no longer argue the structure of the solar system, but ideas about how it was formed change continually. In fact, just this week scientists found what they are calling the oldest known planet in the globular star cluster M4. They say it is a " 'stunning revelation' that will force scientists to revise their ideas of planetary formation."[5]

Contrast science with faith. The core beliefs of Judaism and Christianity have not changed in thousands of years. There is a spiritual aspect to human life that cannot be denied. Spiritual needs must be met spiritually. Nothing else will fill the void.

2. PUT GOD IN THE PICTURE

There's a story of a man driving a convertible on a mountain road who took an unexpected turn too quickly and went right over the edge. As his car fell, he managed to grab on to a tree sprouting from the cliff face as his car dropped a thousand feet to the canyon floor.

"Help!" he screamed. "Can anyone hear me?" An echo was the only response.

"God, can you hear me?" he cried.

Suddenly the clouds rolled together and a voice like thunder said, "Yes, I can hear you."

"Will you help me?"

"Yes, I will help you. Do you believe in me?"

"Yes, I believe in you."

"Do you trust me?"

"Yes, yes, I trust you. Please, hurry."

"If you trust me, then let go of the tree," thundered the voice.

After a long silence, the man cried, "Can anyone *else* hear me?"

If you want to embrace faith, you must let God into your life. No one else is worthy of our absolute and unconditional trust. Theologian F. B. Meyer said, "Unbelief puts our circumstances between us and God. Faith puts God between us and our circumstances." Who

> "Unbelief puts our circumstances between us and God. Faith puts God between us and our circumstances."
>
> —F. B. MEYER

wouldn't like to have the Creator of the universe helping them? James, one of the fathers of the first-century church, advised, "Come near to God and he will come near to you."[6]

3. ASSOCIATE WITH PEOPLE OF FAITH

Comedian Bob Hope once went to the airport to meet his wife, Dolores, who had been doing some charity work for the Catholic Church. When her private plane pulled in, the first two people to step off the plane were Catholic priests. Then came Dolores, followed by four more Catholic priests. Hope turned to a friend near him and quipped, "I don't know why she just doesn't buy insurance like everybody else!"

It's a fact that you become more like the people you spend time with. If you desire to increase your faith, spend time with others who exercise theirs. Learn from them. Find out how they think.

4. EXPLORE AND DEEPEN YOUR FAITH

Developing your faith is very similar to developing yourself physically. Perhaps that's why the Bible contains so many athletic metaphors for spiritual growth. If you want to get into good physical condition, you need to exercise your body regularly. If you don't, you not only don't gain strength and conditioning, you begin to lose what you once had.

D. L. Moody, a nineteenth-century lay preacher who founded Northfield Seminary and the Moody Bible Institute, explained how his faith developed. He said, "I prayed for faith, and thought that some day faith would come down and strike me like lightning. But faith did not seem to come. One day I read in the tenth chapter of Romans, 'Faith comes by hearing, and hearing by the word of God.' I had closed my Bible and prayed for faith. I now opened my Bible and began to study, and faith has been growing ever since."

Reflecting on Faith

St. Augustine of Hippo observed, "Faith is to believe what we do not see; and the reward of this faith is to see what we believe." When I made my faith decision back in 1964, I knew at the time I was doing the right thing for myself spiritually. But I didn't know that I would "see what I believe" played out so dramatically in my life:

In my teens . . .   My faith gave me assurance of eternal salvation.
In my 20s . . .   My faith gave me meaning and fulfillment.

In my 30s . . .	My faith gave me a platform to help others.
In my 40s . . .	My faith gave me a foundation for my leadership.
In my 50s . . .	My faith gives me a peace that cannot be given by others or taken away by them.

I cannot imagine how my life would have played out without my faith at the center of it.

> "Faith is to believe what we do not see; and the reward of this faith is to see what we believe."
>
> —St. Augustine of Hippo

Dreaming of the Heavens

Ever since he was a kid, Rick Husband wanted to be an astronaut. He remembered seeing his first space launch at age four, and he was fascinated by the Gemini and Apollo missions. Patty Ragan, a friend whose family has been close to the Husbands for three generations, said, "Rick wanted to be an astronaut from the time he was in the fourth grade, and he did everything he needed to do that."[7]

When Husband went off to college at Texas Tech, he studied mechanical engineering and became a member of the Air Force ROTC. He completed undergraduate pilot training and then began his career as an F-4 fighter pilot in the air force. Before long, he became a flight instructor and then a test pilot. As a program manager, he helped work on an increased-performance engine. He became an F-15 demonstration pilot, and he participated in a pilot exchange program with the RAF. In all, he had logged more than thirty-eight hundred hours of flight time in more than forty different kinds of aircraft. He was among the best of the best. Along the way, not only did he earn his master's degree in mechanical engineering from Cal State Fresno, but he also got married and had two children. He was respected not only for his skill in his career, but also for his faith and his devotion as a husband and father.

The Right Stuff

In December of 1994, Husband finally realized his dream of becoming an astronaut and began training a few months later. In 1999, he went into space for the first time as pilot of the space shuttle *Discovery,* and he loved it. "One of the most enjoyable things about flying in space is getting to see God's creation from a different perspective," said Husband. "There are just so many different beautiful aspects of the views you get to see out there that it is an awe-inspiring sight, almost no matter in which direction you're looking."[8]

Husband's next trip into space was aboard the *Columbia,* and this time he commanded the mission. As usual, his family watched the launch in Florida. That was always the most nerve-racking time. When Rick's wife, Evelyn, described it, she said that the worst is "in the first couple of minutes because of the *Challenger.* When I saw the rocket boosters come off, that pretty much does it for me because I feel like we're home free."[9]

Little did anyone suspect that the real danger would be when *Columbia* was making its final descent to land at Kennedy Space Center. On February 1, 2003, at about 9:00 a.m., the space shuttle *Columbia* disintegrated over the Dallas–Fort Worth area, just a few hundred miles from where Rick Husband grew up. The entire crew of seven was lost.

Just two days after the tragedy, Evelyn Husband was interviewed by Katie Couric on the *Today* show. She was remarkably composed. She talked about how the families of all *Columbia*'s astronauts had come together to comfort one another, how they were grieving together, and how supportive NASA had been. She expressed her desire that space exploration continue. And she also explained how she was making it through such a difficult time:

> When Rick autographed pictures for people, he always put a Bible verse on it that was Proverbs 3:5-6, which says, "Trust in the Lord with all your heart and do not lean on your own understanding; in all your ways acknowledge him, and he will make your paths straight." And that verse has been a blessing to me and Rick, and now it's a tremendous blessing to me because I don't understand any of this, but I do trust the Lord, and so that's been a tremendous comfort.[10]

If you desire to have the kind of peace that Evelyn Husband has and the assurance that she and Rick enjoyed, then make a faith decision and learn to deepen and live out your faith daily.

FAITH Application and Exercises
Deepening and Living Out Your Faith Daily

Your Faith Decision Today

Where do you stand when it comes to faith today? Ask yourself these three questions:

1. *Have I already made the decision to deepen and live out my faith daily?*
2. *If so, when did I make that decision?*
3. *What exactly did I decide? (Write it here.)*

_____

_____

_____

_____

_____

Your Faith Discipline Every Day

Based on the decision you made concerning your faith, what is the one discipline you must practice *today and every day* in order to be successful? Write it here.

_____

_____

_____

_____

_____

Making Up for Yesterday

If you need some help making the right decision concerning faith and developing the everyday discipline to live it out, do the following exercises:

1. *What has been your attitude toward faith up to now? Has your approach been to ignore it, misunderstand it, discount it, fight it, or delay it? Try to understand your personal barriers to faith. What must you do to remove them so that you can place your faith in God?*

2. *Sometimes when people open themselves up to seek spiritual truth, they can look back at their lives and see the hand of God at work. Think about your own life. Have there been times when God might have been trying to get your attention? Were there times when you seemed to be protected from harm despite your own actions? Ask God to reveal his pursuit of you in your life.*

3. *If you once embraced faith but allowed it to fall to the wayside, per-haps it was because you hadn't deepened it before a time of testing. Go back to your spiritual roots and do some exploring. Approach it afresh. Study the Bible and learn now what you neglected then. Bring God back "into the picture."*

4. *Seek out people of faith whom you respect. Talk to them about their beliefs. Ask them to recommend books and tapes for your growth. And find out where they are connected spiritually so that you can find a community of believers with whom you can connect.*

Looking Forward to Tomorrow

Spend some time reflecting on how your decision concerning faith and the daily discipline that comes out of it will positively impact you in the future. What compounding benefits do you expect to receive? Write them here.

_____

_____

_____

_____

Keep what you've written as a constant reminder, because . . .
Reflection today motivates your discipline every day, and
Discipline every day maximizes your decision of yesterday.

CHAPTER 11

Today's **RELATIONSHIPS** Give Me Fulfillment

When Armand Hammer, the chairman of Occidental Petroleum, died in December of 1990, he was a legend. In his ninety-two years of life, he had done things people only dreamed about. He had become a successful international businessman, a person of influence with presidents and statesmen, and a generous philanthropist and patron of the arts. *USA Today* called him "a giant of capitalism and confidant of world leaders" and "flamboyant crusader for world peace and a cancer cure."[1] An article in the *Los Angeles Times* stated,

> The billionaire industrialist had cut a flamboyant swath throughout his colorful and varied career. A public figure comfortable with royalty, heads of state, the rich and famous, he stirred up controversy among not only ardent admirers of his keen intelligence and bold strategies but also scathing critics who questioned

his ethics and powerful ego. A man of immense wealth, he endowed schools, museums and cancer research centers with gifts totaling tens of millions of dollars.[2]

Most reports cited his many accomplishments: making his first million by age twenty-one, providing humanitarian aid and famine relief to Soviet Russia in 1921, improving U.S.-Soviet relations, and receiving numerous prestigious awards granted by over a dozen countries. The biographies written about Hammer before his death in 1990 describe him in glowing terms. The story was that he saved his father's pharmaceutical company while he was still in medical school, traveled to the Soviet Union in his twenties, made huge amounts of money in business there, bought and amassed a huge collection of priceless czarist artwork and treasures, and made a fortune selling them in the United States. He later went on to buy the small and struggling Occidental Petroleum Corporation, turning it into a multibillion-dollar organization. Most people thought he was a business genius. But after he died, the truth about him came out.

Public Relations Over Human Relations

Armand Hammer's image was the result of a carefully crafted public relations campaign that spanned seven decades. He manufactured much of his personal "history." He continually controlled information about himself, hired ghostwriters to create fictitious autobiographies of his life, and even created a company, Armand Hammer Productions, whose mission was to make films promoting him. All these efforts were made to disguise a greedy, deceptive man who used people like objects and then threw them away like trash when he was finished with them.

Harvard-educated political scientist and author Edward Jay Epstein published a book called *Dossier: The Secret History of Armand Hammer*, which revealed Hammer's real story. Hammer didn't become a millionaire while in his twenties. Nor was he an art collector in Russia. He wanted to make a fortune in business, but he was continually in debt and actually supported himself through government-granted business concessions and by laundering money for the Soviets so that they could finance covert agents. When Soviet officials needed someone to unload the art treasures they had confiscated in the wake of the revolution, they looked to Hammer. He made up the story about his first million to explain how he came by the artwork and treasures. As he sold the objects in the U.S., he received a percentage, but the bulk of the funds were funneled to the Soviets.[3]

Hammer never really had much money—until he married his second wife. His first wife, Olga, and he were married in Russia in 1928. When he first met her in 1925, she was married to someone else, but Hammer quickly convinced her to divorce her husband. In 1929, they had a son, Julian. But when Hammer's aspirations grew and Olga no longer fit the image he wanted to project, he went looking for another wife. He began wooing Angela Carey Zevely, a socialite whose family traveled in the same circles as the Roosevelts. In 1943, three weeks after his divorce from Olga was final, he married Angela. He used her money and her political connections to get a concession from the government so he could make liquor for general consumption at a time when most distilleries were required to produce materials that would help with the war effort. The venture was very profitable, but he also incurred heavy debts.

In the 1950s, Angela had served her purpose, and Hammer was ready to look for another wife. He soon found Frances Tolman, a widow whose husband had left her $8 million. He had already promised his mistress, Bettye Jane Murphy, that he would marry her when he divorced Angela, but he reneged on that promise—even though

Bettye was expecting the child Hammer said he wanted. He had Bettye shipped to Mexico, arranged a phony marriage for her with another man to keep his own name off the birth certificate, and made her promise not to tell the child he was the father when she was born. Meanwhile, when his divorce was finally settled in 1956, he married Frances. He then lent his companies Frances's money to get them out of debt. He also bought stock in Occidental Petroleum Corporation.

A New Role

It didn't take Hammer long to become president and chairman of Occidental. He had already built his reputation (falsely) as a great businessman. His flair for publicity and hype drove up the company's stock price. He then used the inflated stock to buy other companies. To keep absolute control of the company, since he owned only 10 percent of its stock, he forced the members of Occidental's board of directors to give him signed, undated letters of resignation. That way, he could keep them from voting against him.[4] When he saw the potential for a vastly lucrative oil deal in Libya, he bribed his way in.

Meanwhile, he used Occidental like his own personal bank account. In the end, he owned only 1 percent of Occidental's stock, but since he was chairman of the company, he used its resources to subsidize his philanthropic activities, underwrite his parties, pay for his personal lawyers and bodyguards, and provide him with a private jet—a Boeing 727.[5]

Same Old Story

Hammer appears to have burned every relational bridge he ever built. He had no friends at Occidental; he "fired his top executives as though they were errand boys."[6] He allowed his father to go to prison for him (the older doctor took the blame for a botched abortion Hammer performed that led to a woman's death). He neglected his only son, sometimes paying him to stay out of the public eye and forcing him to make an appointment to talk to him on the phone. He hid himself from his only other child, his illegitimate daughter, Victoria. He left a trail of broken marriages. Even his last wife, Frances, gave her relatives evidence prior to her death so that they could sue him for defrauding her of $400 million. And Hammer collected, cast off, and paid off (with Occidental's funds) various mistresses over the years.

Hammer alienated his two brothers' families too. In 1970, when the wife of his brother Harry died, her family asked Hammer to give them the old homestead in Vicksburg, Mississippi, which had been in their family for six generations. Instead, he sold it to a stranger for $22,000.[7] And in 1985 when his brother Victor died, Hammer filed a claim of $667,000 against the $700,000 estate rather than disbursing it to Victor's children and nursing-home-bound wife. Hammer dropped the claim to avoid the publicity only when it appeared that Victor's daughter would make the case public.

It's no surprise that when Hammer's funeral was held on December 13, 1990, it was poorly attended. His son, Julian, did not attend. Neither did the family of his two brothers. His pallbearers were his chauffeur, his male nurse, and other personal employees.

More than anything else, Hammer had wanted to build and protect his reputation. Epstein describes Hammer as "a bullying blowhard with an ego like a Mack truck, whose main aim was to parlay a genius for negotiation (which he had) into a Nobel Peace Prize (which, luckily for the prestige of that award, he never got). His career as humanitarian . . . was loud, insubstantial and based on hype."[8]

In the end, Hammer had nothing. He didn't have the huge personal fortune everyone expected. Within a year of Hammer's death, more than one hundred charities, museums, family members, and other individuals had made claims against his estate. (He had publicly promised large sums to many charitable organizations, but had not followed through on many of those promises.) Within days of his death, Occidental Petroleum distanced itself from him. (The company's Web site doesn't even mention him in its history.) His family was in shambles (not that it would bother him). And his precious image was ruined. When documents in Russia became declassified after the fall of the Soviet Union, his carefully hidden role in Soviet espionage came to light.

Why Relationships Matter Today

Armand Hammer exhibited a drive that was insatiable until his death at age ninety-two. It's difficult to know what fueled it, but I suspect that the absence of fulfilling relationships in his life may have contributed to it. Somehow, he seemed to miss some key truths about relationships:

LIFE'S GREATEST EXPERIENCES INVOLVE OTHER PEOPLE

In *The 17 Indisputable Laws of Teamwork,* the Law of Significance states, "One is too small a number to achieve greatness."[9] All the significant accomplishments in the history of humankind have been achieved by teams of people. We tend to revere rugged individualists, but there are no real-life Rambos or Lone Rangers who do things of great achievement on their own. That truth can also be carried over to a personal level. Most of life's great moments—the ones that resonate in our hearts and minds—involve other people.

Rarely do we experience these times alone. And even when we do, our first inclination is to share them with others.

Think back to the most important experiences of your life, the highest highs, the greatest victories, the most daunting obstacles overcome. How many happened to you alone? I bet there are very few. When you understand that being connected to others is one of life's greatest joys, you realize that life's best comes when you initiate and invest in solid relationships.

YOU'LL ENJOY LIFE MORE IF YOU LIKE PEOPLE

Of the people you know, which seem to have the most fun in life? Think about them a moment. Would you describe them as negative, suspicious, surly, and antisocial? Of course not! When have you known someone with those characteristics who loved life and had a lot of fun? The Scrooges of life don't enjoy much of anything. On the other hand, people who love people usually have a ball. If you like people, then no matter where you go, you'll meet a friend.

YOU'LL GET FARTHER IN LIFE IF PEOPLE LIKE YOU

Consultant John Luther observes, "Natural talent, intelligence, a wonderful education—none of these guarantees success. Something else is needed: the sensitivity to understand what other people want and the willingness to give it to them. Worldly success depends on pleasing others. No one is going to win fame, recognition, or advancement just because he or she thinks it's deserved. Someone else has to think so too."

There's an old saying in sales: All things being equal, the likable person wins. But all things not being equal, the likable person still wins. There's no substi-

> All things being equal, the likable person wins. But all things not being equal, the likable person still wins.

tute for relational skill when it comes to getting ahead in any aspect of life. People who alienate others have a hard time. Here's why:

♦ When people don't like you . . . they'll try to hurt you.
♦ If they can't hurt you . . . they won't help you.
♦ If they *have* to help you . . . they won't hope you succeed.
♦ When they hope you don't succeed . . . life's victories feel hollow.

> "Relationships help us to define who we are and what we can become. Most of us can trace our successes to pivotal relationships."
> —DONALD O. CLIFTON AND PAULA NELSON

Donald O. Clifton and Paula Nelson, authors of *Soar with Your Strengths,* say, "Relationships help us to define who we are and what we can become. Most of us can trace our successes to pivotal relationships."[10] How many positive pivotal relationships have you had with people who *didn't* like you?

PEOPLE ARE ANY ORGANIZATION'S MOST APPRECIABLE ASSET

There are plenty of personal reasons to cultivate positive relationships, but there are also other practical ones. Any organization that succeeds does so because of its people. It doesn't matter whether it's a business, sports team, church, or society. Organizationally, you live or die with your people. That's why Jim Collins, author of *From Good to Great,* writes about the importance of recruiting or, as he calls it, getting the right people on the bus.

Study any successful organization, and you'll see that they value their people. Fred Smith of FedEx says, "Federal Express, from its inception, has put its people first both because it is right to do so and because it is good business as well. Our corporate philosophy is succinctly stated: People—Service—Profits." Appreciate your people as your greatest assets, and they will continually increase in value.

Making the Decision to Initiate and Invest in Solid Relationships Daily

When I was in college in 1965, I took Psychology 101 with Dr. David Van Hoose. One day as he was lecturing, he said something that really got my attention. He remarked, "If you have one true friend in life, you are very fortunate. If you have two real friends, it is highly unusual." I was dumbfounded. As a sanguine student, I thought everyone had lots of friends. Even though Dr. Van Hoose defined friendships as relationships characterized by unconditional love, I was still shocked.

Relationships had always been important to me, and I developed good people skills at a young age. When I was in my early teens, my father encouraged me to read *How to Win Friends and Influence People* by Dale Carnegie. I've always remembered the advice that the master of relationships gave in the book: "In order to make friends, one must first be friendly."[11] I had embraced that recommendation, but after hearing the words of my psychology professor, I determined to be more intentional and take relationships to a new level in my life. That's when I made this relationship decision: *I will initiate and make an investment in relationships with others.*

I think a lot of people don't take responsibility for the relationships in their lives. They simply let things happen to them rather than being intentional about it. But to have the kind of solid relationships that bring fulfillment, you have to change your mind-set when it comes to dealing with others. Here are some ways you can do that:

PLACE A HIGH VALUE ON PEOPLE

Let's face it, if you don't care about people, you are unlikely to make building good relationships a priority in your life. My friend Ken Blanchard, author of *Whale Done* and *Raving Fans*, jokes that the Department of Motor Vehicles evidently seeks out and hires people who hate people.

> "You can't make the other fellow feel important in your presence if you secretly feel that he is a nobody."
>
> —LES GIBLIN

When you go to get your driver's license, you expect to be treated poorly. What onetime national salesman of the year Les Giblin said is true: "You can't make the other fellow feel important in your presence if you secretly feel that he is a nobody."

The solution is to place a high value on people. Expect the best from everyone. Assume people's motives are good unless they prove them to be otherwise. Value them by their best moments. And give them your friendship rather than asking for theirs. That will ultimately be their decision.

LEARN TO UNDERSTAND PEOPLE

Tom Peters and Nancy Austin, authors of *A Passion for Excellence,* state that "the number one managerial productivity problem in America is, quite simply, managers who are out of touch with their people and out of touch with their customers."[12] I think one possible explanation is that some managers don't value people.

> "The number one managerial productivity problem in America is, quite simply, managers who are out of touch with their people and out of touch with their customers."
>
> —TOM PETERS AND NANCY AUSTIN

But that isn't always true. Many people care about others, but they still remain out of touch. In those cases, I think the problem is that they don't understand people.

If you desire to improve your understanding of people so that you can build positive relationships, then keep in mind the following truths about people—and actions you can take to bridge the gap often caused by them:

- People are insecure . . . give them confidence.
- People want to feel special . . . sincerely compliment them.
- People desire a better tomorrow . . . show them hope.
- People need to be understood . . . listen to them.
- People are selfish . . . speak to their needs first.
- People get emotionally low . . . encourage them.
- People want to be associated with success . . . help them win.

When you understand people, don't take their shortcomings personally, and help them to succeed, you lay the groundwork for good relationships.

GIVE RESPECT FREELY BUT EXPECT TO EARN IT FROM OTHERS

One day a man arriving at the airport saw a well-dressed businessman yelling at a porter about the way he was handling his luggage. The more irate the businessman became, the calmer and more professional the porter appeared. When the abusive man left, the first man complimented the porter on his restraint. "Oh, it was nothing," said the porter. "You know, that man's going to Miami, but his bags—they're going to Kalamazoo." People who disrespect others always hurt themselves relationally—and they often reap other negative consequences.

I believe every human being deserves to be treated with respect because everyone has value. I also have observed that giving people respect first is one of the most *effective* ways of interacting with others. However, that doesn't mean you can demand respect in return. You must earn it. If you respect yourself, respect others, and exhibit competence, others will almost always give you respect. If everyone treated others with respect, the world would be a better place.

COMMIT YOURSELF TO ADDING VALUE TO OTHERS

Nineteenth-century English preacher Charles Spurgeon advised, "Carve your name on hearts and not on marble." The best way to do that is to add value to others. Do that by . . .

> "Carve your name on hearts and not on marble."
>
> —CHARLES SPURGEON

- ◆ Looking for ability in others
- ◆ Helping others discover their ability
- ◆ Helping others develop their ability

Some people approach every interaction with others as a transaction. They're willing to add value, but only if they expect to receive value in return. If you want to make relationships a priority, you must check your motives to be sure you are not trying to manipulate others for your own gain.

To make sure your motives are right, take this advice from Leo Buscaglia, who wrote *Loving Each Other*: "Always start a relationship by asking: Do I have ulterior motives for wanting to relate to this person? Is my caring conditional? Am I trying to escape something? Am I planning to change the person? Do I need this person to help me make up for a deficiency in myself? If your answer to any of these questions is 'yes,' leave the person alone. He or she is better off without you."[13]

Managing the Disciplines of Relationship Building

I think a lot of the time we take relationships for granted. Because of that, we don't always give them the attention they deserve or require. But good relationships require a lot of effort. To keep me on track in my relationships so that I'm investing in them as I must to make them successful, I practice this discipline: *Every day I make the conscious effort to deposit goodwill into my relationships with others.*

That means I give more than I expect to receive, love others unconditionally, look for ways to add value to others, and bring joy to the relationships I hold dear. Every evening, I evaluate this area of my life by asking myself, "Have I been thoughtful toward people today? Would they express joy that they have spent time with me?" If the answer is yes, then I've done my part.

If you want to improve your relationships through your everyday actions, then do the following:

PUT OTHERS FIRST

The best way to start off on the right foot is to put others first. The most basic way to do that is to practice the Golden Rule: Do unto others as you would have them do unto you. If you take that mindset into all your interactions with others, you can't go wrong. But there are also other ways to show people they matter and that you are interested in their well-being: Walk slowly through the crowd, remember people's names, smile at everyone, and be quick to offer help. People don't care how much you know until they know how much you care.

DON'T CARRY EMOTIONAL BAGGAGE

Few things weigh as much as old hurts and offenses carried day after day in a person's life. If you want to enjoy your time with other people, you've got to get rid of that kind of stuff. You can't keep score of old wrongs and expect to make relationships right. If someone has hurt you and you need to address it and get it out onto the table, then do it right away. Resolve it and get beyond it. If it's not worth bringing up, forget about it and move on.

GIVE TIME TO YOUR MOST VALUABLE RELATIONSHIPS

Most people give away their relational energy on a first-come, first-served basis. Whoever gets their attention first gobbles up their time and relational energy. That's why the squeaky wheels instead of the high producers at work consume so much attention and why so many people have nothing left to give when they get home from work. Since you've already read the chapter on family, you already know that I believe your family provides the most valuable relationships in your life. They should come first as you plan to spend your time. After that should come your next most important relationships. It's a matter of practicing good priorities.

SERVE OTHERS GLADLY

I once heard an airline executive explain how difficult it is to hire and train people for his industry. He said that service is the only thing they have to sell, but it is the toughest thing to teach because nobody wants to be thought of as a servant.

> "Life is an exciting business and most exciting when lived for others."
> —HELEN KELLER

Helen Keller said, "Life is an exciting business and most exciting when lived for others." I think that's true. The longer I live, the more convinced I am that adding value to others is the greatest thing we can do in this life. Because of that, when I serve, I try to do so cheerfully and with the greatest impact.

EXPRESS LOVE AND APPRECIATION OFTEN

After I had my heart attack, a lot of people asked me, "What was your dominant emotion? Was it fear, panic, questions?" My answer surprised many of them. In fact, it really surprised me. It was love. More than anything else in those moments of pain when I wasn't sure whether I would live or die, I wanted to tell the people closest to me how much I loved them—my family, the people who work with me, longtime friends. I learned that you can't tell the people you love how much you love them too often.

I think many people believe the best way they can help others is to criticize them, to give them the benefit of their "wisdom." I disagree. The best way to help people is to see the best in them. I want to encourage every person I

> The best way to help people is to see the best in them.

meet. I want them to know the good I see in them. I practice the 101 percent principle. I look for the 1 thing I admire in them and give them 100 percent encouragement for it. It helps me to like them. It helps them to like me. And what else could be better for starting a relationship?

Reflecting on Relationships

As I grow older, what I cherish most are my relationships. I've been very fortunate in this area of life for a long time. Over a two-year period when I was in my twenties, I was best man in eight weddings. I can't count the number of friends I have. I enjoy a great marriage. I've built relationships that have lasted for decades. Every week, my assistant receives a call from someone who describes himself as my "best friend." And every day I receive e-mails from people I love. As I look back, I realize:

In my 20s . . .   My relationships filled my days with joy.
In my 30s . . .   My relationships gave me wisdom and insight.
In my 40s . . .   My relationships lifted me to a higher level.
In my 50s . . .   My relationships provide me with wonderful memories.

My greatest moments and memories are filled with the people who mean the most to me. I sometimes observe that one day the inscription on my tombstone should read:

John Maxwell
He was my friend

I say it as a joke because I know so many people. But if I knew others would describe me as their friend after I die, I would be content. Some executive once observed, "It's lonely at the top." To that someone else might say, "It's lonely at the bottom too!" My advice is to put yourself where others are, because nothing else in life is as fulfilling as the relationships we cultivate.

My Model, My Mentor, My Friend

As I sat down to write this chapter, I began to think about the relationships I value most highly in my life. And I asked myself, "Outside of my family, what relationship has been the most impacting and fulfilling?" Very quickly one name came to me. The person who has been the most influential mentor in my life, next to my father, is Dr. Bill Bright, the founder of Campus Crusade for Christ.

Has someone who was bigger, faster, and better than you ever come alongside you and taken an interest in you? That's what Bill Bright did for me. In my circles he was a legend. He's what I call a level five leader, someone who's larger than life; a leader people follow because of who he is and what he represents. In the 1950s, he and his wife, Vonnette, made a declaration that they would become slaves for the sake of their faith, and they have lived out that commitment. His worldwide organization has nearly thirteen thousand employees and more than ten thousand trained volunteers. He has been awarded the Templeton Prize for the advancement of religion. Billy Graham called him "a man whose sincerity and integrity and devotion to our Lord have been an inspiration and a blessing to me ever since the early days of my ministry."[14]

Twenty years ago, Bill took me under his wing and became my mentor. He always made time for me. When I had leadership questions, he graciously answered them. He became a model of visionary leadership to me, challenging me to think bigger, to reach farther, to give more of myself. But he was also my friend. He loved me and gave to me with absolutely no thought of getting anything in return.

A Way to Say Thank You

In 2001, I had the privilege of honoring Bill Bright at one of our conferences with the Catalyst Award for lifetime achievement, for being "a leader, pioneer, mentor, and friend of leaders for fifty years." He was very gracious when he accepted it; he's received so many awards over the decades that it probably didn't mean much to him. But it was a big deal to me. Especially since I knew he was dying.

During the ceremony, I read a letter that I composed and delivered to Bill after I received word that he was diagnosed with pulmonary fibrosis. I remember writing it on a plane and just weeping, and I was embarrassed when the flight attendants asked me if I was okay. I wanted to let Bill know how much he meant to me. In part, the letter said,

> Bill, the greatest deposit you have made in my life is your personal interest in me. Often you have said with affection, "My dear John." Each time those words have touched my heart. It was your belief in me that placed me on a program of a conference in 1983. And as I sat beside Lloyd Ogilvie, Ray Stedman, Chuck Swindoll, John Stott, Chuck Colson, and you, I realized this 37-year-old kid was way over his head. Why would you pick me out of a crowd of leaders in South Korea and ask me to ride in your car in the motorcade . . . ? You honored me when I was asked to speak at your international conference. You lifted me to a higher level when you wrote a chapter in my prayer partner book. Over the years, I've benefited from your notes, phone calls, and personal encouragement. But my greatest moment with you was after a lunch we shared together in the late 80s when I felt the load of leadership and you asked me to kneel beside you. That day as I knelt beside you, you laid hands on me and you prayed for God to strengthen me. We embraced and God did answer your prayer.

What's so remarkable is that Bill poured his life into hundreds and thousands of others, just as he poured his life into me.

In March of 2003, I was surprised by a note I received from Bill. In it he invited me to take his place as the chairman of the Global Pastors Network, an organization he founded to equip leaders around the world. He said, "I would like to . . . bestow upon you a worldwide mantle of leadership to touch and train more than ten million pastors in the next ten years. My desire is that God would catapult you further than you have dreamed possible in your lifetime." It was a great privilege. Not only was he giving me an opportunity to make a difference in the lives of so many people, but he was giving me a chance to give back for all he had given me.

On July 19, 2003, Bill Bright died. I'm grateful that I got to see him six days before he passed away to say good-bye. I'll miss him. But with his passing, the overwhelming emotion I feel isn't sadness. It's fulfillment. The relationship I had with him is one of the great joys of my life. And I think back to the words of my psychology professor, Dr. Van Hoose, from four decades ago: "If you have one true friend in life, you are very fortunate." I know I am fortunate indeed.

RELATIONSHIP APPLICATION AND EXERCISES
INITIATING AND INVESTING IN SOLID
RELATIONSHIPS DAILY

Your Relationship Decision Today

Where do you stand when it comes to relationships today? Ask yourself these three questions:

1. *Have I already made the decision to initiate and invest in solid relationships daily?*
2. *If so, when did I make that decision?*
3. *What exactly did I decide? (Write it here.)*

_____

_____

_____

_____

_____

Your Relationship Discipline Every Day

Based on the decision you made concerning relationships, what discipline must you practice *today and every day* in order to be successful? Write it here.

_____

_____

_____

_____

_____

Making Up for Yesterday

If you need some help making the decision to commit to developing good relationships and practicing the everyday discipline of living it out, do the following exercises:

1. *What is your natural bent when it comes to dealing with people? When you are trying to accomplish a task or facing a challenge, what's more important to you—the situation or the people involved? If you tend to put your agenda ahead of people, you need to learn to place a higher value on people. Begin by making it a practice to ask yourself, "How will this impact others?" every time you begin a new project or make major decisions. (If you are* very *task-focused, then make the question part of your agenda.) Then explore the people factor in your mind and figure out ways to accomplish your goals while keeping people first.*

2. *Take action to better understand and interact with the important people in your life based on these seven observations:*

Characteristic	Action
1. Insecurity	Give them confidence
2. Desire to feel special	Sincerely compliment them
3. Desire for a better tomorrow	Show them hope
4. Need to be understood	Listen to them
5. Selfishness	Speak to their needs first
6. Being emotionally down	Encourage them
7. Desire for success	Help them win

   Pick someone new each week to invest in using this strategy.

3. *Begin writing notes to the important people in your life expressing your love and appreciation for them. When I was a pastor, I used to ask my staff to devote time every Monday to handwriting notes to people. Many of them still make a practice of doing it.*

4. *Begin to add value to people very intentionally. Become a mentor to someone in whom you see great potential. Begin by doing the following:*

   ◆ *Look for ability in them.*
   ◆ *Help them discover their ability.*
   ◆ *Help them develop their ability.*

5. *Xerox did some research and found that "totally satisfied" customers were six times more likely to repurchase Xerox products over the next year and a half than customers who described themselves as merely "satisfied."[15] In business, executing the work well often isn't enough to be successful. You have to build relationships. In your career or profession, what can you do to improve your relationships with your clients, customers, or employees? Begin doing it today.*

Looking Forward to Tomorrow

Spend some time reflecting on how your decision to develop relationships and the daily discipline required to maintain them will positively impact you in the future. What will be the compounding benefits? Write them here.

_____

_____

_____

_____

_____

_____

Keep what you've written as a constant reminder, because . . .
Reflection today motivates your discipline every day, and
Discipline every day maximizes your decision of yesterday.

CHAPTER 12

Today's **GENEROSITY** Gives Me Significance

If your income doubled overnight, how much money would you give away? How about if your net worth were suddenly over $100 million? What if you became the richest person in the world? How generous do you think you would be? Those are questions you could have asked tycoon J. Paul Getty who was once the world's richest man, but I don't think you would have admired his answers.

Getty was born in Minnesota in 1892. After graduating from England's Oxford University in 1913, he followed his father into the oil business. During the summers while he was in school, he had worked in the Oklahoma oil fields as a roustabout. When he returned after graduation, it was as a wildcat driller. He became a millionaire by age twenty-three.

Getty continued to build his fortune. He acquired other oil

companies. He invested in real estate. And he bought a one-third interest in his father's oil company. In the late 1940s and 1950s, he secured oil rights in Saudi Arabia, and huge strikes there made him a billionaire. In 1957, *Fortune* magazine recognized Getty as the richest man in the world. He continued building, particularly in the oil business. It's been said that he saw himself as "a solitary knight in fierce battle with the giant 'Seven Sisters' oil firms."[1] In 1967, his many companies merged to form the Getty Oil Company, which Getty led as president until his death in 1976.

Getty didn't like the fame associated with being named the world's richest man. It wasn't because he was humble. It was because the constant requests for money irritated him. He also thought it unreasonable that others assumed he would pick up the check simply because he was wealthy. He said he thought the "passive acceptance of money" corrupted people, so he rarely gave money away.[2]

The Stingy Billionaire

His stinginess became as well known as his wealth. He wore rumpled suits and threadbare sweaters. And he installed a pay phone to be used by guests in his home—Sutton Place, the sixteenth-century English manor situated on seven hundred acres outside London. But the worst example of his unwillingness to part with money was illustrated by an incident involving his grandson.

Jean Paul Getty III, Getty's sixteen-year-old grandson, was kidnapped by an Italian gang in 1973. The kidnappers demanded $17 million in ransom from the billionaire. The elder Getty stubbornly refused to pay them. Only when part of the boy's right ear was cut off and sent to a newspaper in Rome did Getty relent. He finally agreed to pay the kidnappers. But even then he wouldn't give them the entire amount. He agreed to a fraction of what they had requested—$2.7 million—saying that was all he could raise.[3] Fortunately, the boy was eventually found alive near Naples, but he had endured captivity by his kidnappers for five long months!

When J. Paul Getty died three years later, his children, whom he had long ago alienated, and his former wives (he had married and divorced five times) fought in court over his fortune, which was valued at $4 billion. Most of the money ultimately went to the Getty museum in Los Angeles.

Why Generosity Matters Today

So J. Paul Getty was tight with his money. Does that really matter? Didn't he earn it and have the right to keep it? Don't you have the right to keep whatever money you earn—or inherit for that matter? Of course you do. But what you have the *right* to do isn't the point. What would be *best* for you to do? Ironically, one of Getty's sons, J. Paul Getty Jr., articulated a philosophy much different from that of his father. He received only a fraction of the Getty fortune, yet he gave millions of dollars away. He said, "[I am] privileged to be the heir to huge wealth and I regard myself as custodian of that money for the benefit of people who need it more than I do."[4]

What about us? How should we approach giving? Why should we be generous? I believe there are many reasons, but here are just three:

1. GIVING TURNS YOUR FOCUS OUTWARD

No one likes to be around people who think only of themselves. In contrast, nearly everyone enjoys being around people who are giving. Biographer and literary critic Van Wyck Brooks stated:

How delightful is the company of generous people, who overlook trifles and keep their minds instinctively fixed on whatever is good and positive in the world around them. People of small caliber are always caring. They are bent on showing their own superiority, their knowledge or prowess or good breeding. But magnanimous people have no vanity, they have no jealousy, they have no reserves, and they feed on the true and solid wherever they find it. And what is more, they find it everywhere.

Giving to others naturally changes a person's focus, particularly if that giving is habitual. In fact, generosity can be described very simply as changing one's focus from self to others. When you're occupied with giving to others and

> Generosity is changing one's focus from self to others.

helping them succeed, it drives away selfishness. And that not only makes the world a better place, it makes the giver happier. As the Roman poet Seneca said, "No man can live happily who regards himself alone, who turns everything to his own advantage. You must live for others if you wish to live for yourself."

2. GIVING ADDS VALUE TO OTHERS

One of the most significant things a person can do while on this earth is help others. In this life, the measure of a person isn't the number of people who serve him or the amount of money he amasses; it's how many people he serves. The greater your giving, the greater you're living.

U.S. President Woodrow Wilson said it this way: "You are not here merely to make a living. You are here in order to enable the world to live more amply, with greater vision, with a finer spirit of home and achievement. You are here to enrich the world, and you impoverish yourself if you forget the errand." No one stands taller in the climb to success than when he bends over to help up someone else.

When you add value to others, you do not take anything away from yourself.

3. GIVING HELPS THE GIVER

A panhandler asked a woman for money, and she dug in her purse and handed him a dollar bill. As she did, she admonished him, "I'll give you a dollar—not because you deserve it but because it pleases me."

"Thank you, ma'am," he replied, "but while you're at it, why not make it ten and thoroughly enjoy yourself!"

Doesn't it make you feel good when you do something for another person? Don't you feel especially rewarded when the person's need is acute? Ruth Smeltzer said, "You have not lived a perfect day, even though you have earned your money, unless you have done something for someone who will never be able to repay you."[5] That's one of the reasons many people rush to help when tragedy strikes. When people suffer because of earthquakes, famine, hurricanes, or war, givers are moved to help—and they never expect to receive anything in return.

> "You have not lived a perfect day, even though you have earned your money, unless you have done something for someone who will never be able to repay you."
> —RUTH SMELTZER

King Solomon of ancient Israel asserted,

> The world of the generous gets larger and larger;
>   the world of the stingy gets smaller and smaller.
> The one who blesses others is abundantly blessed;
>   those who help others are helped.[6]

When you help others, you can't help but benefit. You can't light another's path without casting light on your own.

> You can't light another's path without casting light on your own.

Making the Decision to Plan for and Model Generosity Daily

When my wife, Margaret, and I started our life together in the weeks after our wedding, we moved to Hillham, Indiana, where I took my first job. The church that hired me was able to pay only $80 a week, so Margaret worked several jobs to help us make ends meet. Those days were very difficult for us financially, yet they were still filled with great joy.

At that time, my brother, Larry, was tasting early success in the business world and was doing very well financially. Larry and his wife, Anita, saw that we were struggling, and for those first few years, they were very generous to us. The only vacations we had were ones they invited us on and paid for. All my good clothes were the result of their generosity. Larry paid my expenses as I worked on a business degree. We will always be grateful to them.

As I look back on those days, three thoughts are clear to me. First, Margaret and I were never jealous of Larry and Anita's financial success. We were thrilled for them, and not once did we covet what they had. Second, we could see that their generous spirit was a tremendous source of joy for them and a blessing for us. Third, I began to realize the incredible value of having a generous lifestyle toward others. That's when I made another of my life decisions: *I will live to give*. Margaret and I recognized that greatness is not defined by what a person receives, but by what that person gives. True generosity isn't a function of income—it begins with the heart. It's about serving others and looking for ways to add value to them. That's the way to achieve significance in your life.

> Greatness is not defined by what a person receives, but by what that person gives.

If you desire to become generous and make generosity part of your daily life, then do the following:

GIVE OTHERS YOUR MONEY

The way people handle money colors their attitude about many other aspects of their lives. Wherever your money is, that's where your attention goes. Haven't you found that to be true? If you invest heavily in the stock market, you probably check the financial page or your earning statements frequently. If you spend a large amount of money on a house, you probably spend a lot of time and effort taking care of it. If you give a lot of money to a church or favorite charity, you care how the money is used and whether the organization succeeds.

That truth is even borne out in the Scriptures. In fact, there are a lot of insights about money contained in the Bible. Believe it or not, the Bible has more teachings about money than about prayer! One of the most telling observations is this one: "Where your treasure is, there your heart will be also."[7]

If you give money to people, either directly or through a worthy charity, you will care about people more. And that will help to foster a more generous spirit in you. You have to "prime the pump" so to speak, and then the giving will flow. If you wait until

> "No man becomes rich unless he enriches others."
>
> —ANDREW CARNEGIE

you *feel* like it to give, you may wait forever. You become generous by first giving money away. Andrew Carnegie, the steel magnate who gave away millions of dollars, said, "No man becomes rich unless he enriches others."

GIVE OTHERS YOURSELF

What do people often value more than your money? The answer is your time and attention. Think about it. What takes greater effort: writing a check or giving your time? What shows the greater level of commitment? My friend Larry Burkett said, "Where there is no giving, there is no commitment." I believe that is true. The people closest to you would rather have you than your money. Nothing can take the place of a spouse's affection. A child desires to have a parent's undivided attention more than anything else. Even sharp employees with great potential understand that a good mentor is more valuable than a mere monetary reward. Money may buy stuff, but a good mentor buys a better future. When you give the gift of yourself, you are being as generous as you can be.

Take a moment to recall the people who've had the greatest impact in your life. Perhaps you had a teacher who helped you understand that you could think and learn. Maybe you had a parent, aunt, or uncle who made you feel loved and accepted. Or perhaps a coach or employer saw your potential, painted a positive picture of your future, and then challenged and equipped you to reach for something better. They helped you to become the person you were always meant to be. What gift could be greater than that?

Rabbi Harold Kushner said, "The purpose of life is not to win. The purpose of life is to grow and to share. When you come to look back on all that you have done in life, you will get more satisfaction from the pleasure you brought to other people's lives than you will from the times that you outdid and defeated them." When you invest in another person just for the sake of seeing them blossom, with no thought to any benefit you might receive, you will be the kind of generous person others want to be around. And your days truly will be masterpieces.

Some people see giving to others as more than just a kind and beneficial act. They see it as an obligation. Physician and missionary Sir Wilfred T. Grenfell said, "The service we render to others is really the rent we pay for our room on this earth. It is obvious that man is himself a traveler; that the purpose of this world is not 'to have and to hold' but 'to give and to serve.' There can be no other meaning."

Managing the Discipline of Generosity

It's very easy to live only for yourself. In fact, that may be every person's natural bent. I know it's mine. But we can take another path—to be generous. My desire is to be the kind of person *I* would like to be around. To help with that, I practice this discipline, reminding myself: *Every day I will add value to others.*

What does it mean to add value to others? How do you do it? Here is how to start:

- **Value People:** This means treating everyone with respect.
- **Know What People Value:** This means listening and seeking to understand others.
- **Make Myself More Valuable:** This means growing in order to give, because I cannot give what I do not possess.
- **Do Things That God Values:** Since he unconditionally loves people, so must I.

When you value people, you open the door to generosity. And it becomes much easier to plan for and model generosity daily. If you've adopted that mind-set, you're ready to be generous to others. Think about these things as you strive to practice the discipline of generosity every day:

Don't Wait for Prosperity to Become Generous

Because I spent over twenty-five years in the ministry, I know a lot about people's giving patterns and their attitudes about money. One of the things I've heard many people say is that if they ever have a lot of money, *then* they will become generous. People who say such things are usually fooling themselves.

A person's level of income and their desire to give have nothing to do with one another. Some of the most generous people I know have nothing materially. And I know plenty of people who have a lot to give but no heart to give it. Statistics bear that out. The average personal income in the state of Mississippi is the second lowest in the United States ranked by state, yet the state is ranked sixth in charitable giving. In contrast, New Hampshire is ranked sixth in average personal income. Do you know where they rank in charitable giving as a percentage of income? They're forty-fifth.[8]

Prosperity and high income don't help people become generous. In fact, Henry Ward Beecher, the father of novelist Harriet Beecher Stowe, warned that they could actually make people less likely to give. He said, "Watch lest prosperity destroy generosity." People in the United States live in the most prosperous country in the world during the most prosperous time in its history. Yet they still don't give much. Today, 2.5 percent of our income goes to charitable giving. That's lower than it was during the Great Depression (2.9 percent).[9] And 80 percent of Americans who earn at least $1 million a year leave nothing to charity in their wills.[10]

People give not from the top of their purses, but from the bottom of their hearts. If you desire to become a more generous person, don't wait for your income to change. Change your heart.

> If you desire to become a more generous person, don't wait for your income to change. Change your heart.

Do that, and you can become a giver regardless of your income or circumstances.

FIND A REASON TO GIVE EVERY DAY

It may be easy for people to find reasons *not* to give. But it's just as easy to find good reasons *to* give. You just need to look for them. At the beginning of this chapter, you learned about J. Paul Getty, a man who seemed to have many reasons not to give. Yet one of his sons, J. Paul Getty Jr., was his opposite. He gave millions of dollars of his fortune away. Become like the younger Getty. Go out of your way to find reasons to give. Look for a compelling cause. Find an urgent need. Look for a group that is making an impact. Seek out leaders you know and believe in. Give to organizations you respect and trust. They're all around you; you just need to make it a priority.

FIND PEOPLE TO RECEIVE EVERY DAY

D. L. Moody, founder of the Moody Bible Institute, said, "Do all the good you can, to all the people you can, in all the ways you can, as long as you can." When it comes right down to it, the recipients of your gen-

> "Do all the good you can, to all the people you can, in all the ways you can, as long as you can."
>
> —D. L. MOODY

erosity are never causes, institutions, or organizations. Ultimately, the recipients are individual people.

People in need of help are all around you. You don't need to go halfway around the world or send a check overseas to help and serve others, although there's nothing wrong with doing those things. But there are plenty of people closer to home who can benefit from what you have to offer—people in your own town, your own neighborhood, even your own home. Being generous means keeping your eyes open for opportunities to give to everyone, whether it's through mentoring a colleague, feeding a homeless person, sharing your faith with a friend, or spending time with your kids. Civil rights leader Martin Luther King Jr. said, "Life's most persistent and urgent question

> "Life's most persistent and urgent question is, 'What are we doing for others?'"
>
> —MARTIN LUTHER KING JR.

is, 'What are we doing for others?'" How you answer that question is a measure of your generosity. And the more generous you are, the greater your opportunity to do something significant for others.

Reflecting on Generosity

I have a lot to be thankful for. As I look back and think about the idea of generosity, this is the pattern that emerges:

In my 20s . . .   Generosity was modeled for me by my brother and many others.
In my 30s . . .   Generosity became a priority in my life.
In my 40s . . .   Generosity became a joy in my life.
In my 50s . . .   My generosity has begun to return to me tenfold.

In the chapter on finances, I mentioned that the desire for options isn't necessarily always selfish. That's true because you can give only what you have. For Margaret and me, having options frees us up to give more to others. We have tried to be generous for the last thirty-plus years. And we have endeavored to plan our lives so that we can continue to be generous. What we do for ourselves alone dies with us, but what we do for others and the world remains and is immortal.

Gone but Not Forgotten

In January of 2002, news channels carried the story of a leader who had died of liver cancer. In the wake of his death, the network morning shows ran retrospectives of his life complete with film clips similar to ones shown for statesmen and Hollywood stars, though neither of these was his profession. Not long afterward, a resolution of tribute was passed unanimously on the Senate floor honoring him. About him, Senator Carl Levin of Michigan said, "He was a man of vision, action and compassion . . . the fruits of his labor will continue to improve the lives of the multitude of children who seek a permanent home and loving family."[11] Who was this individual and what did he do for a living? He was a self-described hamburger cook named Dave Thomas.

If you watched any television during the 1990s, then you know about Dave Thomas, the founder of Wendy's fast-food restaurants. A survey taken in 1997 indicated that 92 percent of the adult consumers polled knew who Thomas was.[12] The president of the United States might not have rated that high! Thomas wasn't a slick pitchman. He was the common guy he appeared to be, but he made more than eight hundred commercials promoting Wendy's. And he really did start the business and knew it inside and out. But if starting a successful business and becoming a media celebrity had been his only accomplishments, few people would have missed him. What separated Thomas from other successful businesspeople and made him loved was his generosity.

Restaurants Were His Life

Dave Thomas was born to an unwed mother in 1932, and six weeks later he was adopted by Rex and Auleva Thomas. When the boy was five, Auleva died. He spent the next eleven years moving from place to place as his father sought work. The boy's favorite moments often came when he and his stern father went out to eat together. "During meals, I had my dad all to myself," said Thomas. "I also liked seeing all of the families sitting together, enjoying themselves."[13] Thomas began studying restaurants, figuring out their service and menus. It's said that by age nine, he had already acquired a level of expertise, understanding what customers wanted.

Thomas began working when he was twelve. He got his first restaurant job at a family-run establishment in Knoxville, Tennessee. Three years later, after another family move, he landed at the Hobby House Restaurant in Fort Wayne, Indiana. There, he was mentored by the restaurant's owner, Phil Clauss, who taught him everything about the business. From then on, Thomas knew what he wanted to do. He wanted to make a career in the restaurant business.

Thomas joined the army at eighteen, went to cook and baker's school, and became one of the youngest soldiers to manage an enlisted men's club. When he finished his tour in Germany, he returned to Fort Wayne and worked with Phil Clauss again. In 1964, when Clauss offered Dave a chance to revive his four struggling Kentucky Fried Chicken franchises, Thomas jumped in and made them highly successful. When Clauss later sold them, Dave became a millionaire.

In 1969, Thomas fulfilled his dream of starting his own restaurant. He loved cheeseburgers, so a burger restaurant was a natural for him. He opened the first Wendy's Old Fashioned Hamburgers restaurant in downtown Columbus, Ohio, named after one of his daughters. It wasn't long before he owned four of them in Columbus. He was becoming highly successful, and when he was able to make drive-through windows work better than anyone else in the fast-food industry, his restaurants really took off. He opened more stores and continually tried innovative ideas. His idea of franchising cities and regions rather than single stores accelerated growth. In the company's first 100 months, they opened more than 1,000 restaurants. Today, there are more than 6,000.

What Really Matters

When Thomas was running his company, he mentioned occasionally that he had been adopted. At first he was shy talking about it, but he became bolder when he realized it could help motivate his employees. He wanted everyone to achieve. He used to say, "Share your success and help others succeed. Give everyone a piece of the pie. If the pie's not big enough, make a bigger pie."[14] It was simply part of his value system. He always believed in giving something back. In his second book, *Well Done!*, he explained,

> If you're not giving of yourself as much as you're giving of your wallet, are you really generous down deep? We should work hard to make the Virtuous Circle of Generosity the number-one epidemic in the United States—giving of wealth, giving of self. Unstoppable and unending.[15]

In 1990, President George H. W. Bush invited Thomas to give back in a big way. He asked Thomas to head the White House Initiative on Adoption and raise awareness for the cause of adoption. Not only did Thomas do that, but he also fought to reduce the red tape and cost of adoption. More important, it was the catalyst that prompted him to dedicate the last twelve years of his life to the cause of adoption.

In 1992, Thomas established the Dave Thomas Foundation for Adoption. The organization works to promote adoption and make it easier for parents to adopt. It also partners with adoption organizations working to place the more than 125,000 children in foster care with permanent families. When asked about why he started the foundation, Thomas simply said, "I just know everybody deserves a home and love."[16]

But that was only the start for Thomas. He has continued to work for kids waiting to be adopted. He donated the profits from his first book, *Dave's Way,* to adoption causes. He pioneered a program at Wendy's offering adoption benefits, and then he initiated "Adoption in the Workplace" to urge other companies nationwide to do the same. He testified before Congress on adoption and urged lawmakers to institute tax credits for adoption. He even partnered with the U.S. Postal Service to create and promote a set of adoption stamps.

Dave Thomas loved doing things for children, especially those who needed to be adopted, but he did a lot more than that:

- ◆ He established the Thomas Center at Duke University, which houses the Fuqua School of Business Executive Education.
- ◆ He founded the Enterprise Ambassador Program at Nova University to mentor high school students.
- ◆ He supported the Children's Home Society of Florida.
- ◆ He did public service announcements for adoption, the GED program, 911 Emergency Services, the American Lung Association, and numerous local charities.
- ◆ He financially assisted Children's Hospital in Columbus, the Arthur G. James Cancer Hospital and the Richard J. Solove Research Institute at Ohio State University, and the St. Jude Children's Cancer Research Center in Memphis.

The people closest to Thomas have missed him. Jack Schuessler, chairman and CEO of Wendy's International, Inc., remarked after Thomas's death, "He was the heart and soul of our company. He had a passion for great tasting hamburgers, and devoted his life to serving customers great food and helping those less fortunate in his community."[17]

Despite his success and his high profile, Thomas never lost his perspective. He never wanted to be a "big shot." He said, "Everybody only lives so long. The one thing people remember about you isn't how much money you made or the deals you swung. What they remember is if you were a nice guy."[18] Thomas demonstrated just what kind of guy he was by giving his time, talents, and resources to help others. And that, not Wendy's, is what made his life so significant.

GENEROSITY APPLICATION AND EXERCISES
PLANNING FOR AND MODELING
GENEROSITY DAILY

Your Generosity Decision Today

Where do you stand when it comes to generosity today? Ask yourself these three questions:

1. *Have I already made the decision to plan for and model generosity daily?*
2. *If so, when did I make that decision?*
3. *What exactly did I decide? (Write it here.)*

_____

_____

_____

_____

_____

Your Generosity Discipline Every Day

Based on the decision you made concerning generosity, what is the one discipline you must practice *today and every day* in order to be successful? Write it here.

_____

_____

_____

_____

_____

Making Up for Yesterday

If you need some help making a commitment to becoming generous and living it out every day, do the following exercises:

1. *Since giving starts from the heart, that's the first place you should look to assess where you are as a giver. What value do you place on other people? Are they important? Do you believe that every person is worthy of respect and consideration? Or do you value only the people you respect or who can help you? Take an honest look at yourself. (If you're brave, ask others to evaluate you too.) You will not value generosity until you value people.*

2. *To become more generous, begin with the people closest to you. First, you need to know what's important to them. Give it some thought, and then write down what each person values. On your list, you'll want to include your spouse, children, parents, close friends, colleagues, employer, etc. If you are having a hard time deciding what they care about, spend some time in conversation getting to know them better before trying to complete your list.*

   Once you've completed the list, start brainstorming ideas for how you can add value to them. Try to include ideas that draw on your time, talents, and resources.

3. *How generous are you now? How much of your time and money do you give to people and organizations that return no benefit to you? Take a look at your financial records and your calendar. What percentage of your money goes to charity? Is it no more than a few dollars a year? Is it only 1 to 2 percent? In the chapter on finances, I recommended that you give no less than 10 percent. If you're not there, try to begin reworking your budget so that you can get there in the next couple of years. If you've been blessed with financial resources and you're already giving 10 percent, then try to increase your giving.*

   And don't just write a check. If you're not spending time helping people who cannot return the favor, then you're not being as generous as you could be. Pitch in at your church, volunteer for a benevolent organization, or mentor an employee. It doesn't matter where or how you add value, as long as it's someplace you believe in.

4. *If you feel that you have little to give, then work on making your-self more valuable. One way to do that is to take the suggestion of Dave Thomas and "make a bigger pie." If you earn more, you'll have more to give away. But you can also make yourself more valu-able by engaging in personal growth. Good mentors are able to add value because they have much to give. (I'll tell you more about how to do that in chapter 14.)*

Looking Forward to Tomorrow

Spend some time reflecting on how your decision concerning gen-erosity and the daily discipline that comes out of it will positively impact you in the future. What compounding benefits do you ex-pect to receive? Write them here.

_____

_____

_____

_____

_____

Keep what you've written as a constant reminder, because . . .
Reflection today motivates your discipline every day, and
Discipline every day maximizes your decision of yesterday.

CHAPTER 13

Today's **VALUES** Give Me Direction

While I was preparing to write this chapter, two notable things happened. Sam Waksal, former CEO of ImClone, who had pleaded guilty to securities fraud, bank fraud, conspiracy to obstruct justice, and perjury, was sentenced to more than seven years in prison and ordered to pay nearly $4.3 million in fines and back taxes. The judge in the case, William H. Pauley, told Waksal, "The harm that you wrought is truly incalculable," and said he had damaged his company, his family, and investors nationwide.[1] The other notable thing was that Martha Stewart, founder of Martha Stewart Living Omnimedia and a friend of Waksal, was indicted on charges of securities fraud, obstruction of justice, conspiracy, and making false statements to prosecutors and the FBI.[2]

Unless you've had your head in the sand since the beginning of the new millennium, you've grown sick of hearing such stories. Enron admits to inflating its income figures by $586 million over a few years and files Chapter 11 bankruptcy. The Justice Department is still working to find out how much executives knew about the company's status while unloading more than $1 billion of Enron stock.[3] WorldCom admits to overstating profits by $7.1 billion,[4] costing 17,000 workers their jobs, and costing the company's stock 75 percent of its value.[5] News breaks of the Catholic churches covering up improprieties by some priests. The list goes on and on.

What do all of these stories have in common? Values! Every story reflects the incredible damage that can be done when individuals lose direction after failing to embrace and practice good values daily. James B. Comey, the United States attorney for the Southern District of New York, said the indictment against Stewart was a tragedy for her company and its six hundred employees. "It's a tragedy that could have been prevented if those two people had only done what parents have taught their children for eons," he said, "that if you are in a tight spot, lying is not the way out. Lying is an act with profound consequences."[6]

Why Values Matter Today

George H. Lorimer, onetime editor at the *Saturday Evening Post,* said, "Back of every life there are principles that have fashioned it." Those principles that guide your life are your values. After all, a person's core values are nothing more than principles that he or she has internalized. And those core values are critical to success because they function as . . .

> "Back of every life there are principles that have fashioned it."
>
> —GEORGE H. LORIMER

AN ANCHOR

How do you make good decisions during life's inevitable rough times if you don't have values? How do you find direction? People without values are adrift on the ocean of life. When the waves come crashing down, they have no place to rest. Any big storm can threaten to put them under. Any current is liable to take them places they don't want to go. However, when you have strong values, you have something that holds you steady, even when the weather gets nasty.

A FAITHFUL FRIEND

Because your core values are the deeply held beliefs that authentically describe your soul, they become a companion to you throughout your life. That can be very reassuring. U.S. President Abraham Lincoln said, "When I lay

> Your core values are the deeply held beliefs that authentically describe your soul.

down the reins of this administration, I want to have one friend left, and that friend is inside myself."

YOUR NORTH STAR

Just like your circumstances, the way you live your life is constantly changing. You acquire new skills, disciplines, and habits. Practices always change according to the situation. On the other hand, values don't. They are always dependable to guide you. To paraphrase a saying I once heard,

Methods are many,
Values are few.
Methods always change,
Values never do.

Once you have thoroughly examined your values and articulated them, you will be able to steer your life by them. You may add to your list as you become older and wiser, but if something is truly a core value, then it remains one for life.

Over the years, I've taught a lot of lessons on values to leaders because values are critical to any kind of success. In preparing to write this book, I spent some time revisiting my own values. Now that I am in my fifties, I think I have finally created the list that will last me until the end of my life. I used that list to outline this book:

I value my attitude because it gives me possibilities.
I value my priorities because they give me focus.
I value my health because it gives me strength.
I value my family because it gives me stability.
I value my thinking because it gives me an advantage.
I value my commitment because it gives me tenacity.
I value my finances because they give me options.
I value my faith because it gives me peace.
I value my relationships because they give me fulfillment.
I value my generosity because it gives me significance.
I value my values because they give me direction.
I value my growth because it gives me potential.

With the guidance of those twelve values, I hope to fulfill the purpose of my life, which centers on three main areas:

1. **My Family:** to live a credible life so that my values are accepted by my family.
2. **My Work:** to influence as many people as possible in the shortest amount of time.
3. **Myself:** to die with the satisfaction that I have served God, others, and my family.

If you want to be proactive in the way you live your life, if you want to influence your life's direction, if you want your life to exhibit the qualities you find desirable, and if you want to live with integrity, then you need to know what your values are, decide to embrace them, and practice them every day.

Making the Decision to Embrace and Practice Good Values Daily

I grew up in a home where great values were taught and lived out, but I didn't make a conscious decision to embrace good values and live them out until 1970 when I was twenty-three years old. That year I read *Spiritual Leadership* by J. Oswald Sanders.[7] It changed my life. Up until then, I had been a people pleaser and census taker in my leadership. I led people according to what was popular. Ninety percent of the time that was okay. But on the occasions when a *real* leadership decision was required, when I really needed to do something that would be unpopular, I wavered. Reading Sanders's book made me realize that I was not leading according to my values, and it gave me the courage to do the right thing, even if it wasn't popular. I made the decision: ***I will lead others based on the values I embrace.***

I still have my copy of *Spiritual Leadership* because it marked me. Inside the back cover, I wrote three commitments that would shape the rest of my life. The book challenged me

1. **To Be God's Man:** No matter where my work takes me, I desire to be in the center of God's will.
2. **To Develop My Potential to the Best of My Ability:** I will never allow myself to be lazy, indifferent, or noncommittal concerning spiritually lost people.

3. **To Be a True Spiritual Leader:** God is my idol, Jesus is my pattern, and the Bible provides my direction. Too many men are stereotyped leaders. Their whole outlook is warped by their surroundings. I will not, with God's help, be poured into another man's mold or teach what I do not believe.

> At times, my value-based leadership has alienated me from others, but never from myself.

For thirty-four years, I've continually asked myself this question: "Am I leading others according to the values I embrace?"

At times, my value-based leadership has alienated me from others, but never from myself.

Comedian Fred Allen said, "You only live once. But if you work it right, once is enough." How can people work it right? By knowing their values and living by them every day. Do that, and you will have few regrets at the end of your life. Here are some suggestions to help you get started:

CREATE A LIST OF GOOD VALUES

Begin writing down any and every idea you have concerning values. List every admirable character quality you can think of. As an aspect of your life comes to mind, try to capture what's important to you about it. Ultimately, your values should not be determined by externals, such as your profession or your environment, but as you consider such things, you will be prompted to be thorough in your thinking.

When you think you've exhausted every possible idea, set the list aside for a while but keep thinking about it in the back of your mind. When new ideas come, add them to the list. You may also want to do some reading to stir your thinking and see if you've missed anything.

After a few weeks, begin to combine ideas on the list. (For example, "truthfulness" and "integrity" really overlap. So do "commitment" and "hard work." Choose one—or pick another word that better describes both terms together.) Then narrow it down. You can't possibly live out twenty or fifty values, so you need to start eliminating some. Which are based on truth and your highest ideals? Which items on your list truly represent the core of your being? Which will be lasting? What would you be willing to live for? To die for? Start eliminating anything that's superficial or temporary. If you're married, involve your spouse in this process. Your lists of values may not be identical, but they should have much in common. And if any of your values seem to be at odds with your spouse's, beware. You need to talk these values through and find out where you really stand, or there will always be conflict in your marriage.

EMBRACE THOSE GOOD VALUES

Years ago my friend Jim Dobson, the founder of Focus on the Family, delivered the commencement address at Seattle Pacific University. In it he spoke about the midlife crisis that many people experience between the ages of thirty-five and fifty. He said, "I believe that it is more a phenomenon of a wrong value system than it is the age group in which it occurs. All of a sudden you realize that the ladder you've been climbing is leaning against the wrong wall." Clarifying and embracing your values can help you to prevent such an occurrence from happening to you.

MAKE A DECISION TO LIVE THOSE VALUES DAILY

True life change begins when you decide to change your value system, because it's foundational to everything you do. My friend Pat Williams, senior vice president of the Orlando Magic, once told me that when Roy Disney was asked about the secret of Disney's success, he used to say that the company was managed by values, which led to ease in good decision making. The same is true for an individual.

Physicist Albert Einstein advised, "Try not to become men of success. Rather, become men of value." Why would he say such a thing? Because he knew that having values keeps a person focused on the important things. That leads to a better quality of life, a life of integrity. Besides, if you focus on your values, success is likely to follow anyway.

> "Try not to become men of success. Rather, become men of value."
>
> —ALBERT EINSTEIN

Managing the Discipline of Values

Managing your life according to your values isn't easy. Why? Because your values will be tested daily by those who do not embrace them. Negative people may discount you when you display a positive attitude. People without families may not understand your devotion to your family. Unteachable people won't understand your dedication to personal growth. And those whose priorities are different from yours will try to convince you to follow them or make unwise compromises.

The discipline I practice to battle this is simple: *Every day I review and reflect on my values.* To help me do that, I keep a list of my Daily Dozen in my "thinking companion," a little notebook I always keep with me so that I can write down ideas and jot down reminders of things to tell Margaret. Every time I open the notebook, I see those twelve values. I also give myself the twelve-minute test. At the end of each day, I spend one minute reviewing and reflecting on each of the Daily Dozen. That way, I stay on track and am less likely to drift away from living out my values.

To become better at embracing and practicing your values every day, follow these guidelines:

ARTICULATE AND EMBRACE YOUR VALUES DAILY

How do you manage something as abstract as your values? You begin by putting them in concrete form. Once you've created your list of values, write a descriptive statement for each one explaining how you intend to apply it to your life and what benefit or direction that will bring. Keep that document where you can see it every day. Think about your values often to help them "soak in." As you go through your day and face decisions, measure your choices against your values. And whenever it's appropriate, talk about them. It not only cements your values in your mind and helps you to practice them, but it also adds a level of accountability.

Good business leaders understand the importance of speaking about their values continually. Stew Leonard, president of Stew Leonard's Dairy, says that he continually verbalizes the value of the company's customers. "We don't see customers the way you do," he says. "Our people imagine each of our customers with $50,000 tattooed on their forehead." How is that? It's simply a matter of math:

$100   Average amount each customer spends per week
x 50   Number of weeks per year customers shop his store
x 10   Average number of years residents live in his city
= $50,000   The value of each customer[8]

When you embrace your values wholeheartedly and articulate them continually, you dramatically increase your chances of living.

COMPARE YOUR VALUES TO YOUR PRACTICES DAILY

The gap between knowing and doing is significantly greater than the gap between ignorance and knowledge. A person who identifies and articulates his values but doesn't practice them is like a salesman who makes promises to a customer and then fails to

> The gap between knowing and doing is significantly greater than the gap between ignorance and knowledge.

deliver. He has no credibility. In business, the result is that the person loses his job. In life, the person loses his integrity.

In 1995, Girish Shah, an assistant controller for a division of a Fortune 500 company, was charged with embezzling $988,000 from the company over an eight-year period. He pleaded no contest in court, and he was prepared to repay $728,000 immediately and borrow additional money from relatives to repay the rest.

The CEO of the company was outraged. To court officials he wrote:

> I view Mr. Shah's crime as particularly egregious. Not only did he steal from the stockholders of this Fortune 500 company, but he breached the fiduciary duty placed in him by the company and his supervisors. . . . I urge you to impress upon Mr. Shah and those others who commit similar crimes that wrongdoing of this nature against society is considered a grave matter by the Texas Court and will not be condoned.[9]

You know what was ironic about that statement? It was made by Tyco CEO Dennis Kozlowski, the man later charged with looting $600 million from that same company with the help of two other executives.[10] Evidently this disconnection between his stated values and his practices was a pattern. Kozlowski used to brag to people about how frugal he was with the company's money. He often pointed out the spartan offices the company possessed in one location even as he maintained lavishly appointed offices in another.

Discrepancies between values and practices create chaos in a person's life. If you talk your values but neglect to walk them, then you will continually undermine your integrity and credibility. And that will happen even if you are unaware of your behavior and are not doing it intentionally.

Live Out Your Values Regardless of Your Feelings

Many people get into trouble when their values and their feelings collide. When you're feeling good and everything's going your way, it's not difficult to consistently live out your values. However, when your values determine you should take an action that will hurt you or cost you something, it can be harder to follow through.

If one of your values is integrity and you found a bank bag of money on the street that you suspected was stolen, you probably wouldn't have too difficult a time turning the money in to the police. But what if you saw your boss stealing from the company you work for and you knew that calling attention to it would get you fired? That choice would be more difficult, especially if you knew that losing your job might cost you your house or ruin you financially.

Successful people do what's right no matter how they feel about it. They don't expect to be able to feel their way into acting. They act first and then hope that their feelings follow suit. Usually that doesn't involve anything dramatic. The tough decisions are the everyday ones. For example, if good health is one of my values, will I exercise even though I don't feel like it in the morning? Will I refrain from eating a big piece of chocolate cake even though I really want it? To be successful, my values—not my feelings—need to

> "Nice guys may appear to finish last, but usually they are running in a different race."
> —BLANCHARD AND PEALE

control my actions. Ken Blanchard and Norman Vincent Peale wrote in *The Power of Ethical Management,* "Nice guys may appear to finish last, but usually they are running in a different race."[11] Living by your values is running in a different race.

EVALUATE EACH DAY IN LIGHT OF YOUR VALUES

Most people take very little time to do any reflective thinking, yet that is necessary for anyone who wants to live out his values with consistency. Ben Franklin used to get up in the morning asking himself, "What good will I do today?" When he went to bed, he asked himself, "What good did I do today?" He was evaluating himself in light of one of his values. For the last several years, I've tried to do something similar. At the end of the day, I reflect on whether I have added value to anyone's life during the day, because that is something I desire to do every day of my life.

Reflecting on Values

As I reflect on the values decision I made in 1970, I realize that it has provided me direction in my personal and professional life:

In my 20s . . .   My values gave me courage to do the right thing.

In my 30s . . .   My values motivated me to leave my comfort zone and take big steps professionally.

In my 40s . . .   My values enabled me to have favor with other leaders.

In my 50s . . .   My values have given me great security.

For thirty-four years, my values have provided a solid foundation on which I have built my life.

An Audience with the President

Early in 2003, I found myself in one of those situations where I had to make a difficult choice. I do a lot of conferences for business organizations and large corporations. In recent years, one of the organizations that has often invited me to speak is Home Interiors. I was scheduled to speak at their national convention for several days, but a few days before I was to speak, I received the kind of phone call a leader only dreams about. A staff member from the White House called to ask if I could come to participate in a two-hour meeting the president would be having on Thursday.

What an opportunity! I had met George W. Bush once when he was governor of Texas, before he decided to run for president. But meeting him at the White House and having an opportunity to voice my opinion on an issue in a session with him was quite a privilege. There was just one problem. The meeting was at the same time as one of the sessions I was scheduled to teach to the people of Home Interiors. My brain immediately went into overdrive. I'm the kind of person who loves to explore options and solve problems. This was simply an obstacle to overcome. Somehow, I was going to work it out to meet with the president *and* keep my commitment to Home Interiors.

Linda Eggers, my assistant, and I began exploring possibilities. We talked to representatives from Home Interiors to discuss options. They were very gracious and flexible, and they were even excited for me. We tried sliding my speaking slot to another day. We tried moving the time. We explored whether I could rent a private jet to make the trip to Washington and still get back on time. None of those things worked. The only option that seemed viable was to videotape me on Monday and show the session on Thursday. We had finally found something that worked!

But then I got to thinking. That was okay for me, but what about for Home Interiors? Wasn't commitment one of my personal values? And didn't I teach the people at my company, Maximum Impact, to display a 100 percent commitment to excellence in everything we do? I asked Linda to get Home Interiors' representative back on the phone. "Let me ask you one thing," I said. "Which would you rather have? Me live or on tape?" Obviously, the answer was live. "I'll be there Thursday as we promised." I hung up the phone and asked Linda to send my regrets to the White House.

That's the Way Life Is

There's nothing a leader likes better than to meet with other leaders and talk about leadership, so passing on the meeting was extremely disappointing. But it was the right thing to do. I made the decision based on my values. Now, do I *always* do the right thing? No, of course not. But am I always striving to live out my values with integrity? Absolutely. That's the most important part of the process. What's ironic is

> By choosing to embrace and practice good values every day, you may not always *get* what you desire, but you will always *be* the person you desire to be.

that the meeting with the president was canceled at the last minute anyway. President Bush had to meet with Prime Minister Tony Blair on short notice because of the situation in Iraq. How sad it would have been if I had made the other decision, based on how I felt about the opportunity! I would have let down the people of Home Interiors, I would have compromised my values and integrity, and I still would not have gotten to meet with the president.

By choosing to embrace and practice good values every day, you choose the higher course in life. And your life goes in a direction that you will always feel good about. You may not always *get* what you desire, but you will always *be* the person you desire to be.

VALUES APPLICATION AND EXERCISES
EMBRACING AND PRACTICING GOOD
VALUES DAILY

Your Values Decision Today

Where do you stand when it comes to values today? Ask yourself
these three questions:

1. *Have I already made the decision to embrace and practice good
   values daily?*
2. *If so, when did I make that decision?*
3. *What exactly did I decide? (Write it here.)*

_____

_____

_____

_____

_____

_____

Your Values Discipline Every Day

Based on the decision you made concerning values, what is the one
discipline you must practice *today and every day* in order to be successful? Write it here.

_____

_____

_____

_____

_____

Making Up for Yesterday

If you need some help making the right decision concerning values
and developing the everyday discipline to live it out, do the following exercises:

1. *What values have you been embracing up to now? One of the best ways to answer that question honestly is to examine yourself in a few key areas:*

   ◆ *How do you spend your time, especially your discretionary time?*

   ◆ *How do you spend your money, especially your discretionary money?*

   ◆ *Who are your heroes and role models?*

   ◆ *What do you think about most, especially when you're alone?*

   Your answers to these questions will tell you a lot about what you really value.

2. *Who has influenced you most in the area of values? Try to recall as many of the people as possible and write their names here. Then write the value or character quality they encouraged you to adopt. (Note: Some of the values may not be positive.)*

   _____

   _____

   _____

   _____

   _____

   _____

3. *Identify the role models whom you desire to emulate from today forward, along with a one-phrase strategy describing how you will interact with them (meet to discuss values, read their book, study their life, etc.).*

   _____

   _____

   _____

   _____

_____

_____

4. *Go through the process described in the chapter of brainstorming values and then select the values you desire to live out.*

5. *How have you handled your feelings in the past when they made you want to compromise your values? Has that been a difficulty or an area of strength for you? Most people need to develop a strategy to help themselves in this area. Try these:*

   ◆ *Identify the areas where you most often struggle, and then try to avoid putting yourself in those kinds of situations in the future.*

   ◆ *Brainstorm the pros of keeping a value versus the cons of compromising it in an area of weakness. Write the pros and cons on an index card or in your daily planner so that you are constantly reminded of the rewards of discipline and the consequences of compromise.*

   ◆ *Ask someone to hold you accountable in your area of weakness.*

6. *If you don't strategically set aside time and designate a place to reflect every day on how your practices compare to your values, you probably won't follow through. Plan a time and a place to do this on a regular basis.*

Looking Forward to Tomorrow

Spend some time reflecting on how your decision concerning values and the daily discipline that comes out of it will positively impact you in the future. What compounding benefits do you expect to receive? Write them here.

_____

_____

_____

_____

———————————————————————————————

———————————————————————————————

Keep what you've written as a constant reminder, because . . .
Reflection today motivates your discipline every day, and
Discipline every day maximizes your decision of yesterday.

CHAPTER 14

Today's **GROWTH** Gives Me Potential

When I begin working on a book, one of the first things I do is sit down with Charlie Wetzel, my writer, and Kathie Wheat, my researcher, and brainstorm about what stories we might include to illustrate the ideas and principles I want to teach. It's a stimulating process where we all throw out names and stories, and the best idea wins. Usually, in that first meeting we come up with more than half the story ideas. Then off Kathie goes to do the research. And as we make progress writing the book, we keep looking for additional stories and fill in any "holes" along the way.

Over the years, we've discovered that an example of how someone failed to live out a principle sometimes illustrates a concept better than a positive example. You've probably noticed that in *Today Matters,* we've opened each chapter with a negative example of someone who neglected one of the Daily Dozen. But an interesting thing happened as we sought out a representative story for this chapter on growth. We couldn't find a good one.

We were looking for a story about someone who had *fantastic* potential but who clearly missed it and lived an unfulfilled life because he never dedicated himself to growth. There's a reason we couldn't find a really good story about someone like that: You rarely hear about them. People who settle for mediocrity don't stand out. Their stories don't get told.

In your personal experience, you may have known people you thought missed their potential. Maybe there are people you grew up with whom you looked up to and expected to accomplish great things, but they never achieved much. You may even have been surprised to grow past them personally or professionally. Or perhaps you have some regrets yourself. Maybe you quit taking piano lessons as soon as you were old enough, and now you wish you had stuck with it. Maybe you dropped out of school. Or maybe you didn't stick with a tough job that you now realize could have taught you a lot and helped your career. When someone misses opportunities for growth and improvement, he may feel regret. If he goes long enough without growing, he begins to feel he's had an unused life. And that's not unlike an early death.

Misconceptions about Growth

Novelist Robert Louis Stevenson said, "To be what we are, and to become what we are capable of becoming, is the only end of life."

Nearly all people would like to become who they are capable of being, yet I think many people don't. One reason is their misunderstanding of growth:

> "To be what we are, and to become what we are capable of becoming, is the only end of life."
>
> —ROBERT LOUIS STEVENSON

THEY THINK GROWTH IS AUTOMATIC

When we're children, our bodies grow automatically. Also, during that time, there are adults, such as our parents or teachers, who challenge us to grow mentally on a daily basis. So we get used to growing. The problem comes when we stop growing physically and we get out of school. We expect our bodies to take care of themselves as they did the first twenty years of our lives. And we think that our minds will take care of themselves too, even though we no longer have anyone pushing us to improve.

The truth is, if we don't take responsibility for our growth, it won't happen. Growth is not automatic. If you believe it simply comes with age, you might turn out like the subject of singer and comedian Tennessee Ernie Ford's comment, "He started out at the bottom, and sort of likes it there."

> "He started out at the bottom, and sort of likes it there."
>
> —TENNESSEE ERNIE FORD

Personal growth works exactly opposite to compounding interest in a bank account. If someone deposited a sum of money into an account the day you were born, the way to make it grow is not to touch it. But when it comes to your potential, you *must* tap into it to make it grow.

THEY THINK GROWTH COMES FROM INFORMATION

The greatest obstacle to growth is not ignorance. It's the illusion of knowledge. Have you ever known someone who was a font of data yet could do nothing with it to benefit himself or others? Individuals like that are similar to encyclopedias—filled with information, but useless when unused. Life change is the proper measure of whether information makes a difference.

THEY THINK GROWTH COMES WITH EXPERIENCE

Gilbert Arland said, "When an archer misses the mark he turns and looks for the fault within himself. Failure to hit the bull's-eye is never the fault of the tar-get. To improve your aim, improve yourself." A person who believes that

> Life change is the proper measure of whether information makes a difference.

growth comes simply as the result of experience is like an archer who keeps shooting arrows off-target and believes he's improving because he keeps missing in the same place. Experience is good only if it's reflected on and one learns from both his mistakes and successes.

Why Growth Matters Today

Pulitzer prize–winning composer Gian Carlo Menotti said, "Hell begins on that day when God grants us a clear vision of all that we might have achieved, of all the gifts we wasted, of all that we might have done that we did not do." No one wants to look back at life and see time and opportunities wasted. That's why it's important to recognize the value of growth before too much time passes.

With that in mind, allow me to give you four specific reasons why growth matters today:

1. GIFTING WITHOUT GROWTH LEADS TO INEFFECTIVENESS

Missionary physician Albert Schweitzer said, "The secret of success is to go through life as a man who never gets used up." How do you ensure that you will not get used up before your life is done? The answer comes in the way you approach talent. If you draw on your talent but never add to it or sharpen it, you're headed for trouble, because nobody is *that* talented. But when you place a premium on growth, you take whatever talent you have and you increase it. That not only raises your effectiveness today, but it makes your talent greater so that you can be effective tomorrow.

2. GROWTH PREVENTS PERSONAL AND PROFESSIONAL STAGNATION

Have you ever felt that you were just stuck in some aspect of your life? You want to advance in your career, but you seem to have stalled. You desire to improve your relationship with your spouse, but you don't seem able to break new ground. Or you hit a plateau in your health, and nothing you do seems to advance your efforts. How do you overcome such stagnation? I'll tell you what a lot of people do: They make external changes. They look for a different job, leave their spouse, or give up exercising.

The better solution is to pursue internal changes. External changes generally only relieve symptoms of stagnation temporarily. If you get a different job, the newness of it and the fresh challenges it brings may thrill you for a while, but when that wears off—a few weeks, months, or years later—you will be faced with the same old problems. The same is usually true for second marriages. And if you give up exercising, your health will only decline.

However, if you make personal growth your goal, then your focus is on changes you can make on the inside. You become better equipped to face career challenges. You discover new ways to relate to your spouse. You find ways to improve your eating or maximize your exercise. You gain the potential to break the stagnation and improve your situation without some of the losses of career changes, broken relationships, or neglected health.

3. YOUR PERSONAL GROWTH IMPACTS YOUR ORGANIZATION'S GROWTH

What is the lid holding down your business, department, or organization? What is currently limiting its potential? You may face challenges related to technology, capital, cash flow, personnel, or markets. And those may be legitimate obstacles. But no matter what work you do or where you do it, your greatest challenge is you!

For years I've taught leadership conferences for people who desire to grow their organizations. And I've found that many leaders are looking for quick fixes to create growth. One of the things I've taught in those set-

> "In order to *do* more, I've got to *be* more."
> —JIM ROHN

tings is that if you want to grow the organization, you must grow the leader. Business philosopher and author Jim Rohn puts it another way: "In order to *do* more, I've got to *be* more." If you are growing, then your organization has a good chance to grow. If you're not growing, you will be a lid on your organization's growth.

4. ONLY THROUGH CONTINUOUS IMPROVEMENT CAN YOU REACH YOUR POTENTIAL

The Tartar tribes of central Asia spoke a certain curse against an enemy. They didn't hurl words calling for their enemy's swords to rust or for their people to die of disease. Instead they said, "May you stay in one place forever." If you don't try to improve yourself every day, that could be your fate. You will be stuck in the same place, doing the same things, hoping the same hopes for coming years, but never gaining new territory or winning new victories.

Making the Decision to Seek and Experience Growth Daily

In 1974, a critical event occurred in my life that would change it forever. I met Kurt Kampmeir of Success Motivation, Inc. for breakfast in Lancaster, Ohio. While we were eating, Kurt posed a question. "John," he asked, "what is your plan for personal growth?"

Never at a loss for words, I tried to find things in my life that might qualify for growth. I told him about the many activities I was engaged in throughout the week. And I went into a speech about how hard I worked and the gains I was making in my organization. I must have talked for ten minutes, until I finally ran out of gas. Kurt listened patiently, but then he finally smiled and said, "You don't have a personal plan for growth, do you?"

"No," I finally admitted.

"You know," Kurt said simply, "growth is not an automatic process."

And that's when it hit me. I wasn't doing anything intentional or strategic to make myself better. And in that moment, I made the decision: *I will develop and follow a personal growth plan for my life.*

That night, I went home and talked to Margaret about my conversation with Kurt and what I had learned that day. I showed her the workbook and tapes that Kurt was selling. I knew those resources could help us grow. The cost was $745, a huge sum for us at the time. We couldn't afford it—but we couldn't afford not to get it either. Up till then I had always believed in my own potential, but I had never thought about having a way to increase and reach it. We recognized that Kurt wasn't just trying to make a sale. He was offering a way for us to change our lives and achieve our dreams.

A couple of important things happened that night. First, we figured out how to scrape together the money to buy the resources. It would require us to make sacrifices in our already-tight budget for the next six months. But more important, Margaret and I made a commitment to grow together as a couple. From that day on, we learned together, we traveled together, and we sacrificed together in order to grow. It was a wise decision. While too many couples grow apart, we were growing together.

If you're ready to make the decision to pursue growth and experience improvement every day, then do the following:

Answer the Question: What Is My Potential?

I saw a story about a St. Louis doctor who met a young man in high school who had lost his hand at the wrist. When the doctor asked about his handicap, the teenager responded, "I don't have a handicap, sir. I just don't have a right hand." The doctor later learned that the young man was one of the leading scorers on his high school football team.

The greatest handicap a person has is not realizing his potential. What dreams do you have that are just waiting to be fulfilled? What gifts and talents are inside you that are dying to be drawn out and developed? The gap between your vision and your present reality can only be filled through a commitment to maximize your potential.

Make a Commitment to Change

Author William Feather said, "The only thrill worthwhile is the one that comes from making something out of yourself." To make something out of yourself, you need to be willing to change, for without change, there can be no growth. The problem most peo-

"The only thrill worthwhile is the one that comes from making something out of yourself."

—WILLIAM FEATHER

ple have is that they want things to stay the same yet also get better. Obviously, that can't happen. If you truly want to grow, then commit yourself to not only accepting change, but seeking it.

SET GROWTH GOALS

When I first began going after personal growth using Kurt Kampmeir's materials, I pursued a growth plan that was foundational rather than specific. And that was okay then. I was in my midtwenties and I was just getting started. But as I got older, more experienced, and further in my career, I started to focus my growth in a few key areas. One was communication. That made sense for me, not only because I spoke to audiences four or five times a week, but also because I had some natural ability in that area. Another area was leadership—something I needed to do well every day of my life to succeed in my career.

As you plan your growth, it will benefit you greatly to be focused. Peter Drucker, the father of modern management, said, "The great mystery isn't that people do things badly but that they occasionally do a few things well. The only thing that is universal is incompetence. Strength is always specific. Nobody ever commented, for example, that the great violinist Jascha Heifetz probably couldn't play the trumpet very well."[1] In the chapter on priorities, I encouraged you to focus your priorities in three main areas: requirement, return, and reward. You should use the same criteria for your personal growth. Focus on growing in your areas of greatest strength, not your weaknesses. And grow in areas that will add value to you personally and professionally.

LEARN TO ENJOY THE JOURNEY

Eugene Griessman, author of *The Path to Achievement,* says that most grand masters of chess learn and relearn chess moves, gambits, and combinations over a period of fifteen years before they win their first world title. That's a fifth of most people's lives. If you're going to spend that much time learning something, then you had better learn to like it. If the destination appeals to you, but you cannot enjoy the journey it takes to get there, you would be wise to reexamine your priorities to make sure you have them right.

PUT YOURSELF IN A GROWTH ENVIRONMENT

I've often wondered what would have happened, when I came home to Margaret that day in 1974 after seeing Kurt Kampmeir, if she had said she didn't want to grow with me and that $745 was too much money for that personal growth kit. I wonder because I know that her companionship and partnership on the personal growth journey have made all the difference. By working together to improve ourselves, we created a growth environment that helped us to broaden our horizons and live a life that we never could have imagined when we first got married. And that environment continued as we raised our children. When Elizabeth and Joel Porter were growing up, their mental, emotional, and spiritual growth were our highest priorities.

I've been told that certain species of fish will grow according to the size of their environment. Put them in a tiny aquarium, and they remain small even at adulthood. Release them into a huge natural body of water, and they grow to their intended size. People are similar. If they live in a harsh and limiting environment, they stay small. But put them someplace that encourages growth, and they will expand to reach their potential.

Managing the Discipline of Growth

When I finished working through Kurt Kampmeir's materials, my appetite was whetted for more growth. And it was then that I determined to practice this discipline of growth: *Every day I will grow on purpose with my plan.* Margaret and I continued to do much of our growing together, but each of us also began tailoring our growth plans to our individual strengths and needs. One of the results of learning is that you realize how far you still need to go, and the more we learned, the hungrier we were for more growth.

As you prepare to embrace the disciplines of growth, I want to encourage you to do the following:

MAKE IT YOUR GOAL TO GROW IN SOME WAY EVERY DAY

In 1972, high school swimmer John Nabor watched the Olympics on television and was inspired. He was already an excellent swimmer, but he began thinking about making the leap to become an Olympic-caliber athlete. He figured he would have to lower his time by four seconds in four years. For you and me, that might not be too difficult, because we have such a long way to go.

But for someone like Nabor, who was already well trained, that seemed impossible. Elite racers think in terms of improving by fractions of a second. Thinking about that fact, he suddenly figured out how to approach the task. If he planned to train ten months a year for the next four years, he would have to improve by a tenth of a second every month. It was still a great challenge, but he believed he could do it and be ready for the 1976 Olympics.

Nabor had the right idea. And it worked. He came home with five medals, four of them gold. If you and I want to be successful

1. *How do people even approach the idea of figuring out their potential? I think the best place to start is where your dreams and your strengths meet. What do you dream about? Who would you like to be? What would you like to do? For the moment, forget about the obstacles. Write that dream here:*

_____

_____

_____

_____

_____

_____

  What are your strengths? What talents, gifts, and skills do you possess? Brainstorm a bit and write down your answers here:

_____

_____

_____

_____

_____

_____

  Now, how do these two areas intersect? The answer to that question will at least give you a direction to go in your growth.

2. *Look at the closest associations in your life. Whom do you spend most of your time with? Write their names here:*

_____

_____

_____

_____

_____

_____

Now, next to each name write three to five words that best describe each person.

What does that have to do with growth? The people you spend the most time with greatly impact your outlook and direction. If your closest associates are hungry to grow and trying to reach their potential, it will rub off on you. If they have no interest in growing, they will influence you in that direction. If your list doesn't include people striving to reach their potential, then you need to change your environment and find like-minded people with whom to associate.

3. *What is your plan for growth? I recommend that you adopt a plan similar to mine where you listen to lessons and read books on a regular basis. Set aside at least one hour a day, five days a week, for growing time. If you do a lot of driving, you will be able to do even more by listening to messages, seminars, and audiobooks in your car. In addition, plan to attend at least one seminar a year, and make regular appointments with people who can mentor you. Remember, your goal is to focus on your areas of strength.*

4. *Begin creating a filing system. The way to start is to be on the lookout for anything you hear or read that you want to be able to learn from and find later. Capture it in written form, label it by subject, and then file it away. The more you read, the more your resources will grow.*

5. *Find ways to apply what you're learning. Spend an hour a week reviewing your "notes and quotes" to figure out how to introduce their concepts, principles, or practices into your daily life. And if you really want to make an idea a permanent part of your skill set, teach it to others. Nothing cements learning like having to know it so well that you can teach it.*

Looking Forward to Tomorrow

Spend some time reflecting on how your decision concerning growth and the daily discipline that comes out of it will positively impact you in the future. What compounding benefits do you expect to receive? Write them here.

_____

_____

_____

_____

_____

_____

Keep what you've written as a constant reminder, because . . .
Reflection today motivates your discipline every day, and
Discipline every day maximizes your decision of yesterday.

Now, turn the page for one last bit of advice on how to make every day your masterpiece!

Making Today Matter

One of my concerns when I began writing *Today Matters* was that the idea of trying to implement the Daily Dozen might seem overwhelming. At the end of each chapter, I gave you suggestions for improving in an area, but I know it's impossible to tackle all twelve at the same time. It took me four decades to make the decisions and develop the disciplines in all twelve areas! And I'm still trying to keep learning.

So here are my suggestions concerning how to tackle the Daily Dozen and implement them into your life:

Rate Yourself on the Daily Dozen: Look at the following list of the Daily Dozen and rank how well you do them. Put a "1" beside the one you do the best, a "2" beside the one you're next best at, and so on until you've ranked your skill in them from 1 to 12.

_____ Attitude: Choose and display the right attitudes daily.
_____ Priorities: Determine and act on important priorities daily.
_____ Health: Know and follow healthy guidelines daily.
_____ Family: Communicate with and care for my family daily.
_____ Thinking: Practice and develop good thinking daily.
_____ Commitment: Make and keep proper commitments daily.
_____ Finances: Earn and properly manage finances daily.
_____ Faith: Deepen and live out my faith daily.
_____ Relationships: Initiate and invest in solid relationships daily.
_____ Generosity: Plan for and model generosity daily.
_____ Values: Embrace and practice good values daily.
_____ Growth: Desire and experience improvements daily.

Verify Your Self-evaluation: Talk to a friend who knows you well and ask him or her to confirm how you evaluated yourself. If your friend ranks your strengths and weaknesses differently than you do, discuss your differences of opinion and make adjustments to the rankings as needed.

Pick Two Strengths: Pick two strengths from your top six to work on. Make sure that you have made the necessary decision for each area. Then begin practicing the daily disciplines in that area to make it a part of your life. Use the exercises at the end of the chapter to help you if desired.

Pick One Weakness: Choose a weakness from your bottom six to work on. Again, make sure you have made the decision for that area and begin practicing the daily disciplines that go with it.

Reevaluate: After sixty days have passed, reevaluate yourself in the three areas in which you've been working to improve. If you have made significant progress in an area, move on to something new. If an area still needs more work, remain focused on it for another sixty days. But don't work on more than three areas at a time, and never work on more than one weakness at a time.

Repeat: Keep working on areas until you have the entire Daily Dozen under your belt.

Once you have made all the key decisions and each of the disciplines has become a habit in your life, then the Daily Dozen will be second nature to you. When these disciplines are woven into the fabric of your life, you will be able to make today your masterpiece. And when you do that, tomorrow will take care of itself.

Notes

Chapter 1

1. Judith Viorst, *Alexander and the Terrible, Horrible, No Good, Very Bad Day* (New York: Atheneum, 1972), 5.
2. M. Scott Peck, *The Road Less Traveled* (New York: Touchstone, 1978), 15.
3. Ambrose Bierce, *The Devil's Dictionary* 1906 (New York: Oxford University Press, 1999).
4. Seth Godin, "'Slowly I Turned . . . Step by Step . . . Inch by Inch . . . ,'" *Fast Company,* May 2003, 72.
5. Amanda Ripley, "Shadow of a Falling Star," *Time,* March 10, 2003, 56.
6. Dale Witherington, "The Lifebuilders's Creed," e-mail to author, 24 April 2003.
7. Karen Kenyon, "Oscar Wilde: One of the Greatest Wits of the Victorian Age, Wilde Fell Victim of the Harsh Justice of His Day," *British Heritage,* http://britishhistory.about.com/library (accessed April 17, 2003).
8. Oscar Wilde, *De Profundus,* 1905, www.upword.com/wilde/de_profundis (accessed May 8, 2003).

Chapter 2

1. John Wooden with Steve Jamison, *Wooden: A Lifetime of Observations and Reflections On and Off the Court* (Chicago: Contemporary Books, 1997), 11–12.

2. Wooden, *Wooden*, 64.
3. Swen Nader, used by permission.

Chapter 3

1. Armand M. Nicholi Jr., *The Question of God: C. S. Lewis and Sigmund Freud Debate God, Love, Sex, and the Meaning of Life* (New York: Free Press, 2002), 109.
2. Ibid., 102.
3. Ibid., 110.
4. Denis Waitley, *The Winner's Edge* (New York: Berkley, 1983).
5. Ecclesiastes 5:10 NKJV.
6. John C. Maxwell, *The 17 Indisputable Laws of Teamwork* (Nashville: Thomas Nelson, 2001), 107–8.
7. Lance Armstrong with Sally Jenkins, *It's Not About the Bike: My Journey Back to Life* (New York: Berkley Books, 2000), 257.
8. Ibid., 27.
9. Ibid., 50.
10. Ibid., 110.
11. Ibid., 95.
12. "Lance Armstrong: Champion Cyclist Beats Testicular Cancer," www.abcnews.go.com/sections/living/Daily News, February 16, 1999.
13. Armstrong, *Not About the Bike*, 185.
14. Ibid., 114.
15. Ibid., 257.

Chapter 4

1. R. C. Gano, "Howard Robard Hughes, Sr.," *The Handbook of Texas Online*, www.tsha.utexas.edu/handbook/online/articles/view/HH/fhu16.html (accessed July 24, 2003).
2. Michael Sauter, "Howard Hughes: Billionaire, Daredevil, Playboy, Madman," *Biography*, August 2003, 68.
3. "Howard Hughes," Las Vegas Strip History Site, www.lvstriphistory.com/hughe.htm (accessed July 24, 2003).
4. Adapted, original source unknown.
5. Myers Barnes, "Executive Time Management: A Guaranteed Solution," Housing Zone, www.housingzone.com/topics/hz/sales/hz01ea605.asp (accessed July 25, 2003).
6. *Target Marketing*, April 1996.
7. Alec Mackenzie, *The Time Trap* (New York: Amacom, 1997).

8. "Betsy Rogers Wins 2002 National Teacher of the Year," www.talkingproud.us/Education043003.html (accessed May 12, 2003).

9. www.alsde.edu/general/Rogers_Application.htm.

10. "Betsy Rogers," www.talkingproud.com.

11. Mary Orndorff, "Leeds Educator Named National Teacher of the Year," *Birmingham News*, April 29, 2003, 2A.

12. Gannett News Service, "Teacher of the Year Urges Focus on Helping Poor Children," *Tucson Citizen*, May 5, 2003, www.tucsoncitizen.com.

13. www.alsde.edu/general/Rogers_Application.htm.

Chapter 5

1. "Leading Causes of Death—2000," and "International Cardiovascular Disease Statistics," American Heart Association, Statistical Fact Sheets, www.americanheart.org (accessed July 18, 2003).

2. Bernie S. Siegel, *Peace, Love and Healing* (New York: HarperCollins, 1995).

3. "UC Berkeley Epidemiologist Wins Olympic Medal for Studies Showing Exercise Protects against Heart Disease," news release, July 1, 1994, University of California Berkeley Public Information Office, www.berkeley.edu/news (accessed December 8, 2003).

4. "Idols Among Us," www.actionforlife.com/fitness.htm (accessed May 8, 2003).

5. "Jack LaLanne," 2003, Interview, *Bottom Line Personal*, February 15, 2003, 14.

6. Ibid.

7. "Jack LaLanne," 2002, Interview by Dick Foley, *Health Talk*, www.healthtalk.com/celb/lalanne/02.html (accessed May 7, 2003).

8. Ibid.

9. Dennis Hughes, "An Interview with Jack LaLanne," September 26, 2002, www.shareguide.com/LaLanne.html (accessed May 7, 2003).

10. Dinah Gold, "10 Ways to Save Your Life: Practical Advice from the Surgeon General," *Biography*, August 2003, 60–65.

11. Sanjay Gupta, "Why Men Die Young," *Time*, May 12, 2003, 84.

Chapter 6

1. "The Jukes in 1915," Disability History Museum, www.disabilitymuseum.org/lib/docs/759.htm (accessed April 4, 2003).

2. "Jonathan Edwards: America's Humble Giant," Christian History Institute, www.gospelcom.net/chi/glimpsef/glimpses/glmp097.shtml (accessed April 28, 2003).

3. Ted Goodman, ed., *The Forbes Book of Business Quotations* (New York: Black Dog and Leventhal, 1997), 407.

4. Samuel Osherson, *Finding Our Fathers: The Unfinished Business of Manhood* (New York: Free Press, 1986).

5. Nick Stinnet, *USA Today,* January 29, 1986.

6. "Building a Better Dad," *Today's Health and Wellness,* 26.

7. "New Report Sheds Light on Trends and Patterns in Marriage, Divorce, and Cohabitation," National Center for Health Statistics, www.cdc.gov/hchs/releases/02news/div_mar_cobah.htm (accessed June 19, 2003).

8. "Profile for United States: Indicators of Child Well Being," Kids Count, www.aecf.org (accessed June 19, 2003).

9. Matthew Cooper, "Going to Chapel," *Time,* June 10, 2002, 31.

10. Executive Leadership Foundation, Inc., *Absolute Ethics: A Proven System of True Profitability* (Tucker, GA, 1987), 18.

11. Ron Suskind, "Mrs. Hughes Takes Her Leave," *Esquire,* July 2002, www.esquire.com.

12. Richard Dunham, "Karen Hughes and the Courage to Quit," *BusinessWeek,* April 29, 2002, www.businessweek.com.

13. Suskind, "Hughes."

14. Ibid.

15. Bob Costantini, "The President's Right-Hand Woman: Hughes Decides to Leave the White House," www.evote.com/features/2002-04/042402hughes.asp (accessed April 9, 2003).

16. Ibid.

17. Suskind, "Hughes."

Chapter 7

1. "Great Atlantic and Pacific Tea Company, Inc." http://shop.store.yahoo.com/scripophily/greatatandpa1.html (accessed August 19, 2003).

2. Avis H. Anderson, *A&P: The Story of the Great Atlantic & Pacific Tea Company* (Charleston, SC: Arcadia, 2002), 63.

3. William I. Walsh, *The Rise and Decline of the Great Atlantic and Pacific Tea Company* (New Jersey: Lyle Stuart, Inc., 1986), 77, quoted in Jim Collins, *Good to Great* (New York: Harper Business, 2001), Chapter 2, note 2, 269.

4. Jim Collins, *Good to Great* (New York: Harper Business, 2001), 67.

5. Ibid.

6. Ibid., 259–60.

7. "The Great Atlantic & Pacific Tea Company, Inc. Announces Results of First Quarter 2003," Press Release, July 25, 2003, http://biz.yahoo.com/bw/030725/255096_1.html (accessed August 19, 2003).
8. Claude M. Bristol, *The Magic of Believing* (New York: Pocket Books, 1994).
9. Adapted from "The Matter of Fax," Clay Road Baptist Church, April 23, 1999.
10. Gerald Nadler, *Breakthrough Thinking* (Roseville, CA: Prima Lifestyles, 1994).
11. Norman Vincent Peale, *The Power of Positive Thinking* (New York: Ballantine Book, 1996).
12. James Allen, *As a Man Thinketh* (Camarillo, CA).
13. *Leadership,* Spring 2001, 83.
14. John C. Maxwell, *Thinking for a Change: 11 Ways Highly Successful People Approach Life and Work* (New York: Warner Books, 2003).
15. Anne Lamott, *Bird by Bird: Instructions on the Writing Life* (Landover Hills, MD: Anchor, 1995).
16. *Leadership,* Spring 2001, 84.
17. Philippians 4:8 NRSV.
18. Rebecca Murray, "The Real Antwone Fisher Talks About the Movie, 'Antwone Fisher,'" http://romanticmovies.about.com/library/weekly/aaantwonefisherintc.htm (accessed July 25, 2003).
19. Antwone Quenton Fisher with Mim Eichler Rivas, *Finding Fish* (New York: Perennial, 2001), 122.
20. Ibid., 125.
21. Ibid., 127.
22. Rebecca Murray, "The Real Antwone Fisher."

Chapter 8

1. Lewis Early, "Mickey Mantle Mini-Biography," www.themick.com (accessed July 29, 2003).
2. Ibid.
3. Jack Mann, "Decline and Fall of a Dynasty," *Mantle Remembered* (New York: Warner Books, 1995), 79.
4. Mickey Mantle with Jill Lieber, "Time in a Bottle," *Sports Illustrated,* April 18, 1994, 69.
5. Ibid., 74.
6. "A Baseball Reader's Journal: Mickey Mantle: America's Prodigal Son," www.baseball-almanac.com/books (accessed July 29, 2003).

7. Mickey Mantle with Jill Lieber, "Time in a Bottle," 77.
8. Bob Costas, "Eulogy for Mickey Mantle, August 15, 1995—Dallas, TX," www.themick.com (accessed July 29, 2003).
9. Frederic F. Flach, *Choices: Coping Creatively with Personal Change* (New York/Philadelphia: J. B. Lippincott, 1977).
10. "The Fall of France," www.leesaunders.com/html/FoFrance.htm (accessed August 15, 2003).
11. Winston Churchill, *The Wit and Wisdom of Winston Churchill,* edited by James C. Humes (New York: Harper Perennial, 1994), 121.
12. Henry W. Longfellow, "The Ladder of St. Augustine."
13. Warren Wiersbe, *In Praise of Plodders* (Grand Rapids: Kregel, 1991).
14. Arthur Gordon, *A Touch of Wonder* (Jove Publications, 1991).
15. www.nytimes.com/learning/students/scholarship/index.html (accessed August 15, 2003).
16. "Succeeding on Her Own," ABC News, December 17, 1999, www.abcnews.go.com/onair/2020/2020_991217_homelessscholarship_feature.html (accessed April 24, 2003).
17. "A Chat with Homeless to Harvard Inspiration Liz Murray," April 11, 2003, www.lifetimetv.com/community/chat/lizmurray_transcript.html (accessed April 24, 2003).
18. Randy Kennedy, "Six Whose Path to Excellence Was on the Mean Streets of Adversity," *New York Times,* March 3, 1999, www.nytimes.com/learning/students/scholarship/scholarship1.html (accessed July 28, 2003).
19. "A Chat With Homeless to Harvard Inspiration Liz Murray."

Chapter 9

1. William Atkinson, "Drowning in Debt," *HR,* August 2001, www.findarticles.com (accessed July 22, 2003).
2. Christine Dugas, "Bankruptcy Filings Set Record in 2002," *USA Today,* February 17, 2003, www.usatoday.com.
3. Christine Dugas, "Bankruptcy Filings on Record Pace," *USA Today,* August 27, 2001, www.usatoday.com.
4. Dugas, "Set Record in 2002."
5. Christine Dugas, "Debt Woes Nearing Record," *USA Today,* November 26, 2002, www.usatoday.com.
6. Dugas, "Bankruptcy Filings on Record Pace."
7. Dugas, "Debt Woes."
8. William Atkinson, "Drowning in Debt."
9. Ibid.

10. James Patterson and Peter Kim, *The Day America Told the Truth: What People Really Believe About Everything That Really Matters* (Prentice Hall, 1991).

11. Polly LaBarre, "How to Lead a Rich Life," *Fast Company*, March 2003, 74.

12. Proverbs 22:7 NASB.

13. Quoted in Leslie E. Royale, "Debt Free is the Way to Be," *Black Enterprise*, October 2002, www.findarticles.com (accessed July 22, 2003).

14. Ibid.

15. Quoted in Ron Blue's seminars from *USA Today*, January 7, 1997.

16. James Surowiecki, "People of Plenty," *Fast Company*, March 2003, 32.

17. Robert Frick, "If You Knew Suze . . ." *Kiplinger's*, November 1998, www.findarticles.com (accessed July 22, 2003).

18. Lynn Andriani, "The Dollars and Sense of Suze Orman," *Publisher's Weekly*, February 24, 2003, 44.

19. Frick, "If You Knew Suze."

20. Suze Orman, *The Laws of Money, The Lessons of Life* (New York: Free Press, 2003), 11.

21. Ibid., 13.

22. Andriani, "Dollars and Sense," 47.

Chapter 10

1. Unknown, "The Ship," in *The Columbia Granger's Index to Poetry in Anthologies*, Nicholas Frankovich, ed. (New York: Columbia UP, 1997), 520.

2. Source unknown.

3. Harold G. Koenig, Ellen Idler, and Stanislav Kasl, "Religion, Spirituality, and Medicine: A Rebuttal To Skeptics," *International Journal of Psychiatry in Medicine*, 29-2, 1999, 123–31, www.eathingbythebook.com (accessed June 24, 2003).

4. Christopher Reeve, speech at the 1996 Democratic National Convention, August 26, 1996, www.lib.uchicago.edu/nrd13/hd/reeve.html.

5. John Noble Wilford, "Oldest Planet Is Revealed, Challenging Old Theories," *New York Times*, July 11, 2003, www.nytimes.com.

6. James 4:8 NIV.

7. "Shuttle Commander Called 'True American Hero,'" CNN, February 2, 2003, www.cnn.com/2003/US/02/01/sprj.colu.shuttle.husband/index.html.

8. Chris Kridler, "Husband Had Dreams of Space Since He Was a Child," *USA Today,* February 1, 2003, www.usatoday.com/news/nation/2003-02-01-husband-bio_x.htm.

9. Evelyn Husband, interview by Katie Couric, *Today* show, February 3, 2003, National Broadcasting System.

10. Ibid.

Chapter 11

1. "Armand Hammer Dead at 92; Industrialist and Philanthropist," *USA Today,* December 11, 1990, pqasb.pqarchiver.com/USAToday/56038152.html (accessed July 23, 2003).

2. "Armand Hammer Dies; Billionaire, Art Patron, Industrialist," *Los Angeles Times,* December 11, 1990, www.latimes.com (accessed July 31, 2003).

3. Edward Jay Epstein, *Dossier: The Secret History of Armand Hammer* (New York: Random House, 1996), 128.

4. Joel Stein, "Bosses from Hell," *Time,* December 7, 1998, www.time.com.

5. Epstein, *Dossier,* 7.

6. Ibid., 17.

7. Ibid., 349.

8. Robert Hughes, "America's Vainest Museum," *Time,* January 28, 1991, www.time.com.

9. John C. Maxwell, *The 17 Indisputable Laws of Teamwork* (Nashville: Thomas Nelson, 2001), 1.

10. Donald O. Clifton and Paula Nelson, *Soar with Your Strengths* (New York: Dell, 1996).

11. Dale Carnegie, *How to Win Friends and Influence People* (New York: Simon and Schuster, 1936).

12. Tom Peters and Nancy Austin, *A Passion for Excellence: The Leadership Difference* (New York: Warner Books, 1989).

13. Leo Buscaglia, *Loving Each Other: The Challenge of Human Relationships* (New York: Ballantine, 1990).

14. "Bill Bright: A Life Lived Well," Campus Crusade for Christ, http://billbright.ccci.org/staff/multimedia, 2.

15. *Harvard Business Review,* November/December 1995.

Chapter 12

1. "J(ean) Paul Getty," www.biography.com/print_record.pl?id=21530 (accessed May 9, 2003).

2. Clifton Daniel, ed., "Billionaire J. Paul Getty Dies in Britain," *Chronicle of the 20th Century* (Liberty, MO: JL International Publishing, 1992), 1110.

3. "What Else Happened Today: December 15," www.historychannelcom/tdih/today/1215.html (accessed May 9, 2003).

4. "Sir J Paul Getty Dead at age 70," www.msnbc.com/news, April 17, 2003.

5. Ruth Smeltzer, quoted in Erik Kolball, *What Jesus Meant* (Louisville, KY: Westminster John Knox Press, 2003).

6. Proverbs 11:24–25 *The Message.*

7. Matthew 6:21 NIV.

8. "Numbers," *Time,* January 13, 2003, 17.

9. "Numbers," *Time,* December 6, 2002, 21.

10. *U.S. News and World Report,* December 22, 1997.

11. "Dave Thomas Praised in Senate for Adoption Advocacy," February 1, 2002, Dave Thomas Foundation for Adoption, www.davethomasfoundationforadoption.org (accessed August 8, 2003).

12. Bruce Horovitz, "Wendy's Icon Back at Work But Scare Makes Chain Consider the Inevitable," *USA Today,* March 31, 1997, http://pqasb.pqarchiver.com/USAToday, July 23, 2003.

13. Dottie Enrico, "Roots of Ambition Childhood Experiences of Orphaned, Adopted Ignite Drive to Thrive," *USA Today,* September 5, 1997, http://pqasb.pqarchiver.com/USAToday (accessed July 23, 2003).

14. Dave Thomas, "In His Words," www.wendys.com/dave/flash.html (accessed August 8, 2003).

15. Dave Thomas with Ron Beyma, *Well Done!* (Grand Rapids, MI: Zondervan, 1994), 203.

16. Linda D. Reeves, "Wendy's Adoption Plan Hits Home with Thomas," *USA Today,* August 31, 1992, http://pqasb.pqarchiver.com/USAToday (accessed July 23, 2003).

17. "Wendy's Founder Passes Away," January 8, 2002, Dave Thomas Foundation for Adoption, www.davethomasfoundationforadoption.org (accessed August 8, 2003).

18. Horovitz, "Wendy's Icon Back,"

Chapter 13

1. Erin McClam, "Waksal Sentenced to Prison," *Atlanta Journal-Constitution,* June 11, 2003, D1.

2. "The ImClone Scandal," *Atlanta Journal-Constitution,* June 11, 2003, D4.

3. "Chronology of a Collapse," *Time,* January 21, 2002, 31.

4. "Hall of Shame," *BusinessWeek,* October 7, 2002, www.business-week.com.

5. "World-Class Scandal at WorldCom," CBS News, June 26, 2002, www.cbsnews.com/stories/2002/06/26/national.

6. Constance L. Hays, "Martha Stewart Indicted by U.S. on Obstruction," *New York Times,* June 5, 2003, www.nytimes.com.

7. J. Oswald Sanders, *Spiritual Leadership.*

8. Roger Dow, *ICSA Journal.*

9. Associated Press, "Tyco's Kozlowski Took Hard Line Against Embezzling Crimes," *Seattle Times,* January 1, 2003, www.seattle-times.com.

10. Barbara Ross, Roberty Gearty, and Corky Siemaszko, "The Great Tyco Robbery," *New York Daily News,* September 12, 2002, www.ny-dailynews.com.

11. Ken Blanchard and Norman Vincent Peale, *The Power of Ethical Management* (New York: William Morrow, 1988).

Chapter 14

1. Peter Drucker, Quotes on Focus, www.leadershipnow.com (accessed November 24, 2003).

2. Mike Abrashoff, *It's Your Ship: Management Techniques from the Best Damn Ship in the Navy* (New York: Warner Books, 2002).

3. "From Poverty to Public Health Expert," *Biography,* August 2003, 61.

4. Ibid.

5. National Medical Fellowships, www.nmf-online.org/Development/scholars/PrintVersion/richard_carmona.htm (accessed August 14, 2003).

6. "From Poverty," *Biography.*

7. Robert Pear, "A Man of Many Professions: Richard Henry Carmona," *Puerto Rico Herald,* March 27, 2002, www.puertorico-herald.org/issues/2002/vol16n13/Carmona-en.shtml (accessed July 29, 2003).

8. National Medical Fellowships, www.nmfonline.org (accessed August 14, 2003).

About the Author

JOHN C. MAXWELL, known as America's expert on leadership, speaks in person to hundreds of thousands of people each year. He has communicated his principles to *Fortune* 500 companies, the United States Military Academy at West Point, international marketing organizations, the NCAA, and professional sports groups such as the NFL. He is the founder of several leadership organizations, including Maximum Impact. A *New York Times* best-selling author, Dr. Maxwell has written more than thirty books, including *Developing the Leader within You, Thinking for a Change, There's No Such Thing as "Business" Ethics,* and *The 21 Irrefutable Laws of Leadership,* which has sold more than one million copies.

Begin
your new
daily
agenda
today!

Now that you have read the book *Today Matters,* you can begin to prepare a daily agenda that will steer you toward success. Your first step should be to visit **www.TodayMatters.com** and take advantage of the **FREE** training lesson, *Living Life Usefully.* You will learn valuable techniques to make sure every day of your life is being used to its greatest potential.

Living Life Usefully is available to you both in streaming audio format online and on CD (for a minimal shipping charge of $2.00).

REAL

RELATIONSHIPS   EQUIPPING   ATTITUDE   LEADERSHIP

Understand what it means to become a REAL Success.

You have already learned a large number of principles and practices to help you become a success simply by making today the most important day of your life.

Let seasoned leader and accomplished teacher John C. Maxwell guide you through a lifestyle process that promises REAL success — being loved and respected the most by those closest to you.

In *How to be a REAL Success,* John radically redefines success as the art of helping others. Through insightful lessons, challenging exercises, and daily applications, you will learn everything you need to attain lasting success while you help those around you accomplish the same feat. Divided into four training sessions, you will learn critical principles that will shape your growth and development in these key areas:

- **R**elationships
- **E**quipping
- **A**ttitude
- **L**eadership

Every successful person is surrounded by other successful people that they have helped shape and mold. This incredible series helps you become the one to lead others and yourself to true success.

GROWTH APPLICATION AND EXERCISES
SEEKING AND EXPERIENCING
IMPROVEMENTS DAILY

Your Growth Decision Today

Where do you stand when it comes to growth today? Ask yourself these three questions:

1. *Have I already made the decision to seek and experience improvement daily?*
2. *If so, when did I make that decision?*
3. *What exactly did I decide? (Write it here.)*

_____

_____

_____

_____

_____

_____

Your Growth Discipline Every Day

Based on the decision you made concerning growth, what is the one discipline you must practice *today and every day* in order to be successful? Write it here.

_____

_____

_____

_____

_____

_____

Making Up for Yesterday

If you need some help making a commitment to become a person who grows daily, do the following exercises:

that I want to do, so many things I see in my community I think I could help to improve. Where many see obstacles, I see opportunity."[8]

Why does he believe he can do so much to help his community? Because every day he has more to give. That's what happens when you seek and experience improvements daily. Your potential grows, and so does your ability to make an impact on your world.

munity College and graduated with an associate's degree. He also got married to his high school sweetheart, Diane Sanchez, the daughter of a New York City detective, whom Carmona hadn't even been allowed to date after dropping out of high school. The couple then moved to California. Carmona became a registered nurse and began working on his bachelor's degree at the University of California, San Francisco. He was the first member of his family to graduate from college.

At each stage of Carmona's journey, he continued to pick up momentum. He earned his bachelor of science degree in 1976 and then enrolled in the university's medical school to fulfill his dream of becoming a doctor. He finished medical school in three years, finishing as the top graduate in his class, and then went on to a residency in surgery. But of course, Carmona still wasn't finished learning and growing. He knew he still hadn't reached his potential, so he completed a fellowship in trauma, burns, and critical care. Then he moved to Tucson, Arizona, where he went on to create the city's first trauma center. In 1985, he became director of the University of Arizona and Tucson Medical Center's trauma and emergency services.

Most people would be content with those accomplishments and think about resting on their laurels. Not Carmona. Besides fulfilling his duties as a director and professor, he also worked to become a deputy sheriff, a SWAT officer, and the medical director for the fire department. And in 1998, he added a master's degree in public health to his résumé. "My wife says I'm overcompensating for not doing well the first half of my life," explains Carmona. "It's my sense of having to make up for lost time."[7]

Boy, has he succeeded! And he's still going. Five months after receiving the phone call from the White House, he was sworn in as the nation's surgeon general. Now he is working to make an impact on a larger scale. "If it ended today," says Carmona, "I have achieved much more than I expected. But there is so much more

What would cause a respected surgeon and professor of surgery, public health, and family and community medicine at a large teaching university to be so surprised by the question? The answer can be found in Carmona's unlikely personal history.

Richard Carmona was born in Harlem, New York, in 1949 to a poor working-class family. His parents were kind, but they drank too much. One of his childhood memories was coming home from school at age six to find the family's belongings on a Salvation Army truck. They had been evicted. For a year he, his parents, and three siblings lived with his grandmother in a housing project— eleven people in one small apartment.

As a kid, Carmona was interested in medicine and dreamed of being a doctor, but he was a poor student. "I was distracted by family problems and hunger," he says.[4] In sixth grade he made things worse when he started skipping school. In his senior year of high school, he finally dropped out. "It was my own fault," Carmona explains. "I didn't go to class. I wasn't a bad kid, but I was bordering on juvenile delinquency. I was a street kid."[5]

In 1967, Carmona enlisted in the army after being impressed by a Green Beret in his neighborhood. When he realized that he would need a GED to join the Green Berets, he earned it. He thrived in the army. And he went to Vietnam with the Special Forces as a medic, where he earned two Purple Hearts and a Bronze Star. His time in the military changed his life. Carmona says, "They taught me about responsibility, accountability, staying focused, accomplishing missions, and using resources effectively. They gave me the platform for my life."[6]

A New Man

Carmona used that platform as a launching point for tenacious personal growth. After his military service, he enrolled in Bronx Com-in our growth, we must adopt a similar mind-set. If we desire to improve a little every day and plan it that way, then we can make great progress over the long haul.

HAVE A TIME AND PLAN TO GROW

One of my favorite personal growth quotes is from author and speaker Earl Nightengale. I came across it more than twenty years ago, and it made a pro-found impact on me. Nightengale said, "If a person will spend one hour a day on the same subject for five years, that

> "If a person will spend one hour a day on the same subject for five years, that person will be an expert on that subject."
> —EARL NIGHTENGALE

person will be an expert on that subject." After I read that quote, it changed how I planned my personal growth. I started spending an hour a day, five days a week, studying leadership. Over time, that practice changed my life.

To make your growth intentional, strategic, and effective, you need to think it through and plan it well. To give you an idea, I'll share how I plan my growth:

- ♦ **I Listen to Audio Lessons Every Week:** First of all, I'm always on the lookout for good teaching on tape or CD. Every week, I listen to seven audio lessons. Usually, their contents break down like this: Four are average, two are good to excellent, and only one may be outstanding. (If a lesson is bad, I hit the eject button after five minutes.) For every tape, I try to determine what the "take-away" is—the one item I can immediately apply—and do some thinking to try to capitalize on it. And I have every outstanding lesson transcribed so that I can read it, mark it up, and extract every bit of gold from it.

◆ **I Read Two Books Every Month:** If you were to go to my office, you'd find two stacks of books on the worktable near my desk. Those are the books that are "on deck" waiting to be read. They are sorted into two groups, and I read one of each every month. The first stack is of excellent books that I expect will make a strong impact on me. During the month, I spend a lot of time with that kind of book, digesting its ideas, marking the pages, pulling out ideas, and thinking about how I can apply the concepts to my life. (I also file what I learn— I'll explain that in a moment.) The second stack contains average books I intend to speed-read. They may offer just a few concepts that I want to get at quickly but don't warrant a careful reading.

◆ **I Set an Appointment Every Month:** One of the things I look forward to most is listening to and learning from others. So every month, I set an appointment with someone who can help me grow. Prior to the meeting, I prepare a list of questions that correspond to an area where I need to grow and where the person has achieved success. I also do any other homework that I think may be necessary, such as reading any books the person has written, but the success of the interview is determined most by the questions I prepare. My conversations with John Wooden, which I told you about in chapter 2, were the result of one of those appointments. It was a time of empowerment for me. Whenever I spend time with great people, I expect to learn great things from them.

> Whenever I spend time with great people, I expect to learn great things from them.

As you plan your strategy for growth and set aside time for it, don't forget that the more you grow, the more specific the growth should be to your needs and strengths. And anytime you discover that a book, tape, or conference doesn't possess the value you'd hoped for, move on. Don't waste your time on anything of low value.

FILE WHAT YOU LEARN

I have to admit it: I am a compulsive filer. Whenever I find something that I think will be valuable to me in the future—for learning, teaching, or writing—I file it. When I hear a great tape or CD and have it transcribed, I file quotes from it. If it's really good, I might even file the whole transcript. When I read a book, I mark every quote I want to capture and jot down what subject to file it under. If you look in the front of every good book I've read, you'll see a list of page numbers and subjects written in it. When I'm done with the book, I give it to my assistant, who copies the material and files it for me. I've been doing this for forty years!

I want to encourage you to file quotes, stories, and ideas that you find as you learn. Not only will this habit yield a great harvest of material for your future use, it will also keep you more highly focused, force you to evaluate what you're reading, and help you to bypass the junk and go for the good stuff that will stimulate you and help you grow.

APPLY WHAT YOU LEARN

Mike Abrashoff, author of *It's Your Ship*, says, "Up is not an easy direction. It defies gravity, both cultural and magnetic."[2] Often the most difficult part of the upward climb of growth is putting into practice what you learn. Yet that is where the true value is. The final test of any learning is always ap-

> "Up is not an easy direction. It defies gravity, both cultural and magnetic."
>
> —MIKE ABRASHOFF

plication. If what you're learning can be used in some way to help and improve you or others, then it is worth the effort.

Reflecting on Thinking

In each chapter of *Today Matters*, I have shared the decisions I've made, the disciplines I've strived to practice, and my reflections on each of my Daily Dozen. Of the twelve, I'd have to say that personal growth has probably been the strongest. I marvel at what has happened to me as my daily practice has compounded over the years:

In my 20s . . .   Growth became the foundation for my lifelong learning.

In my 30s . . .   My growth began to separate me from my peers.

In my 40s . . .   My growth became the source for my books and tapes.

In my 50s . . .   My growth has taken me to higher levels than I thought possible.

> The greatest of all insights is that we cannot be tomorrow what we do not do today.

The greatest of all miracles is that we need not be tomorrow what we are today. The greatest of all insights is that we cannot be tomorrow what we do not do today. That is why today matters.

Unlikely Path to Potential

In March of 2002, Richard Carmona received a phone call asking if he would consider accepting an appointment to become the surgeon general of the United States. His response? "I was floored," says Carmona. "I thought they had the wrong Rich Carmona!"[3]